Shiva's Rain

Peter Taylor

An autobiographical account of that dark period of 1984, when the world stood armed for nuclear warfare, nuclear waste was being dumped in the oceans, and Greenpeace took on the might of British and French government programmes that threatened world peace and the environment. Being also a spiritual quest through dark world's of the psyche.

Published by

ETHOS-UK
14 Kingston Court
Oxford
www.ethos-uk.com
email: info@ethos-uk.com

First published in the UK by
ETHOS-UK

ISBN 0-9547064-0-4

Printed and bound in the UK by
Short Run Press Ltd., Exeter, Devon.

‘

Preface

I am moved to publish this manuscript by the death of Dr David Kelly, government scientist, expert on Iraqi weapons of mass destruction, worker for the good of humanity and follower of Bahá-u'lláh, an Arab master who believed in the unity of all faiths. I am moved do so not because I knew Dr Kelly, but by the circumstances of his death. He is reported to have said to colleagues, 'there are dark forces at work' and that he would not be surprised if he 'were found dead in the woods'. Which he was.

I am also a scientist, sometimes working for governments, mostly against, but believing in that one humanity and unity of faith. I also follow a spiritual master, and but for him, and some very strong friends, I would likely be as dead as Dr Kelly and by my own hand.

I relate to you here my own experiences of 'dark forces' and leave it to you, the reader, to make what conclusions you may as to the circumstances of Dr Kelly's death. This is my own story. It is as true as I can make it to the time of 1984, to which most of it refers – though I know more now than I did then.

It is a story that weaves the scientific, the political, the personal, and spiritual. It would have been easier to have separated these elements to make each more accessible (or acceptable). I have kept this weave because I believe that science is seldom separate from politics, and politics never separate from the personal. Spiritual realities are always present in all three realms, but seldom acknowledged and often deliberately secret. And whatever dark forces may be at work in the Universe, I am convinced they start and end within the personal mind. Thus, I have worked here to end this separation, and one day, perhaps, that unwholesome secrecy.

**This book is dedicated to my friends,
including my family.**

Contents

1

Prologue
Begun 5th September 1994

I have waited for understanding, but it becomes less with the years. Now I am driven by a necessity that this must come to some form. I will be as true as I can to the events surrounding that particular year of 1984. It is now ten years on. I chide myself constantly that I have not written this down before and sought to publish. I know that for some years after, the events were too raw, wounds unhealed, and, also, some fascination that was unhealthy. The years have seen to that. Now I can be more matter-of-fact, although the poet in me will out in places, and for that, I crave your indulgence, for this is meant as autobiography, whatever that may be. Perhaps, behind the need to understand, there is some need to be understood.

This beginning begins on a fresh bright day, a new moon, at that turn of the year when summer's last promise of dryness and heat leaves these hills. The ocean from my window is deep blue, with pale dunes piled before over-green fields. Behind the cottage is a crescent of ancient woods, here on an escarpment steep and rocky enough to have had only the odd meadow since the last glaciation. Woods here in Arthur's time and when Glyndwr had his rebellion, and whose castle I see grey between the trees. The neighbouring farmer, Ellis Wynne, shares his name with a distinguished Welsh poet, whose house, visible from this window and for years derelict, is being renovated by grants from the European Union. There is a slow turning.

Our poet farmer has kept these woods and meadows free from efficiency. There is bog for alder and iris, the oak are horny, older than any road, of a time when the sea covered the plain of Morfa Harlech, and when no mechanical clatter would sound the morning mists. This year the Union will be offering money for the farms to restore their old stone walls, to replant hedges, to keep the meadows in flower and plant more trees. We have been fortunate on the land of the poet's kin, for these treasures were never lost, at least not here on the mountain that overlooks the rye-grassed plain. Whatever is now re-created elsewhere will not have this unbroken lineage and will be restored by will and plan rather than the chaos of nature, and done not of a true homage, of a poet's eye, but because it will pay.

Still, there is a turning, and I too easily carp. We have been blessed here by Harlech's woods. There has been an education that was lacking in 1984. I will do my best not to introduce it, whatever wisdom it holds, to how I was then, for the sake of historical truth, however embarrassing.

I was educated in Natural Sciences. I held an Open Scholarship at Oxford University. Scholars wore longer gowns and got an extra grant for books. If Oxford in the late 1960s was an elite of the University class, itself then less than 10% of each generation, then the scholars were an elite of that. As a natural scientist I studied biology and geology, and the chemistry and physics relevant to those disciplines. I was very unhappy. I had lied my way into the system. Of course, I had the mind for the task, or at least that part needed to tackle the rational quest, and had distinguished myself in the entrance exams. But my main interest in life was not biology, not science, not even a career. It was women. Their presence gripped me then as it does not now. They held me unfree, for which I blamed them, albeit not consciously, whereas in truth, of course, it was I strangling myself, hating the lust, the magnet, the flicker of flesh. It was not even the pull of a Muse, or of mystery, or of the thousand graces woman holds separate from man, but something rather simple, base and needing, the pull of an energy, an electric, into which I could assuage some dire thirst, or the promise of such.

For all that, there were fears barely felt.

> Capture the half-harsh half-light hair-strewn
> full mouth sensual shadow of her gaze.
> Cage it with irony, steel-meshed heart of the cat.
> Let it leach you of the love of the world, world-wise man,
> no gods are great,
> a woman's gaze needs only,
> heeds only, you.

> Free me of the lizard that crawls
> along the slippery floor of my mind.
> Her fat, round-bellied sleekness, scaly, shiny,
> draws reluctant kisses.
> Thin nails scratch the glass, sound like dreams, tickle behind the ears. She moves pregnantly slow, long tongue, forked, snakes around my palate, flickers across my eyes. She can no longer run, slithers with the sins of her youth,
> winds round my innermost spring,
> choking, snake-like seductive, heavy,
> like a pillow that takes away the day
> mimics the warm claustrophobic night.

I didn't say anything about this at the interview. If I recall, I wanted to be a Game Warden, in Africa. But I did not conceal my interest in the human condition entirely. It had to be Oxford. I had already secured a University place at Edinburgh to study Ecology and Resource Management and I turned to Oxford because I wanted the Secret of Life Itself. At 19, I trust I can be forgiven such romance and naivety. Although perhaps not, for none of my contemporaries had the same quest. Nor any of my Tutors. I thought I would find it somehow in the maze of studies of Man, of The Brain, of Evolution. Somewhere in Psychology. Somewhere in the how and why we began to walk upright. Surely, someone in Oxford, rather than Edinburgh would direct me. I am not sure now why I thought there was a secret.

I know that when I was thirteen I had walked the length of Dane's Dyke, an earthwork that once protected to landward the promontory that is Flamborough Head. I had walked out to the northern part, overgrown by gorse taller than twice my height, and there, surrounded momentarily, with nothing but blue sky above, a huge falcon glided across that circle, so low it met my eye, surprised, with but a flicker of its wings, rising a little, but no more, as if it knew I was friend not foe. Something imparted forever in that meeting, a knowledge, a certainty that though life plays out our roles of separateness, there exists a space where all dimensions merge and all forms cease their playing.

At that time I had my first 'girlfriend', Margaret. She was older by a year or more and interested in birds and mystery. I remember sitting on another part of the Dyke, well wooded, dappled light, when we talked of life. She said then, you must go to Oxford. For some reason we thought that was where philosophers go. I also remember walking along the path atop the wild cliffs, gannets out to sea, guillemot and razorbill whirring below, and looking at her legs, her calves below the dark blue skirt, and wanting not where they led, but that she did not have such a hooked nose. I remember the conversation inside that insisted the legs were perfectly adequate, and if only....

I don't know for sure, but sometime the year before, out on the same headland, when the wind had been up and a driving rain, I had retreated to a farmworkers' hut no bigger than a privy, but stacked high with girlie magazines. I had poured over them for hours while the rain persisted. I can't think it was any other source, something then ingrained about proportion, nothing else. It was in the days before pubic hair was photographed for general consumption. When the rain lifted there was a Wood Sandpiper on the farm pond, which I had not seen before. It must have been autumn, this time of year.

There was also my mother. When I was young she was perfectly proportioned. And for my father, she was his prize. He had won her by persistence and, I suspect, not a little pathos. She was a nurse, and he, back from the front in Burma with near-fatal sandfly fever, struck by beauty.....and need. So there it was, for whatever the aetiology of my disease, driven by conceits I barely knew, genetically or environmentally, possessed by beauty in the eyes, in the skin, in slender limbs and subtle movement of woman.

By the time of Oxford I had had closer contact. Ripe heady scents from that secret forest. One fumbled penetration with a promiscuous but erotic someone I didn't know and who obviously expected more than the microsecond of friction that was all my over-excited member could tolerate before it spilt numbly into the little rubber teat of the condom. No mystery, no pleasure, no words, just excitement and humiliating detumescence.

Thereafter, the carnal came late, and I became acquainted with passionate and forlorn romance, borne of that bewitchment of beauty, of pale skin and dark hair, and all that the sixties girls did to their eyes and lips. The itch was there, but the fundament was that she was on my arm, that the guys' heads spun, that in the quiet of the river valleys, the fair Glamorgan meadows of my school youth, she'd listen captivated, a reflecting glass to my soul.

Oxford was a disappointment. In science I found no answers. I was, in any case, a year advanced of my contemporaries, except in the dreary reaches of biochemistry deemed essential to the course. The University had an Expedition Club, and here I caught the fever for wilderness. In a year I had organised a sortie to Africa, to Kenya's northwest frontier. Our one University staff member, our leader, pulled out, and I, by default, led the six scientists in the team, some already postgraduates. It was a major undertaking. Tons of equipment, three months in high altitude rainforest, hire of Land Rovers, trackers and skinners, collecting of specimens. We discovered a new orchid, white and pale, deep in the darkest of the ravines, the only flower on the forest floor, bright like the moon. Africa kept me alive. A leopard's cough ten paces behind, never seen. Thick bamboo with the buffalo dung still steaming, looking slowly round, peering between the shafts for the merest hint of black hide, heart pounding.

We encountered levels of material depravation I had not imagined. Children with no more than an old sack for clothing. Two came to our camp fire one cold day at 11,000 feet in the Cherangani Hills, and haunted my vision,

> I would think back to that timeless morning
> woodsmoke heavy and low
> the smell of Africa
> how they came
> no words spoken
> no sounds of their feet on the hard earth
> how they watched every move we made
> ready to run
> unsettled white eyes
> two frail black leaves on the white bough of Africa
> that cold plateau Africa.
>
> The wind took what warmth they gained
> shivered huddled close
> pulling the goatskins over their knees
> and watching
> lips ugly spread and open
> teeth protruding
> blood veined eyes
> skin more yellow than black taut over the bones
>
> Enduring the long hours of Africa
> the long hours of mist and absent sun
> they watched us
> until dusk when I glanced to the forest
> after some animal sound
> and looking back
> they had gone

We were not accorded the status of alien gods, despite our wealth and power to move so freely. For although many of the people we encountered obviously strove for material betterment, there was also a contentment, an irrepressible joy in life, and a bemusement at the oddity of our scientific pursuits.

Without Africa I would have left Oxford. On return I tried to change course, from Zoology in the final year with its Animal Behaviour, Ecology and Genetics modules, to Philosophy, Politics and Economics. Africa had made its mark, not in the spectacle of its wildlife, but in the simplicity of its people, in their wisdom, and in their perception of the North. Once, on the edge of the desert I had stumbled on a village gripped by famine. On return, I remember walking down Cornmarket in Oxford and counting the shoe-shops. I could no longer go into restaurants. The late sixties saw the birth of Third World politics, of Oxfam, and of a consciousness of our oppressions. I read Fanon. Chomsky came to St Catherine's College and lectured on American power. Fortunately, Alan Bullock, master of the College, counselled me to stick with what I knew and get a degree, for doubtless, I would never have made it through Berkeley, Locke and Hume. There was nowhere to go, no source.

That was when I married Susan. We had met at a dance shortly before I left for Africa. When I had asked her to dance I had not heard her 'no thanks', and she was too polite to leave the dance floor. I was entranced. She was shy, curtains of hair hiding her lovely face. She came to dinner in the college hall. She was most obviously a really nice girl. I had decided that I definitely did not need a nice girl. I needed someone decidedly naughty, decidedly sexual, and who did not want commitment to relationship. Sue was a virgin. I might as well have been, better I had been, already plagued by doubt as I was.

Maybe it was her quest that I shared. There was a sadness in her, an isolation, a door upon which no one had knocked. I wrote to her from Africa. We married before our Finals. We lived in Western Road, not quite South Oxford, a short walk across the bridge to Carfax and the centre of town. I had six months to do my degree, for there had been little study by then. We loved each other within that romance of living together. I will trace its course later, for it is integral to the events of 1984.

Something then was driven underground, something in the falcon's eye, something in the shyness of that woman I married, something in the touch of Africa, and it would lie dormant until the holocaust of feeling that was to culminate in the year to which I will draw you.

Biochemistry had cracked the first whip. Encountered in the sixth form, 'it would', patronised my biology teacher, whom I greatly liked and respected, 'not so much answer your questions about life, as take away the very need to ask them'. I fell for it. Ribonuclides ruled, everything was electrons. My world turned into essays on building-blocks and metaphors of cellular building sites. How proteins were made in the cell. How the genetic code was cracked. The magic of the double helix was the only magic one needed to postulate. All was explainable, would be explainable.

While I got Africa under my skin, Robin McCleery got self-assembly systems under his, and a First in Zoology. The Universe didn't need explaining, it assembled itself. It is no disservice to Robin to say that as a fellow undergraduate he was boring, because he said so himself. He listened to music no one else could listen to and played disharmonies on the saxophone. That, and study for his degree. He is still there in Oxford, although now a Don.

Before then I had held the apparently naive perception that the Earth had a kind of force-field of life energy that surrounded it like a halo, and that living creatures imbibed this energy at conception and released it at death. This was the soul of the earth, an energy that connected all things, a being, no less, that was all things. Other than that fleeting look into the peregrine's eye, I had nothing to substantiate my thought. And so it was lost.

As for her shyness, I know now she was waiting for love and got me instead. She was not schooled to know the difference, and I not initiated, brought first romance, then need. Love came too late for us. And in the touch of Africa there was wildness which also was lost, a wildness of wisdom and heart and love and passion that was lost to politics and righteousness.

I left Oxford with a good degree. I had to leave then. Study and further research were on offer, although not now among the elite, that post having been bagged by the boring biochemist, but it was all unutterably dry and deathly. I taught for a year at the College of Technology in Birkenhead and greatly enjoyed the contact with students. I taught geology and biological sciences. I wore the same green combat jacket I wore in Africa, and jeans. Some kind of naive statement I'm sure, but it miscommunicated. Where I could not bear to spend money on fancy clothes, my colleagues scented a whiff of Mao. There were parallels. I could not fathom why just because someone was more intelligent, academically at least, they should be privileged. All around I could see how we, the professionals, could prosper. Better pay, better pensions, bigger houses. The less clever tended to stay put, with less security, worse housing, health care and diet. It didn't seem to help my sense of justice that in our democratic freedom any one born clever could by dint of application enter a professional class. I was born to a bus-driver and his nursing wife, loving parents more perplexed than pleased, but not unpleased, that their eldest son should go to Oxford. They were saved from Bolton's back-to-backs by the military career my father then followed.

I could not stomach the atmosphere in the college. Lecturers who would talk to the wall as a device to deal with unsympathetic students. I had to have eye contact. There had to be meaning. The best times were field trips up here in the Gwynedd mountains, looking for patterns in the Silurian. I left after a year. Sue and I crossed the Sahara with two others in a single Land-Rover, continuing the love affair with the continent and that vehicle.

There began a certain dilettantic interlude. I had no wish to contribute. Western society was sick. I wished to play no part,

They penetrate
How they damnwell penetrate
and your body wastes
in the oppressing knowledge
that they'll win

at night you wake
and the faces pass before you
godless or gods long dead
in adoration now of the steel and concrete
fabrications of superior mind

they've seen the film
how you roll the cigarette to one side
and light it one hand on the wheel
looking at the thighs of women

somewhere at the back
blackmen laugh
at a future not theirs

at night you wake
urinating the poison from your body
and not sleeping not thinking
hate

On return from the African adventure Sue and I hitch-hiked to southern Germany with fifteen pounds to our name, where a friend from the Oxford Zoology intake had a job and told us there were many more. Mark Rowlands and I had certain similarities. At the back of the lab we boiled up stingrays in acid to extract the exquisite skeleton whilst the rest of the class carefully dissected their specimens' blood systems, nerves and other bits. We worked for IBM. I told them I had a degree in Physics, which was a little stretch of the contents of Oxford's degree package, but the work was easy to master and involved little more than creeping inside room-height computer cabinets and altering bits and pieces according to two-dimensional technical drawings. Each mission was an interesting challenge.

It was bearable as a life-style because I could get to the Alps. By pushing on the doors of death, I got the jolting fix of life I needed, and the time was spent bagging peaks.

We had married in December 1969. Sue had also taught for a year. By 1975, she was ready to resume her profession and we moved to North Germany where she enjoyed the kind of prestige that her competence deserved. I had decided to become a writer and a poet.

IBM Germany had had its influence,

From morning darkness to night
it takes away the very time of living
you sit and watch the clouds moving across your little patch of sky
the sun melting the frost on your square of grass
and that is it
your contact with life
your sole indication of time and movement
for the whole day
for five days a week
twenty days a month
two thirds of your life.

I knew I could not endure office life in the concrete blocks. And everywhere, the Teutonic powerhouse was being rebuilt,

Its now August 73

men everywhere
scurrying yellow helmeted antlike
slaves of the white skeletal monster
antmen brown and foreign
blind instincts of a blind and impoverished homeland
blind to the power they recreate
blind to history.

Buried
beneath the clays of a thousand glaciations
the seed that is me.

But poet I was not to be. I had a passion for birds. It had grown since Flamborough days. There was nothing so thrilling as something new, something way off track, from Siberia, or Arctic Canada. I can still see in

13

my mind's eye two little pale Arctic Redpolls next to our darker streaky species, tiny jewels longblown to my humble patch of headland. And that May morning with the sun not long up, a huge white-under-sided eagle taking flight from my familiar hawthorns on the gorsy hill, circling above as I looked up to a pale-rimmed eye, and its majestic lazy flight off to the east. It would be 10 years before I would see that form again, in the Atlas mountains, *Circaetus gallicus,* never before seen in Britain and not since.

First it had been birds, that obsession with rarity and beauty, then women, then mountains, now birds again. After a brief return to England and Oxford in 1974 and some months at an isolated cottage near Corwen in North Wales, we found ourselves once more in Germany. This time it was North Germany and I discovered the quiet beauty of an empty quarter of that crowded land - Der Hümmling - heaths and peat bogs, silver birch and stunted oaks, with that winter continental light that makes everything pale and crisp, especially the buffs and browns of fallen leaves and dried sedge. I discovered a small lonely mere, supposedly a Nature Reserve, but suffering farmers' drains and ditches all-around, its lifeblood ebbing - Das Theikenmeer. It was a magnet for wintering harriers, magnificent kite-like hawks.

I set about its restoration. I had been befriended by a Lutheran pastor and his family. His two young boys saw in me some small hero and found me followers, a teenage guerrilla force that engaged the local government, united local arch-Catholics with the protestant incomers, and brought welcome relief from the parental fears of drugs, sex and rock-and-roll. We had a project. The boys built a magnificent 'hide' out of recycled telegraph poles. They blocked dykes and ditches, raising water levels, cut down invading brushwood. Slowly the marshland rejuvenated. I taught them about the migrants, succession of trees, we caught and reared dragonfly larvae together.

By then, mystery had re-asserted its presence. I had dabbled with Hatha yoga in college. The asanas or yogic postures had been little more than ways of staying supple. The mountains were now far away, although in the autumn of 1975 I trained with a daily thirty lengths of the open-air pool right through September, swimming 'til I was blue and shivering, and in October ventured to the summit of the Eiger. My climbing partner, from IBM days, one Peter Robertson, with whom I have long lost contact, had a duvet jacket, and I a humble sweater and anorak. We miscalculated and spent a night below the summit, twelve hours of shivering while he slept soundly. Fortunately, there was no wind and a bright moon. Always something outside of me to excite, to thrill, to keep me away from what was inside.

After several months of intensive yoga and days spent quietly by the mere, with little writing work coming my way, some strange sensitivity began to grow. I could feel a vibration in the land, something touching not my skin, or my tympanic ear, nor visible, but enough to chill the spine.

Our first scent of corruption had been with what the Germans call 'Flürbereinigung', loosely translatable as 'cleaning up the landscape'. Farmers were pressured to amalgamate their dispersed possessions into single large fields on the grounds of efficiency. New boundaries were made, not by hedges but ditches. Old boundaries, usually trees and hedges and meandering streams, must be cleared away. Everything ends up neat and square and featureless. The remaining sward is ploughed and re-sown and fertilised. All herbs and flowers disappear. No butterflies, no dragonflies, few birds.

To save the mere this process had to be halted well away from its small boundaries. We did it. I suspect one not insignificant factor was our prying into the local record books on land purchase. There were obviously things better left hidden from the Common Agricultural Policy funding officials. Whatever, we had won our first reprieve.

The second occurred whilst visiting a government office and looking at maps of my dearly-loved marshland where I noticed a planned new road. It was odd, it seemed to curve in a bow toward 'my' small mere. More prying revealed some buying and selling of land just where the road juxtaposed the mere, strangely marked as open water. It was a small local corruption. A cafe-stop and mini-golf, with a little boating pond, and the road could bend a little that way. The regional authorities were alerted and the developers backed off.

The third encounter was more fateful. The isolation of the marshes had an unsuspected advantage. A group of Federal Government officials arrived in the village to explain. They booked the school auditorium, which was packed. We need not fear, it would be a completely safe installation. It would transform the local economy and bring much-needed jobs for the young people who would otherwise leave. Wiederaufarbeitungsanlage. An Again-Working-Over-Plant. A Nuclear Fuels Reprocessing Plant. Six hundred million investment. Yes, there were emissions, but these were harmless. You could sit at the fence and safely eat your lunch.

I had no reason to disbelieve them. Not on scientific grounds, and my politics had been but briefly engaged by Africa and a spell working in Oxfam's office. I knew nothing of nuclear power stations. I was surprised they talked of emissions. From my University studies I recalled radionuclides being used in ocean circulation experiments, and how they concentrated in food chains. But it was not so much thoughts about health risks, as the people these visiting officials had made contact with. These were, after all, people who would be handling a future German stockpile of plutonium, and they were very friendly with certain nefarious characters known locally as 'schwarz', black hangovers from the nazi era. The chilled-spine reaction had been to certain areas of the land where masses of Germans had died in winter workgangs building the Ems-canal. These were no Jews, but ethnic Germans with whom Hitler's state had quarrels- its communists and any others who dared to oppose. There had been hundreds of thousands at nearby Esterwegen, a concentration-camp few outside Germany have heard of. Everyone here knew which locals had taken the jobs and wielded the clubs and rifle-butts. After the war, this empty quarter of Germany had been a natural retreat for some of the lesser characters who could not depart for South America, or South Africa, or who were not prized and spirited away by Soviet and US science programmes.

My political imagination was born. Here were ex-nazis in high places planning a manufacturing operation for the world's deadliest weapons material. Security would depend upon exact accounting. It was widely known that the old nazis had metamorphosed into a modern business mafia, with connections in Brazil, Chile and South Africa, countries which at that time had clandestine nuclear programmes. At the public meeting however, I restricted myself to a few rather naive questions about the radiation doses that would be experienced at the perimeter fence. The answer patronised. The man was obviously lying and knew far more than he was willing to talk openly about. I had raised my head above the parapet, and a fateful course was sealed.

After the meeting a young physicist from Bremen University approached me. There was an underground, an opposition. They knew all about the technology of reprocessing. At the next meeting they would be there in force. In the village there formed a less covert opposition and I, as the only technically literate local, became their advisor. I liased with Bremen, and returned briefly to Oxford to contact scientists there. In Oxford nobody in my circle of botanists and wildlife ecologists had more than the faintest idea on emissions, food chain bio-concentration processes, and the health risks of low level radiation, whereas in Bremen, effectively run as a socialist city-state within the state of conservative Germany, there were professors and students not only actively monitoring the risks of the industry, but dogging the apologist's every step in the communities where an ambitious national programme would place dozens of American PWR reactors, as well as their own make of Fast Breeder (using plutonium fuel produced as a by-product of the ordinary reactors). In addition, there was a plethora of fuel fabrication plants, reprocessing operations, and final waste disposal sites. It was known collectively as the future 'plutonium economy'.

In 1975 there were no publicly accessible documents showing the risks. All decisions had been taken by a technocratic elite in knee-jerk response to the oil-price hike (then known as a crisis, as if the oil was actually on the point of running out). Within two years I came to have an obsessive dislike of the whole nuclear industry, and sought to curtail if not its expansion, which then seemed impossible, then at least its cavalier attitude to radio-active emissions. I put my unexercised brain cells on overdrive, and rapidly acquired expertise in the scientific and legal backgrounds necessary to enter what became a gladiatorial contest. In truth, it was a simple visceral dislike. It is not explainable in scientific terms. It is a matter of the clash of worlds. Mine was a small remote but hauntingly beautiful marshland landscape, where the occasional intruding tractor soon disappeared again into the morning mists, farmers ferrying bales of straw in the winter, muckspreading, cutting the hay; where curlew and snipe brought off their broods amid the slow feet of cattle; where life could speak softly in the whisper of dragonfly wings......and I felt then that something was being spoken, that I was rediscovering a listening I had not felt since the age of fourteen. I would envision the monstrosity on the horizon, a white cement fortress with its stacks and towers and security fences, access roads with six hundred smart new cars every morning....white coats and high-waged pale faces, another world.

The birds would still come to the marsh. I'd seen that before. On the Suffolk coast, when I was sixteen, I'd tasted the exquisite beauty of Minsmere with its wild heaths surrounding hundred of acres of blowing reed, refuge of bittern and marsh harrier. The birds were still there, but I could never go back. The horizon is now dominated by four nuclear reactors and the steel webs of transmission lines. The wilderness has gone. The bond that can exist between human and animal is broken, an intimacy is lost. This cannot be explained to the nuclear mind, which will detail how the edifice may enhance the wildlife interest, heating the water, increasing species diversity, even preventing other developments from encroaching on the reserve. Many conservationists have nuclear minds.

I was not alone in my gut reaction. The Lutheran pastor and his children formed the nucleus of the action-group. Before long, the conservative Catholic farmers were as one against the Anlage. The government had expected to be greeted with open arms, and became ever more patronising and dismissive, running roughshod over local democratic sensibilities. This latter was to prove their undoing. After Hitler, there is a deep fear of losing what has been regained, of not seeing the insidious approach of oppression until too late. The opposition coined the term Electrofascism. The Fast Breeder became a nazi Phoenix. Der Spiegel began a series of revelations on the network of business deals between Germany's nuclear industry, with its smattering of ex-nazi physicists, and their contemporaries in the bolt-holes of Chile, Argentina, Brazil and South Africa. In 1994 we may easily forget the nature of those regimes in the 1970s.

I gained regular contact and inspiration from the group of 'dissidents' in Bremen. Led by the Professor of Physics, Jens Scheer, and of mathematics, Rudiger Schaeffer, and with the support of the department of International Law, they had taken out a series of injunctions against the string of reactors planned for the Weser River, as well as the Fast Breeder at Kalkar. Their undergraduates were all working on socially relevant theses such as environmental health and industrial risk, often in the local communities, and as back-up to the legal teams. They had formed an 'Arbeitsgruppe Politische Okologie' - a Political Ecology Working Group. Ecology in the service of the community, direct and relevant to ordinary life, and more importantly, to political life in the broadest sense. At Oxford I had completed a mini-thesis in my final year on the species diversity of tree-hole communities, you know, the bits where branches have broken off and the rain forms little pools.

Scheer was sacked for espousing Maoist doctrines, but the other distinguished professors were not so easily labelled as communists and subversives. Many of Germany's foremost scientists, philosophers and sociologists were speaking out against what Robert Jungk called the Atom-State. The Federal Government tried the mailed-fist throughout 1975 and 1976. There were fortifications at all the sites and pitched battles ensued with gas, water cannon and mounted cavalry. Demonstrators were imprisoned and fined crippling amounts. However, back in the Hummling marshes, the government were routed. Fifteen hundred farmers occupied the site with tractors, their digging forks raised like prehistoric beasts in defiant threat posture. The industry backed-off to Gorleben, an equally remote forested region astride the border with the East, where at least half of those at risk would have no means of protest.

That year was a year of intense and emotional meetings. I spoke at village halls full of angry, frightened and bewildered country people, unable to articulate their fears, conscious of their ignorance, suddenly aware by what delicate strands their democratic system held together, and by what lengths their supposed representatives in the State and Federal parliament would go to override their view. At one point all of the regional parliaments (the equivalent of our county and district councils and their administrations) threatened to close if they were over-ruled by the State or Federal Government. When the State gave way to this pressure, but moved the project to Gorleben, the farmers of the Hümmling hired 4 coaches and travelled the two hundred miles to rally the locals there against the plant.

I had found some part of myself. Looking down a long table crowded by ruddy faces, in faltering German, and close to tears, sensing the vulnerability of these formidably conservative people with their clearly defined families and roles, I became their articulateness. Not that I was alone. The rebellion was led by the Lutheran pastors, and thoroughly backed by the university students. They were the ones gassed and truncheoned at Brokdorf, Grohnde, Kalkar, Wyhl and Brunsbuttel. My only taste of the action was on a march to the Fast Breeder site at Malville in southern France. Susan and I were gassed, but not before the site was occupied in the face of several hundred armed and black-shirted, jack-booted French troops. The reactor was called Super Phenix, although quite what France wanted to resurrect thereby I do not know.

I wrote a small semi-sociological piece in 1977, which was published in the Ecologist. It became a standard text for the Open University course on the control of technology, and opened contact for me with the radical technology movement as it then was in Britain. Godfrey Boyle, Peter Chapman and David Elliott were beginning to provide a philosophical and technological basis for an Alternative Britain. Their work led to the creation of the National Centre for Alternative Technology at Machynlleth in mid-Wales. If I missed the sixties rock revolution, and the student upheaval of 1968, I was in the thick of the seventies' reaction to techno-centric and anti-democratic futures, part of what was then lamely called, 'the alternative movement'.

The 'movement' was to prove naively irrelevant to the coming 80s, but then it felt like the 'resistance' that would one day overcome the oppression. The new fascism was the technocratic mindset: progress equals complexity and control, bigger, faster, more economic...its features were high dams, turbines, uranium and plutonium fuel cycles, motorways, industrial agriculture, and of course, ever more sophisticated weapons systems. The neutron bomb was in vogue in France and being tested in the Pacific. None of this could possible last. The oil would run out. The soil would be exhausted. The nuclear hair-trigger would get pulled.

The scientific opposition was busy formulating the 'alternative paths', alternative energy sources, alternative agriculture, alternative medicine, whilst laying bare the hidden risks of contamination, radioactivity and pesticides, or of eventual world desertification and starvation. There was plenty to grapple with as a scientific ecologist. This was the final battle to stave off Armageddon. The very fate of Mankind was at stake.

As you might appreciate, I was not much of a lover. Or any kind of companion for that matter. People avoided me at parties, which were in any case, few. I had become serious and obsessive, tight as a coiled spring. In 1976 we moved back to Oxford. I enrolled for a Diploma Course at the

Institute of Social Anthropology. Oddly enough, to study religion, or to be more exact, religious perceptions of the world. There was a battle-weariness, but also a deep questioning. It had become clear to me that 'the opposition' were motivated by a particular emotional response to the world, to existence, just as we, in the resistance, were motivated by feelings we quickly learned to hide. The battle had been fought on some coldly rational no-mans-land of risks and benefits, legal rights, projections of demand, limits to growth, pollutant feedbacks....all rational debates focussed upon physical survival, a material debate. Yet on both sides there were deeper symbols of the divide, kept well out of the court-rooms, public hearings, and the debating forums from schools to parliaments.

I felt the need of sociological training. In Germany there had been radical sociologists active in the movement. They had been alive to the use of symbol and hidden motivation. My scientific training had left me unprepared for the use and abuse of factual evidence. I had been brought up to view science as an objective pursuit of knowledge, of the establishing of agreed truths, as value-free and apolitical. The German experience had been a political baptism. No scientist was free. Each had their paymaster. Few could dictate the questions to be asked, the choice of project, few controlled the publication and dissemination of research. The great edifice of science served the technocratic machine like some modern-day priesthood. Most disturbingly, the scientists did not see themselves as lackeys to a particular political system, they were religiously but unconsciously devoted to its values, which they saw as an ultimate truth of human progress.

Much as I felt the alternative philosophy was a truer one, I did not champion it and restricted my combat to the right for a fair hearing, and access to that suppressed body of information without the suppression of which the technocrats could not hope to hold their power. Uranium and plutonium fuel cycles presented horrific risks - the scarring of sacred lands in the winning of the ores, the potential melt-down of reactor cores, leaking or exploding waste tanks, and bioaccumulation of discharged radioactivity in food chains. These were hardly the only risks of a technocratic future, and not even the worst, but the nuclear industry had become the flagship. If it could be sent down, then the whole lot could be turned around.

Apart from the need for a secure base, for the Institute might prove a springboard into University teaching, Susan and I needed to settle and recuperate from what had been a dark time. My psyche had been full of nazi-plots and networks, agri-mafia and corruption, and we both needed a rest from that. I launched myself into Africa, but this time in the pages of Evans-Pritchard and Godfrey Lienhardt, of the Dinka and Nuer peoples and the mystic language of nomads. African witchcraft provided a study point for systems of perception, of cause and effect, illness and health, God and spirits, so divergent from our own that the counterpoint would begin to highlight the cultural roots of our own high-blown perceptions of reality. I also read Castaneda.

My tutor at the Institute was the linguistic anthropologist, now deceased, Edwin Ardener. I had the greatest difficulty understanding any sentence he uttered, but somehow the effort was rewarding in un-measurable ways. I had the feeling all social anthropologists wanted to be another Malinowski or Durkheim and that most knew they would never be and displaced this upon a hope they would tutor the next Durkheim or Malinowski and gain the honour that way. They had fixed ideas of what would constitute greatness, related, of course, entirely to what had gone before.

As long as I produced essays on these great names and their thoughts, especially critical essays, I was a contender. I enjoyed the first year of doing that, but most especially prided myself on spotting Castaneda's fictions before it was more widely suspected. The problem was that I approved whole-heartedly of his deceptions, and especially that he had been awarded a Doctorate for field work he made up. I can readily accept that Castaneda had some remarkable encounters, and probably did have a teacher of the stature of Don Juan, but the works were constructed and all the more brilliant for that. And all the more acceptable to me as a poetic art of interpreting cultures. He had presented 'non-consensus reality' in the only way it would penetrate the techno-culture, as factual encounter in the journey, however personal, of a qualified scientist.

However, my leanings toward study could not break the psychic tautness that held me to the nuclear industry. The newspapers reported that British Nuclear Fuels had applied to build a new Reprocessing Plant to augment its already dilapidated operations at Windscale. The plant, known as THORP after the 'thermal oxide' spent fuel it would take from the next generation of reactors, was identical to the German operation. I called on Friends of the Earth to offer my help. FOE had little interest. Walt Patterson and Amory Lovins were handling the brief and engaging lawyers for the Public Inquiry. They were only interested in proliferation of nuclear material, and arguing for an alternative energy programme. Discharges were not an issue.

I was disturbed. I had seen the figures for Windscale's discharges. For the last year in which details were available, which was 1974, the emissions were thousands of times higher than the German plant would be licensed to emit. Particularly disturbing were the massive releases of plutonium into the marine environment, a metal that would remain radio-active for tens of thousands of years, and of which one-millionth of a gram was a fatal dose. Quick perusal of Ministry of Agriculture records revealed BNFL had begun discharging huge amounts in 1970, and within a few years had topped a quarter of a tonne. The nuclide would have sedimented and remained in the vicinity. Theoretically, it could be reworked by currents, loosened by storms, spray-blown to shore, or accumulated through shell-fish adhering to the mud. None of this appeared in BNFL's application. Nobody seemed interested in the issue and I started to write in the press. By the summer of 1977, I had been joined in my concern by other scientists, in particular Dr Brian Wynne, a metallurgist turned sociologist at Lancaster University, and with local concerned citizens and the ecologist Edward Goldsmith's rather more flush and famous brother James offering expenses, we scoured the planet for experts: Prof. Edward Radford on the hazards of low level radiation (then chairman of the US National Academy of Sciences specialist group on the subject); Dr Vaughan Bowen, radiochemist and oceanographer at Woods Hole Oceanographic Institute, Massachusetts, and leading expert on the fate of plutonium in the marine ecosystem, and Dr Sadao Ichikawa, a leading Japanese geneticist studying the cellular effects of emissions from the nuclear industry.

I left the Institute, with apologies, before the Diploma exam. Fortunately, with what we had saved, we had not used public money and I could simply postpone things. But Susan was unhappy in deeper ways that I could then know. We were expecting a child, Matthew, who came in December of that year. I committed myself to the Inquiry of 100 days. She wanted to come, to live nearby, to give up her own studies (for a new teaching qualification in English as a Foreign Language). I could not agree to it. Fateful nobility. I was convinced the whole Windscale environment was polluted and no place for a pregnant woman. It was not just the radioactivity- we would hardly be exposed to that, but the whole negativity of the battle, and what it did to me. I did not expect to return. Like some bloody hero riding into the sunset, a real sense of doom, an ending. It is pathetic in retrospect.

I had an entirely pessimistic expectation of the consequences of taking on the British establishment. No career seemed possible. I wanted Susan safe. She had her own circle of friends. As an insanely jealous, possessive and self-doubting unreconstructed male, the bravest I could manage in response to her intimations of an open marriage, was 'I don't want to know anything'. For all the growing estrangement, she was my refuge, my sacred spring, fountain of beauty and source of love.

At the Windscale Inquiry we made radioactive discharges a public issue. I cut my legal teeth. Other opponents were firing their expensive lawyers because they foundered under the weight of technical facts. It was easier for us to imitate the silks, and within weeks, the press had grown to appreciate that. In the public at large there was a sizeable literate audience who, if they would not or could not articulate their own opposition, were thankful someone was doing it. This number included not only academics, but government officers and scientists afraid to give voice to their own criticisms of the corruptions they encountered in their own profession. At the end of the Inquiry I had a reputation, a small group of committed colleagues, and a foundering marriage. Matthew was borne into an atmosphere of uncertainty, doubt and tension, of questions not asked, of a struggling physical love devoid of real communication, fear of asking and looking small, fear of answers and acting even smaller.

Economically we were kept free by the Rowntree Charitable Trust's grants to my new organisation: the Political Ecology Research Group, PERG for short, and pronounced 'purge' by the cantankerous establishment lackey, Lord Justice Parker, who served as a supposed objective Inspector at the Inquiry. I embarked on a book of the play, for it had been pure theatre, and re-enrolled for the Diploma. Susan kept her secrets.

In all of this a certain darkness of our dearly beloved State had also manifest. Voices on the telephone. Articles in the Daily Telegraph about PERG and others being funded by Moscow. Visits from Special Branch on the pretext of searching for aliens - foreigners, that is, for these were the days before David Icke. Nothing very severe and totally mild by the standards of other countries, but it had its effects. 'They' made it obvious they knew our movements, the content of letters and phone calls. I had nothing to hide and made no concessions, but it left an atmosphere of oppression, the more so because they were probably free-lancers for the nuclear establishment's special police force, building up their files on the pretext of preventative medicine. For certainly, in the days of Baader-Meinhof, I had come close to such nihilistic persuasions, and we had come to know things of use to terrorists, such as the vulnerability of high-level liquid waste tanks to small explosive charges the consequences of which would outdo a minor nuclear weapons attack.

This brings you to 1978. The year of my first contract as a self-employed critical scientist. The year Susan's secret broke. The year of my breakdown. The year I began to recover my selfhood. I will not elaborate now. This started out as a prologue, to introduce myself as a rather traditionally educated person possessed of the rational faculty and a sharp intellect. I was not a flower-child of the 60s, which at its outset I spent birdwatching, then studying for A-Levels, haunting the discos and loving the Beatles, and taking nothing more mind-expanding than Coca-Cola and an Oxford Degree. I was an old-fashioned democrat. I believed in our Parliament, not because it was effective, but because I did not know of a workable and likeable alternative. By 1978 I believed in its potential for improvement, to give MPs more power, more research facilities and less theatricals, and to weaken the power of secret cabinet committees, dealers and fixers between Ministers, bankers, industrialists and the military.

Between 1978 and 1983 I made thorough use of my legal and scientific skills. PERG became known internationally as a reliable source of technical support for citizen's initiatives, local and regional government, and to such august bodies as the professional planners' Town & Country Planning Association, which published my book on the Windscale Inquiry, and above all the newly growing environmental lobby groups such as Friends of the Earth and the activists at Greenpeace.

A precarious living evolved as we gained credibility and contracts. Our team consisted of the engineer, Gordon Thompson, a brilliant mind fresh out of Balliol, with a doctorate in plasma physics that had been sponsored by the Atomic Energy Authority; Martin Stott, fellow Oxford graduate in geography who did his Master's degree on sociological aspects of the Windscale Inquiry; Robert Jones, undergraduate biochemist; Kate Davies, doing a PhD in biochemistry; Roger Kayes, Cambridge marine zoologist with a smattering of economics from Yale and a spell as a county planner; Alan Francis, ex-Atlas Laboratory computer specialist; Charlie Arden-Clarke, Oxford zoology graduate (when not radio-tagging otters for his Masters degree in Natal). We had a formidable array of brain-power and could within a matter of a few months match the expertise of any industry or government scientific lobby. By 1983, I had produced, with Ian Sanderson, one of our Doctoral associates based at Leeds University, a major review of Alternative Energy Strategies for the European Parliament, given seminars in Strasburg and at the Commission in Brussels. We had good press in the science journals, and I spoke regularly on TV and Radio.

During the five years from 1978 through to Christmas 1983 two major elements of what happened in 84 need to be introduced. I will do so but briefly and then craft into the narrative what details may illumine that year. Firstly, I became chief scientific advisor to Greenpeace, working on ocean dumping of radioactive waste, in which Britain was the world's major culprit, as well as Windscale discharges and the aftermath of the French testing at Mururoa in the Pacific.

Secondly, my emotional world collapsed into turmoil at the beginning of this period as Susan and I began a long and drawn out process of separation. We had lovers and the patina of new age aspiration cracked rather quickly into jealousies and accusations, argument, distance and hurt. I still clung self-righteously to the Christian concepts of marriage and our vows of lifelong commitment, but Susan lived separately by 1983, and I suffered an agonising exile from the daily rhythms of the children. Owen was born in the middle of this, in 1981.

The emotional upheaval of these years was a double-edged sword. I had entered a mire of stress and torment, blame and bloody-mindedness. My body was tense and irritated, my mood obsessive and depressive, unable to unleash my angers because I judged them unfair. It was I who could not reach the ideals of selfless love and unpossessive behaviour, or magnanimous support of Susan, who by the end of the five years of turmoil lived in west Oxford in a neat little two-bedroom house, whilst I slept on my office floor off the Cowley Road, manfully but foolishly paying all the bills. During those years before 1983 we had lived together, although seldom sleeping together, and for all of the growing forces pulling our psyches apart, there was a determined effort to stay committed. Our difficulties opened us to new people and sources of help that I doubt I would have contacted otherwise.

In the mid-1970s I had been part of a small group of Oxford intellectuals, several of whom had been the scientists working in PERG, who helped lay the foundations of what was to become the Green Party. Anthony Cheke was a driving force, science-trained at Cambridge and I had been with his Zoologist brother in Kenya. I knew that in addition to his ecological work, he was involved in Co-Counselling networks, forms of self-help therapy. I needed more than therapy, but he was my first port of call, and he quickly realised he would need to pass me on to more impartial hands. One Dave Wilmott and his lady, Cathy Sunshine, came into my life.

It was hard to believe they could help. Firstly, he was undeniably happy. Not for him the woes of eco-catastrophe. Cathy was the first Earth Mother I had encountered. Serene, concocting the most brilliant dishes out of the most mundane roots and leaves, pulses and seeds. Dave salvaged my psyche and taught Susan and I to communicate and see each other. There was little theory or practice, just a steady unlocking of the heart aided by his ample flow. One late night he left the flat he shared with Cathy on a sudden mission and with the parting words, 'if you want to sleep with Cathy its alright with me'. I did want to sleep with Cathy. She was hugely pregnant and exuded an aura of peace, an energy that was tangible to my jaded spine and caused a bulging erection if I came within five feet of her. She had been most clear about her boundaries, she only had sex with Dave. We laughed at my desire, a celebration not an embarrassment. I left the next morning supercharged with life-force, without a wink of sleep, and polished off the Diploma Exam in Social Anthropology. That more than anything began the shift in my sexuality, hitherto always dark, needy, apologetic to itself, always ejaculated and relieved, never stored and savoured, and always without innocence.

I needed other expert help. Peter Mole, St,Catherine's graduate and now a doyen of acupuncturists, lived around the corner and was newly qualified. My first encounter with alternative medicine began, 'I'm glad you have come, another few months and you would be seriously ill, probably dead'. He talked of a polarity reversal, a build-up of negative energy discernable in the electrical patterns of the skin and in the delicately mapped meridians that channel energy from organ to organ. The pattern was always the harbinger of serious and often fatal illness such as cancer. The diagnosis, a stake-out of needles across the back, was also the cure as the energy was drained away and healthy polarity resumed.

My irritability ceased. Moreover, haunting obsessive thoughts about Susan's lover, which repeated at five minute intervals every day for three months, disappeared within a week. I took up squash and running. The course of acupuncture lasted several months, but Dave was the mainstay of my recovery process.

I had wondered from what source he gained his irrepressible well-being. On the wall of their flat was a picture of a ridiculously dressed shiny-cheeked fat man, little more than a boy but got up like a king. Kitsch in reds and golds. The Guru Maharaji. I dismissed it. But then Dave and Cathy had something that I wanted, and that was not apparent in any of the circles I moved in. One day I looked a little closer. The eyes were mischievous behind the disguise. For Dave, 'gumraji' was Jesus and Buddha and Krishna all rolled into one, the avatar of our age. He laughed at the get-up, the Rolls Royce and the Mansion in Florida....'everyone's expecting another carpenter to walk out of the desert in rags and poverty. When Jesus came, they were all expecting a King, in splendid clothes and riches....but the Divine will never meet expectation. Expectation kills the Divine. This time he's come as a King, and of course those who want a beggar from the desert will turn away, and those who can see will draw closer'.

I approached the Guru. The essence was to become a Premi, a Lover. Not of him, but of the ultimate Great Teacher or Master, which was the Divine Light within. The Guru led you toward that light. But the light was not readily accessible to the likes of me. It would have to be worked for. First came Initiation, a process of gaining, or being given 'Knowledge'. To get that you had to attend 'Satsang', meetings of devotees who would share their experience, one at a time, while everyone listened. It was horrible. Sycophantic nonsense. Intolerable hour after hour of romantic slush, mostly from women who surely had missed the point and were in love with the dancing fat man.

I had to get to him, usually spelt Him, yet only those with 'Knowledge' were allowed to have 'darshan', a microsecond of an audience.

Nevertheless, I joined a long line of shuffling devotees at Birmingham's National Exhibition Centre, the only place big enough to fit all ten thousand of the queue at once. The place was silent, permeated by a peace, a solidarity, not solemn but quiet, abiding, waiting for something both infinitely joyful and infinitely poignant. Maharaji was at the end of a tented tunnel of yellow canvas, on either side of the queue were the Initiators, who, sensing any un-readiness, quietly pulled the odd person from the line and led them away. If I got past them then I was ready.

Nearing his presence the air was electric and my skin and spine tingled. His eyes met mine only momentarily. I was pole-axed, my knees gave way and I had to be carried sobbing from the tent. I had looked not into the eyes of a simple fat and happy boy, but the depth of love in the Universe. I felt recognised and known. That Love knew 'me'. This sudden realisation went like a knife through the layer of superficial consciousness that was my personality, to a deeper place, a me that was a part of that love as surely as my arm was a part of my body. It was a homecoming and an irresistible grief overcame me.

The formal initiation escaped me until a year later. I could not stomach the devotees, the most precious of whom were celibate and lived in ashrams of semi-detached, suburban houses with the curtains drawn. My judgemental side took some time to subside and the Initiators kept telling me I was not ready.

Things I was not accustomed to, began to happen. I had my first lover, Gillian, and for a couple of months lived separately from Susan in a bedsit. Gillian brought my sexuality back to life. The deadness I had felt in my system evaporated in her presence. She had approached me after a lecture I had given at Oxford Polytechnic, and began to attend strategy meetings of the embryonic green party. Not finding the voice to break through the formal talk I had scribbled her a note, folded and pressed into her hand,

> Would that I in times of gentle dark
> could close the space between
> and listening silent to your heart
> would not fear
> clarity power death.

She came close to me in those awkward years. As a student of international politics, active in the anti-nuclear movement, she understood and respected my work, although I had little need of that. I was captivated by proportion, once more, and a delicious pheromonal scent of skin that would raise my spirit in ethereal salivation. Perhaps this awakening was also a trigger for other phenomena. One morning she had not long left my

27

bed. I was dozing, when suddenly the mattress inverted and was instantly stuck to the ceiling, with me looking down at where I had been and impervious to gravity. I was bemused rather than frightened and re-imposed normality by insisting 'this is not happening' repeated about three times before the Universe suddenly complied.

If that was a test, the ordeal was to follow. New Year's eve 1979, we had a party in the house Susan and I were once more sharing. My sister had come. I should introduce her, and the rest of my siblings, two brothers. My sister was also called Susan. I saw little and knew little of her after she had left my parents home at 19. As a teenager she had experiences which we took little notice of, contacts with spirits in her room, and had now for several years been in training with Wiccans. My younger brother Ron had also been a remote figure, having spent the last year or more circumnavigating the Mediterranean on a bicycle. He had just returned and we had been in strained discussion about Knowledge and Maharaji, whom he felt distinctly hostile to. He talked of his own contact with spirit, a spirit of Nature, that to me at once seemed dark and treacherous compared to the simple source that was Divine Light. My middle brother Robert was teaching English in Spain at this time and caught in a tempestuously incompatible marriage, after flirting with ascetic Buddhism in the jungles of Thailand, an affliction he picked up as a romantic student at Durham University.

As far as I am aware, my parents never did anything in this lifetime deserving of such strange karmic consequence as brought by the four of us. They did not read books. They did not go to church. My father liked cars and aeroplanes and to his great credit, after being a thoroughly right-wing foil to all of my student rages against Britain's imperial legacy, and having spent his technical life maintaining either nuclear-tipped missiles or army helicopter gunships, became chairman of Andover's branch of the Liberal Party.

I was telling of another party. The bells of Jericho's church were tolling midnight. Our room was momentarily quiet. Someone dimmed the lights and we waited to raise a toast. I looked across the room at Susan, my wife, whose face, and only her face, had turned a deep blue. Tricks again. Then the room began to move, or rather sway, and my knees felt decidedly unsteady. Had I been slipped something? Sister Sue had earlier given me a powdery substance to chew. 'Moroccan black' she had called it. Harmless cannabis. They had all had some. I never smoked the stuff and knew only that it could make you laugh at jokes that were not funny. I had surely been slipped something stronger, perhaps in the drinks. I was furious. I hated the thought of any drug, kept my body as pure as I could. I wobbled discretely to the kitchen where I found a friend and PERG associate, Andy Sluckin, who by now must surely be a professor somewhere, but then was studying for his doctorate in psychology, and knew about these things. I asked him to follow me upstairs, said I was beginning to hallucinate. I sat on the bed, held his hand, told him not to leave me, that I would shortly let go....

At first there was a pleasant kaleidoscope of colour, patterns spinning around, and I thought, 'oh, this is fun, all that stupid resistance and this all that happens'. Then it was as if unseen hands gripped mine, forcing them together and pressing them into the floor. I opened my eyes but the room went white, leaving me completely engulfed in a blizzard of light. My hands stayed pinned to the floor by an external force, and I sat helpless and expectant. There was a presence in the room. My spine chilled. I could see no shape or form, just a sense of unmitigated evil. I strained to pull my hands apart and work against the force. If I could get them apart, get them free, I could place them in 'mudra' as protection against what was to come. I sweated with the effort, eventually working against the energy that pinned them and forming a triangle of fingers, tips touching. It seemed to take an age to get the last finger in place, a huge effort of will to direct it into position against the invisible pressures around it. Once achieved, I felt immediately stronger. Then suddenly my body disappeared. I could not feel it and looking down at my hands, could see nothing. In reaction, my hands shot up to my face in horror. They passed over the surface of the skin but I could feel nothing except my lips, as if they were the only part of me still materialised. The 'presence' laughed. My triangle of forces had been easily broken by this simple trick. I issued a scornful challenge. 'Games! So what! I know what's real'.

The forces redoubled their attack, trying to rip my hands apart and bearing down on my body like a vastly increased gravity wave. I felt sick, as if I would be crushed. My whole spirit and will raged against the onslaught. I would not give in. The energy came at me in repeated waves, a lull as if to catch my defences down and then a surprise attack, then rose to a constant penetrating scream to submit, to give in, to surrender. The evil presence seemed to dance wildly behind the white-out, dashing close to my ear, urging my surrender, confidant of winning.

In one of the lulls, Matthew, then just able to toddle, entered the room. I could hear his voice to one side, and Sue inquiring if it was alright for him to come in. The energy about me was now like a sheet of luminous yellow flame. I could see nothing beyond it, yet as Matthew came in and walked about the room I could see him clearly through the flame, as if his body parted the waves. I knew he was untouched and that his innocence kept him safe. He came close and looked at me and I could see him clearly, though no one else.

There was one more bout of strong pressure waves, which I again fought to resist. Then a calm. Momentarily the force field about me disintegrated and I came back to normal vision and cool reality. I was drenched in sweat from the enormous effort. Andy was there, hand on my knee, concerned, as I related what I had experienced. I knew it was not over and gathered my strength for the next bout. It must have taken hours. The house felt quiet. There was only Andy in the room.

Again my vision was wiped out. But this time I felt as if I was sinking. All about me was sea-blue. I was at some great depth and being drawn down into an ever deepening and darkening abyssal prison. I did not know how to resist. A hand grabbed mine. Looking along my outstretched arm, to his outstretched arm, I saw Maharaji's face. He held me fast and started to ascend. Suddenly there was a look of doubt across his face. How could this be? Maharaji, the master, in doubt? In a moment I was back in the depth alone. There seemed no hope, no way of getting back. I felt on the verge of resignation. Love had been conquered. The ruling power was force and evil. I began to affirm that love was at the heart of the Universe. The presence mocked in response.

'Your master is nothing more than a beginner. Love is an illusion'.

I strengthened my affirmation. 'I have seen. I have seen. I have seen that there is love in the Universe.' It was enough for me that love existed. To love I owe my allegiance.

'Do your worst. I have seen God. Love exists. Love exists. Love exists'.

Slowly the power of the mantra broke the forces holding me down and my body began to ascend through the dark blue waters, through paler blue-greens to the light. I came out of the spell. Andy was still there in front of me. He smiled. 'You're out'.

'I think so. I think its over.' I was helped to my feet and down the stairs. The ordeal had lasted four hours. Hot soup and bread was laid before me. My taste buds exploded with delight. The party had broken up swiftly. Roz, one of Sue's Wiccan friends, had attempted to come and help, but had been forced back and had commented, 'Not even a priest could go in there right now', such was the overwhelming sense of evil.

It took a week to integrate. The world was as the Catholics had always said, a war-zone of Good and Evil. The Devil was real. I had met him. But I hated to capitulate, and slowly sense re-asserted. I had met my projections and fears. I had been tested. I had been strengthened, though chastened. The Devil was simply that which must test our faith. How could love grow strong on a diet of syrup? The Universe became One again.

I do not know when I first read Yogananda's 'Autobiography of a Yogi', or even why. Perhaps it was about this time. Certainly Susan and I had been practising Hatha yoga but had taken things no further than health and positivity. Gillian joined me in breathing and stretching exercises and Maharaji promised initiation into deeper secrets. Dave had been a flower-child. Groups and communes, Acid, sex and Elvis Presley (his other Guru! He never seemed to explore the darker developments of Rock), and having seen the lot, settled for the peaceful meditative life. He arrived late one Sunday evening and insisted I join him for a week in London. He had met an American by name of Leonard Orr, who had discovered 'rebirthing'. Whatever Orr had to offer, if it moved Dave, then it had to be extra-ordinary. But a week, and at a cost of £85 excluding meals, it was out of the question. As it happened I had a television interview that Monday and would be in Town. On the coach from Oxford the next morning I began opening my post. An envelope from a client contained some expenses I had not been expecting....exactly £85. Being by then not impervious to such nudges, I went to see Leonard that evening at the October Gallery.

I have normal sight. I do not see auras or ghosts or disembodied divine masters. But Leonard had a white halo. I ignored it. A trick of the light. He began to talk of his encounter with the immortal yogi, Babaji, who lived in a cave in the Himalayas. Yogananda had met and been taught by an immortal who appeared to him out of a ball of light, and who had held a physical body last in 1922. Could this be the same Babaji? Leonard was convinced it was he, and retold the villagers' story of finding a young sadhu in Babaji's cave by the river where he had last taught before disappearing into a ball of light in 1922. When the old men were fetched from the village, they saw an old man they recognised as Babaji, whereas to everyone who didn't know the old master, they saw a man of youth and beauty. He arrived in 1970 and was now still there, and Leonard had become his pupil. Someone at the back interjected, 'what colour is your aura?', to which Leonard replied it was usually white. I decided to stay for the week.

2

The Warriors

In the approach to Christmas 1983 I found myself in the London office of Greenpeace for a meeting with brother Robert. On his return from Spain I had persuaded him to enlist. He had, by now, some considerable experience of 'toxics' campaigns, having worked in the Amsterdam, Vancouver and Hamburg offices on these issues. He was near the end of a long and successful battle against Tioxide, a multinational producer of Titanium Dioxide for the paint industry and a major polluter by discharge and dumping into the North Sea.

Robert had taken a double honours in Botany and Geology from Durham University. He, too, was no flower child, and although rather more flamboyant than I, only marginally less repressed on the feminine and intuitive side of his nature. There was an unspoken tension between him and Pete Wilkinson, campaigns director, whom he greatly admired but could not emulate. The office generally was a tense place. The old-guard in Greenpeace were largely left-leaning macho males and sexism was evident in the clear demarcations of campaigners, male, and their assistants, female. Elaine Lawrence was an exception, sometime campaigner, sometime board member, but right now keeping her head down until the new age could dawn.

Robert had been baptised several times in the effluent of the paint industry. The technique had been to wade up to the waste pipes from the seaward end and plug them with a bung. Quite spectacular on film, as the pressure would create a massive fan of liquid. The effluent was largely acids and heavy metals and Robert joked frequently on the potential side-effects on his sensitive brain. He had been close to death as a child, poisoned by a proprietary talcum powder containing mercury salts.

Our paths did not cross professionally. I was deeply embroiled in the nuclear dumping issue. Pete Wilkinson had worked hard on the shipping unions to black the dump ships, and I had busied myself with the UN forum for international treaties on ocean dumping, known as the London Dumping Convention, where a concerted legal and scientific campaign through 1982-83 had forced a moratorium. The British government then said it would not abide by the majority vote. However, after a spectacular campaign orchestrated by the Rainbow Warrior off the Spanish coast had brought the matter to public view and international opprobrium, the National Union of Seamen had forced a momentary compliance.

Ron had not escaped the family affair. Knowing his taste for adventure and love of deserts, Robert and I invited him in the summer of 82 to take a short walk into Nevada as part of a select international gathering of three among the rocks and gravel of the US nuclear test site. They held out undetected while British tests were postponed and the protest made in Parliament. Few people knew Britain tested its weapons there. He then began training Greenpeace teams, and in the summer of 1983 we had all spent a night in Cannon Row jail following a little-known failed attempt to climb Big Ben from rubber boats floated across the Thames. The police had bugged and otherwise penetrated the UK office and the team never made it across the river. Prime Minister Thatcher had been well-pleased, but Ron was now working on the return match.

Robert's compartment of the open-plan office is immediately apparent. There are plants everywhere. Nothing very exotic, spider-plants draping down over the filing cabinets, Monsteras and rubberplants, the usual haul from the corner-shops in Islington. The other compartments are bare by contrast. Everyone busy. A campaigner's life is ninety percent telephone conversation.

Robert looks serious. I have always had the sense when I watch him that he is acting, and he has done his whole life, like a movie, conscious of the camera, a self-conscious bad actor. When he is acting serious it shows even more. I have come to like and appreciate the added colour. He is flamboyant. Red necktie, calf-length boots, hair to his shoulders. He reminds me of Jack Nicholson, the broad forehead and a fleeting wildness. The rest of the office is comparatively Spartan, each compartment with piles of files and paper, pin boards and schedules, and every available space carries personal postcards, dolphins and whales, pictures of the boats in action. Every phone is busy. Waves and nods acknowledge my entrance. Robert gestures for me to sit down, and when I do, gestures me up again while he listens intently on the phone, and points to the next compartment. As I peer over, there is the beaming face of youngest brother Ron.

I go round the mountain of filing cabinets and forest of Robert's plants and we hug affectionately. At these moments when the three of us are together, all the office seems to be smiling. Ron and I talk quietly about the 'return match'. The international office has just given its approval. There will be training sessions at our hide-out in North Wales. That is as much as he will say. From now on, everything will be on a need-to-know basis. No one else in the office knows that the 'Ben' climb is on again, and no one except Ron knows the route in. But Ron is here to discuss Robert's targets. Chimney climbs for a coming Acid Rain campaign. There are arrays of photos of power stations and chimneys along the Thames and in

Yorkshire. Choices have to be made and carefully reconnoitred for access. Robert is planning a spectacular. There will be eight climbs in different European countries, including one behind the Iron Curtain in Czechoslovakia. Each team will unfurl a banner with a letter S,T,O or P, and then a slogan in the native language of the country. Ron is stretching his brain trying to work out the combinations of success and failure that would still spell STOP for the front pages.

Robert is off the phone and we exchange questions of family. It is months since I have seen him. It is a testing time emotionally. He has a son the same age as Matthew, now six, and he and Kim Narayan, his wife, have been living apart and at times coming back together for several years. He asks after Sue. I sense that he holds me responsible, not out of a real knowledge of our difficulties, but out of a sense that the older brother should have been wiser, less egotistical. He always disapproves of my anger. There is a wooden Buddha on his desk and pictures of North American Indians among the pasted-up press cuttings.

Robert needs to talk business, and since nothing is ever discussed in the office anymore, two bugs having been removed from the wall the previous week, we leave for the local pub.

'The guy on the phone just now has information on an illegal dumping operation off the Cornish coast. We've arranged to meet this evening and I'd like you both to come and meet him. We've met once already but I'd like you to meet and see what you think. The ships are dumping barrels of nuclear and chemical wastes'.

'How do they know there's nuclear waste involved?', I asked.

'There has already been a massive kill of mussels. That's how they got involved. They heard of the mussel kill and they have a special interest in Cornwall. I've already confirmed with MAFF (Ministry of Agriculture, Fisheries and Food) that the kill took place, and there is a local naturalist who is monitoring the situation, a man called Trevor Beer. He actually saw some barrels on the shore, but they disappeared before he could get back with a camera'.

I was sceptical of the nuclear angle. 'But how do they know its nuclear waste?'

'It contains both Cadmium and, we think, radioactive material. We have a code YE 72 and/or 45 from a white label with orange markings on red brown forty-five gallon drums. The Y means 'extinguishing' agent and the E means protective clothing is necessary'.

Apparently the mussel kill occurred at the end of September through to the middle of October. Official estimates were of 500 tons washed up on that coast. The location was the North Devon coast near Hartland Point. Beer found the barrels at Croyde and reported them to MAFF.

I still could not get a clear picture. Robert had had no success with checking the label in hazardous chemical manuals, nor a name on one of the barrels, MEZERIUM. He talked of a poisoning affecting the byssel threads that attached the mussels to the bottom. MAFF believed the whole event could be explained by storms, but local fisheries officers had seen nothing like it and there had been no severe storms in the weeks prior to the wreck.

'I wanted to show you we had corroboration first. The initial information did not come from Devon. It came from a group here in London. In particular, a guy called John Taylor. You'll meet him tonight. He's a martial artist. N'th Dan Shotokan *and* he's a Tai Chi master. Both the yin and yang so highly developed in one individual. Quite incredible. He and his students had reached a certain level and wanted to do something for the planet. John read about the mussel kill in the press. He meditated. Contacted his teachers. He was told the mussels had been killed by a poison acting on the byssel threads. The poison had been dumped. It contained cadmium and radioactive material. He sent one of his students, he calls them 'the warriors', out on the astral plane, he doesn't go himself, and he saw barrels at the bottom of the sea - described them, red-brown, labels YE 45 and got the letters ME EZIUM. They were leaking'.

Ron and I looked at each other and said in unison, 'astral plane?'.

'Astral surveillance. Martial artists when they reach the higher levels of training can enter the astral plane and carry out surveillance. Some can actually move physically. Ninja used to penetrate defences and carry out assassinations that way.'

Robert would often talk as if he were addressing journalists who knew nothing of these things. It slightly irritated. Of these things I had been aware from a passing interest in martial arts, in which I trained for a year when in Germany, and that yogic masters could operate on the astral plane. Babaji would sometimes appear to people and had been reported bi-locating and materialising his body from light. As a brown belt in Karate himself, Robert was also no stranger to these potentials. Ron took more convincing.

We went over the material carefully. John Taylor's astral work had first indicated there was a dumping operation. Robert had checked out the press reports and tracked down the local naturalist, Trevor Beer. He had written and now had copies of correspondence between Beer and MAFF.

'We needed Beer to get confirmation of the barrels. We thought we knew the port for the ship - the name Appledore had been given. Then the astrals saw some barrels on the beach. It was the middle of the night. They had to get to Beer without spooking him. So one, Charlie, I think, you'll meet him, went out and reached Beer's garden in Barnstaple. There was a hedgehog on the lawn, so he entered the hedgehog and shuffled and scratched at the door, woke Beer, who came out to the garden and looked straight at him, that is, the hedgehog. He communicated the idea to go down to the beach, even though it was the middle of the night. Beer went, saw the drums, got the name MEZERIUM - which we had not got exact until then, and one of the codes YE 72 and colour, they all fitted. Unfortunately the drums had gone by morning so no photographs. Beer told MAFF but they've done nothing so far'.

'Cosmic fucking hedgehogs', was all Ron could say, still appearing decidedly dismissive. 'That's all we need. Who else have you told about this?'

Robert continued. 'The warriors expect us to do something, but I can't go to the board with any of this astral stuff, obviously, we've nothing very concrete'.

I doubted the nuclear connection. Nuclear waste was too strictly controlled. But then the legal dumping operations had been blocked and maybe they had material that was rotting and needed to be dumped quickly. Cadmium was intriguing. It was a neutron absorber, the kind of chemical one just might use to mop up a mess in a waste tank that had gone critical. But such waste would require shielded containers, too large and heavy for this manual dumping operation. There had been rumours at the Windscale Inquiry of a criticality accident at one of the military research bases. That could have been mopped up with cadmium, although boron would have been more usual. It would mean plutonium contaminated wastes, probably some fission products. The plutonium could be shielded by ordinary drums, but the fission products would emit penetrating gamma rays that would place the dumping ships' crews in serious danger. Taking such a risk was not likely, as it would also endanger the personnel wherever the waste was stored prior to dumping.

Ron and I left Robert shortly afterwards. He had to tidy up his office work and we would meet to visit the 'astral warriors' later that evening. We walked around Islington talking mostly of my difficulties back in Oxford. He was less judgemental than Robert. After his return from Africa he had also made a strong connection with Guru Maharaji. He, Robert and I had begun working closely together after we had spent three days at a workshop on the North American 'medicine path', with a Chippewa medicine man called Sun Bear. It had been a homecoming of sorts. Sun Bear held a sacred pipe ceremony in the grounds of a park in Ealing. A soft magic had descended on the group. For a moment I saw us all, ages ago, the same ceremony, elders from different tribes, peace before the holocaust that eventually was to engulf us. A sparrow hawk weaved over the trees and the doves scattered, then a stillness and again that sense of unity, of a dimension that stretched out between all living things as if each had no boundary.

Ron had moved to Oxford and joined our monthly rebirthing gatherings. We had worked now for two years or more on the energies that flowed, or didn't flow, between us, on how we reacted to each other as brothers, on his patterns of holding himself small in relation to me, on mine of acting superior, expecting to be followed, as if I was always right and of his need to keep himself independent, to prove himself in my eyes, in his own eyes.

Once, following an emotional encounter with Sue, I had gone to his room late at night. My energy had been draining rapidly as if someone had thrown a central switch. I lay on his floor in a feotal position and went into a deep trance-like state, barely breathing. I felt I could simple decide to die. I *had* decided to die. The thought surfaced, that if I could not be with the children I did not want to live. That thought had a deep hold upon me and now appeared to be ordering the life to leave me. Ron did not persuade me otherwise.

He simply stated, 'if you want to go it is alright by me. You have to decide whether you want to live'.

It had gone very deep. At its sump I held on by no more than a feather breath, and the decision to live began to make its journey back to the surface. He had held me then without judgement or interference.

In the three years since meeting Leonard we had set up a rebirthing group in Oxford. Anthony Cheke and Dave Wilmott both gave up their jobs to take on the task of full-time barefoot psychotherapists and rebirthers. Each member of the group paid for individual sessions and for a monthly gathering when we would pay someone to come in from outside. Several Americans had led our group. There were about twenty of us. Even Sue had joined for one year. She had also been drawn to Maharaji. For all our difficulties, we had worked together on the emotional patterns that raged between us. Robert had also gone through the rebirthing process, although less intensely. There was a common bond. Dave had likened it to the water-brothers of the book, 'Stranger in a Strange Land'. The more advanced rebirthing sessions had taken place in hot-tubs, the warm pulsating redwood-coloured waters of which mimicked the womb.

We had been opened at levels we had not been open before, our bodies more sensitive, our minds now conscious of their negative thought patterns, of how thought itself was a creative force and created each individual reality. The process involved the simplest of breathing techniques, a gentle merging of the inhale and exhale such that subtle but powerful tensions and holding patterns in the breath are released. The aftermath of modern western birthing techniques had left all of us with chronic breathing tensions, mostly simple holding and pausing, as if laid down by the first frightened grasp of air and freezing shock of light and cold.

Such a simple technique, yet it liberated enormous amounts of energy, heat and muscle tension locked in the chest. With the release of the breath, would often come visions of the birth canal and feelings and impressions of the first entry into the world. Once that trauma had been 'healed' by re-experience and integration, it acted as a passport to experience in the womb and beyond that into an unfurling of past incarnations.

Leonard Orr had fallen upon the technique by 'accident' in the late 1970s and then began experimenting with friends. Soon he had a group of 'new age rebirthers' and had founded a therapy. Into this unsuspecting Californian community of 'conscious breathers' came one night an ethereal visitor, manifesting in Leonard's study from a ball of light, the yogic master we now know as Babaji, Himalayan patron saint of all yogic breathing. He simply pointed and said, 'You friend'. It took two years before a student of Leonard made contact at the Himalayan ashram and Leonard travelled out there to be taken under Babaji's wing.

The breathing did more than liberate physical energy. The tightness in the breath, once released, seemed also to correlate to negative life patterns and the release to then feed back and begin to free up the mental apparatus of the mind. It was as if the breath had become life-affirming and the bodymind no longer tolerant of behaviour that was in any way counter to that. For many that negativity was represented by jobs, marriages, relationships to drugs, alcohol and tobacco. That simple technique literally turned lives upside down. Orr had emphasised the need for support groups, a kind of spiritual community.

Out of this community and its teachers, grew, however, subtle forms of spiritual ambition. We had little critical appraisal at the onset, everything was new, and the energy changes were exciting and eventful. In retrospect, some of us became rather materially focussed. Negative expectations were weeded out and replaced, mostly thoughts about what we did and didn't deserve in the ways of motor cars, clothes, sexual partners and money. I had no doubt of the reality shifts that could occur from observing my twenty or so fellow travellers. On a more philosophic level there were deeper implications. Reality itself now seemed no more than a collective or consensus reality, albeit hard to break out of. Dave gave me Richard Bach's 'Illusions' as yet another contribution to my conscious evolution.

I had begun to examine all of my expectations and deeper thoughts and unconscious conditioning, particularly about women, and was beginning to see why life had brought me such pain and turmoil. There, in my unconscious mind was the menu and it had been delivered faithfully. And was still being delivered. It was not enough to know the programming. The deep structures had to be reprogrammed with discipline.

I told Ron I had reached some limit, some threshold of how far I could go with the help that was available. I had been working with a Dutch rebirther, a former actor called Paul Romer, also a student of Babaji. He had been given the name of Tukaram by the master and sent out to run workshops. Tukaram's workshops were like no other. He worked very differently to Leonard Orr. Where Leonard had systematically classified thought patterns and their karmic consequence, identifying what he called the five 'bigees' or major negative conclusions about life - starting with the first breath and 'life is a struggle', Tukaram worked entirely with intuition, with humour, dance, poetry and drama. The name meant 'arrow that does not hurt'. His insights would come suddenly and penetrate layers of the unconscious, precipitating releases of grief or anger.

In the last workshop with Tukaram I had built a thought picture in a process where all of the mind's negative patterns are painted into the form of a personal monster. Many in the group had received quite simple animal pictures. Mine was amorphous. It had no edges, it stretched in every direction. There was no way to tackle it. If I could name it, it was called 'self importance'.

I had seen the extent of my ego. I could not go further. Tukaram could not help. I had to get to Babaji. I had been petitioning. Each time he would answer telepathically......'you have everything for your learning exactly where you are now'. I had hungered for retreat, to go to the ashram in Herakhan, to purify my mind and body, fasting, yoga, chanting, I would need months of it, years of it. Yet every time I was told to stay with everything here. To keep working in both worlds.

Ron also had contact with Babaji. Firstly as a gentle presence during rebirthing sessions, and then, most strongly, at the turn of the year, he had been motoring across Westminster bridge in the VW camper, returning from a chimney-scouting operation along the Thames, and looking up at Big Ben, seeing the scaffolding newly erected to clean and refurbish the stonework, when Supertramp had come on the radio....they had a single, 'Babaji, why don't you come to me...', one of them had contact, maybe was a devotee. Ron had suddenly seen it clearly... climbing the Ben, and a banner, 'Time to stop Nuclear Testing'. He was sure it was Babaji urging him. Yet that operation had ended ignominiously in Cannon Row jail!

On that night of action there had been Babaji devotees everywhere. Martin Jackson was Ron's co-climber, Maida Suarez was look-out. I had been there on the South Bank that night. How cocksure the police had been. When I had called at the station to see what had happened, they calmly arrested me without even asking if I had been involved. My first time in a jail. It was 5.00 am and cold. Breakfast and a cuppa came seven hours later. The cell smelt of urine and had dried blood smeared on the walls, as if someone's head had been banged and dragged across it. Tiles and cold concrete. By the time we came before the magistrate the appalling prospect of another night there had sapped any revolutionary fervour and I did not embrace the prospect of my honesty being tested by the conditions of release.

Fortunately, I had only to agree to be bound-over 'to keep the peace'. Was that not what we were doing, all along! In clear conscience I could reply, 'certainly, your honour, when you put it like that, I do so agree'.

Ron was now planning the return match. He laughed, mischievously. How, then, the coppers had laid out all the climbing gear. I recalled they had been most impressed. One copper had said, 'You guys really mean business but this is the Houses of Parliament. You could get yourselves shot. Why don't you go to Birmingham, lots to climb there. We had to get the PM out of bed for this!'

Birmingham! We laughed again at the thought.

One of them had leant over to me, showed me a photocopied map, the plan of attack, and whispered, 'You need to watch your backs. Someone in the office'.

Ron had a new plan. 'This time we don't use the river. We come from the street. Total security. That's as much as I am saying. But we do need to know more about what we will encounter on the other side of the wall. I'm wondering if the 'astrals' could check it out for us.'

We would soon find out. We met Robert and headed for John Taylor's house in Greenwich. Delafield Road, down-market semis but respectable. A short blond-haired rather unassuming astral traveller, Charlie, led us to the kitchen. The hall was cluttered with all manner of bric-a-brac, as if collected from flea-markets but never used or sold on. Every shelf was occupied. Pebbles, potted plants, books, shells, children's toys. The house was dark, curtains drawn except for a large window out onto a small garden. In the middle of a patch of grass was a pole with a fibre door-mat wound round at man-height, tied in a tube it simulated a body and was used for practising kicks. John Taylor sat on a high stool behind the kitchen table, hidden initially by the door through which we entered.

'So, the three brothers! Welcome. Robert, I trust you have good news. Things are moving rather quickly.'

Robert had little to report. Beer had been writing to the authorities, had reported the drums. He hadn't got much further with the haz-chem codes. He had other projects and didn't have any resources for this one, not even to make a visit to Devon. There was no way Robert could explain to the Greenpeace board that astral surveillance was involved.

John was irritated and impatient. He could appreciate that Greenpeace needed evidence to act, but the dumpers were still operating. They had more information now, of a store somewhere in the Midlands, near Worcester, or Dudley. They had seen the drums stacked in a warehouse. The navy was involved. He then went into a trance-like monologue, not much of which I can relate because I could not follow. The images came thick and fast. There was much mention of Arthur and Pan. I had had little contact with the Arthurian New Agers, seldom went to Glastonbury, and the language and images were lost on me.

Taylor himself was obviously genuine. He had cat-like grace, a disconcerting hybrid of a strong masculine face, bordering on the ugly, with long feminine hair which he threw aside with womanly flicks of his head. His forearms were wiry and finely muscled and ended in hammer-like fists. There was a sense of deadly speed and accuracy, the lightning grace and competence of an accomplished fighter. His 'warriors' however, did not look the part, and I found it hard to believe they had reached high levels of competence. Charlie's body appeared untoned and unready. I have only a feint recollection of two other men present. Then there was Charmayne, his wife. She taught Tai Chi at the same dojo. She was dark-haired and dark-eyed giving a slightly oriental appearance.

Tea was made on a primitive bottle-gas stove, whilst Robert gleaned more detail from John. There were names of a ship, the port, location of a warehouse, the involvement of the navy. Taylor admitted they were green-about-the-ears, that they didn't know the rules 'on the other side', that Pan was tricky to work with. He agreed to reconnoitre Big Ben.

I had to leave for Oxford, and left as Charlie was to 'go out' to look at the scaffolding around the clock tower.

Robert gave me a lift in a hired van, and we left Ron with the astrals. We talked as he drove me to Victoria coach station. Money was short and I wasn't then running a car. Trains were more comfortable but expensive. We shared about our women. I was less forthcoming than with Ron, wishing to avoid the high-minded lecture about how I ought to know better than to get angry. He had great affection for Sue and the two boys. He spoke also of an eerie feeling of being watched and for the first time had a sense of foreboding and personal danger. He reminded me how all three of us had met on the first day of this year in the woods at Shotover Hill near Oxford, how we had lit a candle and left it burning, a symbol of our commitment to work together. What we were now moving into felt dark and threatening in a way that former campaigns had not. He felt vulnerable, unable to martial his own energy, drained as he was by the turmoil with Kim. As he talked I had fleeting vision of Sue's house in Oxford, from the rear, looking down into the unlit patio and garden.

We embraced and parted. We would meet briefly again at our parents on Boxing Day, a family custom. On the coach I mused over the past year or more. How when Ron had been arrested after the Nevada action, a local reporter had rigged up a phone contact with Ron in the jail, and the sheriff, and then phoned Dad. He'd asked what Dad thought of it all, to which Dad had replied he approved, that Britain didn't need nuclear weapons, nor for that matter, an Air Force to deliver them.

When asked, 'and Mr Taylor, may I ask what kind of work you do', Dad said simply, 'I work for the Ministry of Defence' and declined to say more.

He now worked as a civilian instructor at the Army School of Aviation, as well as being chairman of Andover's Liberals. Maybe we had had some effect over the years. But if 'home' in Andover was harmonious, Oxford was far from it. I would be spending Christmas with Sue and the children. Things were very tense. We had lived apart since October 1982 and I had not yet accepted it. There was a constant clash of wills, of perceptions and judgement. I felt she could not and would not see me clearly, that all of the work I had done since meeting and working with Leonard and Tukaram had changed me fundamentally yet she saw only the old me.

She had finally forced the separation at a time when my work had begun to penetrate the established ways of thinking on energy policy. That October, I had been invited to give a seminar to the European Commission and had travelled over with Ian Sanderson and Roger Kayes. Susan had made her move the day before I was due to leave, and my body was still in shock at what I felt as a betrayal of the past years of effort and progress. It was a grace to have colleagues with me who were also friends.

In the seminar I was on auto-pilot. At some point in the middle, I took a break for a pee. Whilst at the urinal I had a sudden vision. A pair of large sharp scissors cut through what was my umbilical chord, and it was Susan doing the cutting. I felt the emotional shock in my gut, as if death would engulf me. The clarity and suddenness of the vision set me reeling, and I took a few minutes to let the message sink in. On some energetic level, I had made Sue my mother, my sustenance.

I had to gird myself for the second half of the presentation. I have no idea how it kept together.

I was incredibly busy at this time. Only now can I appreciate how unbalanced I still was. In the previous month I had been twice to Strasbourg, once to Rotterdam, once to Copenhagen. I was negotiating to represent the National Union of Mineworkers at the Sizewell Inquiry, working on the radwaste dumping moratorium, the International Water Tribunal's indictment of Britain's nuclear reprocessing operations for polluting the North Sea, the Greater London Council were also keen to mount a case against Sizewell, and we had just finished a the review of Alternative Energy Strategies for the European Parliament. I had given seminars and lectures on energy policy at the Universities of Cambridge, Oxford, Birmingham and East Anglia and was teaching a course at the City University in London.

In November, a Greenpeace diving team checking the Windscale pipeline for a potential bunging operation had been contaminated by a waste spill. The oily discharge had formed a slick and the Geiger counters had gone off scale. I had been involved in the debriefing. The divers were worried (Grace O'Sullivan, one of the team in the Zodiac inflatable was later to give birth to a Down's Syndrome child). I had just completed the first scientific review of the Windscale discharge operations from material garnered at the 1977 Inquiry and it had been requested by marine labs all over the world. The government had ordered fifty copies.

In addition, Charlie Arden-Clarke had worked for me ferreting about in the regional health records of South West Cumbria. We had published a report showing evidence of excess cancers and it had been roundly attacked by various professorial advisors to the County and to the government. Our data indicated a slight excess for the region as a whole, but we could not get access to data which would show the whereabouts of each cancer case, and in particular the childhood cases. If the slight excess was spread evenly over the county, then nothing was likely to be wrong. If they were clustered around Windscale, that would be another story. The government had refused to divulge further data, or to mount a proper survey.

We had worked for six months with a team from Yorkshire TV, led by James Cutler. Their programme went out in November just as the Greenpeace team made the headlines over the contaminated boat. The TV researchers had painstakingly gone from door to door tracking down the cancer victims, as they had done in their previous award-winning documentary on the asbestos industry. The programme, under the 'First Tuesday' series, demonstrated a tenfold excess of childhood leukaemia and brought immense scientific controversy. The government had just announced it would set up an Inquiry into the 'alleged' excess, to be headed by the respected medical professor, Sir Douglas Black.

The nuclear industry was now under intense pressure from all sides. Its land-based search for 'repositories' of waste had stalled through local opposition. The county councils of Powys and Bedford had already employed me to provide sources of alternative expertise. The reactor programme was now subject to a Public Inquiry at Sizewell and a consortium of local authorities and metropolitan councils had also employed us to provide evidence of engineering risk and accident consequences. The miners wanted a health risk comparison of the nuclear and coal fuel cycles. The Fire Brigades Union and the National Union of Public Employees wanted the emergency planning reviewed and compared with other countries.

Thus, my workload had expanded much further than Greenpeace and now stretched from the European Parliament and Commission, through national government, to local councils. The financial pressures promised to be alleviated, although as yet, there was little extra money on the table.

This was also a time of consistent action against the nuclear weapons programme. Greenham Common had been circled by the womens' camps. Cruise missiles were being flown in. Many of my woman friends at that time were either involved or strongly affected. I had been close to the writer Leonie Caldecot, who had just published an interview with me in one of the upmarket trendy womens' magazines. Close also to Manami Suzuki, a journalist I had met when invited to Japan the previous year to take part in the annual pilgrimage to Hiroshima. In Japan I had also undertaken a lecture tour aimed at building opposition to the transfer of Japanese spent fuel to Windscale for reprocessing. I had a friend in Oxford too, in Tine Andersen, a Danish PhD student now involved with the womens' peace networks.

These intimate friendships exposed me to deep sources of feminine wisdom and love and nurtured me greatly. Outside of the Oxford rebirthing circle, there was little appreciation by the men of the deeper questions of life. Most campaigners, scientists or activists were male and had a hard political motivation, a driving sense of injustice and anger, an emotional attachment to success, and an acute lack of self-nurturing. I would come away from the endless strategy meetings drained, only to be further stressed by the impossible situation in Oxford.

Gillian had given up her advanced studies and left for the United States where she had joined a rather strange yogic cult of ill-repute known as Ananda Marga. I had met her briefly in Philadelphia in one of their ashrams. She was distant. There had been pain in separating. She had gone partly to escape the feelings around our relationship, in particular my loyalty to Susan. I greatly felt the loss of her presence. There had been many encounters with women from the rebirthing groups. A journey of sexual awakening had begun, but there was no one person who was present in the way I needed. On return to Oxford I would be spending nights on a futon on the floor of my office-bedsit. If my be-suited opponents in the legal conventions could have witnessed my nights in that forlorn little room in unfashionable East Oxford!

It was Thursday 20th December and Christmas was on a Tuesday. Work would cease on the Friday evening. Tine was in Denmark. Manami in Japan. Handel's Messiah was on in Oxford and Maharaji was in Brighton that weekend. I would visit the boys and have supper with them and then go to Brighton. As I switched on the office light I thought I heard a voice say 'You Come'. I looked around. There was nobody.

The voice said again quite clearly, 'You come'. There was a photograph of Babaji on the mantelshelf and it had definitely summoned me.

That was how it had been with him. Out of the blue he would come as a disembodied voice. This time there was no doubt. On other occasions I would request little confirmations. The first time had been a trial. Whilst still sharing the house with Sue, and shortly before an important Greenpeace strategy meeting I was going to attend in Amsterdam, I had begun a rebirthing process in the bath. After breathing in slow connected rhythm for about half an hour, I had submerged my body slowly until all the 'chakras' were under water, head tilted back to get the forehead and crown under but nose still able to breathe. I reached a deep and peaceful place of stillness, with no need to breathe for several minutes, and sank down under the water.

A voice whispered, 'you are now in a place of power, what do you want?'

There had been many 'rebirthing' games with the power of creative thought. This or that kind of car, or lover, or job. I didn't feel wise enough to create such visions of desire.

I asked for 'guidance'. Then the voice hit with stunning rapidity, 'Wise choice. Don't go to Amsterdam. The death of one of your children. You will lose Susan, but not in the way that you think.'

I was reeling from the impact, rose from the bath, when the voice added, 'this is a process, remain standing, allow the water to dry slowly on your body'.

After an hour or two's hesitation I shared the process with Sue. I cancelled out on the Amsterdam mission. That night Matthew went into high fever. We called the doctor who prescribed anti-biotics. At that time Sue and I were moving rapidly away from conventional medical approaches and embracing homeopathy. It was not obvious to me that Matthew had a bacterial infection. We obtained the prescription, but held off using it. Having spent the previous five years investigating government cover-ups on radiation effects, the inadequacies of science, the absence of organised epidemiological research, I had come to regard the massive over-subscribing of anti-biotics as a potential causal factor in the development of childhood leukaemias.

Sue and I lost each other several times in argument over whether to use the antibiotic. We were not able to contact our homeopath and that caused her to waver. That night I stayed close to Matthew, lay my hands on his back and breathed with him gently and in unison. He slept deeply and by morning he was bright and free of any sign of illness. I waited another day and a night. All was well. I went to Amsterdam. Whilst away Matthew's fever returned and Sue used the anti-biotics. It seems a small thing now, but at the time it symbolised the gulf between us.

The second 'guidance' began after a series of petitions for help. The pace of political and scientific work in the three years of 1980-1983 had been immense. Yet these were also the years of intense energy changes as a result of the rebirthing process. The internal work required large commitments of time for week-end retreats and sometimes week-long workshops. The body processes were deep and unpredictable. Each breathing session liberated layers of energy and this might be followed by feeling lighter and freer, or a period of complete lack of energy, bouts of dizziness and 'lights out' experiences where the only thing to do was to lie down and go into a breathing session known as a 'spontaneous rebirth'. Such had occurred in the middle of the lecture tour in Japan, shortly before a meeting, and much to the consternation of my hosts who presumed I was ill.

I became confused as to the appropriate path to follow. Should I give up the unequal struggle and pursue the path of inner growth, or give up the attempts to work on myself and increase the political work. Doing both seemed to be a recipe for failure in either endeavour. I asked Babaji directly for help, but insisted I didn't want any disembodied telepathic messages. I couldn't trust that not to be coming from the recesses of my own mind. I needed somebody out there, somebody I would recognise as his messenger.

The voice replied, 'I will send you a messenger. The messenger will be very small'.

I interjected, 'What? Like a dwarf?'.

It repeated, 'Very small. Green. And Foreign.'

Great! All I needed was to look out for a little green man from another planet. Babaji was playing with me. Yet, I knew to trust him and kept alert. It took two weeks before my messenger manifested. I had attended a meeting on energy policy at South Bank Polytechnic. My friend Leonie Caldecot was chairing a conference of feminists, 'Women for Life on Earth' in what was then the Greater London Council building, and the first day was open to men. I entered the hall where about four hundred women were seated and listened for a couple of hours to diatribes of anti-patriarchal propaganda.

'Where was Love?', I thought. How could this amount of congealed anger possibly lead anywhere?

A sudden realisation dawned and my spine tingled, here everyone was 'green'. My teacher was here! I sat upright in anticipation as Leonie took the microphone and began to introduce 'three sisters from the North American Continent'. Onto the stage walked three Hopi women, one a silver-haired 'grandmother elder' about four feet tall. The younger women talked briefly of ancient Hopi prophesies, of the End-Times to be marked by the spiders' webs across the land (the electricity pylons), of the desecration of the sacred sites for the minerals that should be left in place, (uranium mines in the South West), minerals that balanced the earth and the heavens, of fire from the great Gourd of Ashes (the nuclear bomb), of the Eagle building his nest in the sky (the US space programmes' sky-lab) and the Eagle landing on the moon, and how three times the Hopi would go to the 'great glass tower in the East' to talk to the nations and not be allowed to speak (the Hopi nation had sent delegations to the UN in New York to negotiate over land rights).

Finally, the grandmother spoke. Her voice like crystal reverberated around the hall. There was a palpable hush and then stunned silence as she uttered that dreaded word....

'Love. Love in the heart. Without love in the heart no political work was of any value. You must strengthen the love in your heart. You must work in the world and you must work to strengthen the love in your heart'.

In the melee afterwards I came close to her, and silently sent my thanks. She didn't seem to notice. I marvelled at the wonder of my Babaji. He had crossed the frontiers of time, of race and culture, to offer me this simple confirmation of my path.

From then on, 'colour-coded' messengers became a bit of joke between us. The next had been 'red-and-white'. Again there was a gap of many days. I had been sitting in Tine Andersen's flat relating a dream about skiing down a slope, as if I was in a ski-jumping contest and then skiing over a cliff and falling into the sea and then Tine swimming out to rescue me. I had one interpretation about the need for woman's support, when she began to say, 'this is about the whole male trip....'

Behind her head was a large plant in a pot and sticking out of the compost a Danish flag. The red and white flag signalled... 'listen, Peter, listen to this!'.

Tine's interpretation was that my whole spiritual journey was simply an extension of the male hero's trip, the skiing down the slope was a metaphor for that, as would be skiing off the cliff, and woman would be there to rescue me from the inevitable crash.

It was hard to hear that.

I was now awaiting the third messenger, this time 'yellow-and-blue'.

Sue and I went to Handel's Messiah, which we both found deeply moving. The next morning I went straight round to my travel agent and booked the next available flight to Delhi, which thankfully was after Christmas. I then went down to Brighton to see Guru Maha Raji.

My initial contact with him had waned as a result of the unbearable soppiness of his devotees. However, after meeting Leonard, who had also been initiated by him, and after several months of intensive rebirthing, I had softened, become less judgemental, and had often sat for hours listening to his 'premies' and their stories of adoration and insight.

I had been initiated sometime in 1981, along with Sue and Ron. Initiation consisted of four rather simple but 'secret' meditation techniques, which we were placed under oath not to reveal. The techniques were not in themselves the 'knowledge', but they helped reveal and strengthen it, opening the congested neural pathways to experience the cosmic flow of 'nectar' an energy you could almost taste that seemed to trickle down behind the palate, and divine harmonics, like a celestial choir, a sound that seemed leftover in the Universe after all had been built and could be heard when all else was sufficiently still, and a divine light that would blaze like a beacon behind the eyes. But most nourishing of all, 'the holy name', not a name but a vibration that began in the chest and rose through the trachea to suffuse the whole head. Perhaps this was the 'gnosis' of the Essenes. A certain knowledge that God was love, that love was real, tangible, a force that dwelt within.

In my first rebirthing session I had understood what Jesus had meant by 'The Kingdom of Heaven is within you'. In that week in London with Leonard we had paired off and retired to various flats and houses for evening breathing sessions. My rebirther was a middle-aged woman with red hair and many resemblances to my mother as she would have been around my own birth. We were alone in a small bedroom and thankfully her motherly vibrations meant that no carnal energies disturbed my session. After a few minutes of the connected breathing I went into a deep trance-like state. I needed no exertion to keep the breath going, as if I 'was being breathed' and as if a powerful hand was holding me, enfolding me on all sides. I entered bliss. For two hours there were no thoughts.

'Only if you become as a child, can you enter the Kingdom', and for the first time I knew what 'child' meant. No thoughts, no preconceptions, just the moment, the breath and that surrounding sense of love, the presence of a universal being, the being of a universal presence.

That was the first session. The second had been a catharsis of writhing and struggling, visions of the birth canal, a crescendo of hyperventilation culminating in a back-arched tetany and released by a primal scream. Dave was my rebirther, and he was superbly calm through it all. The body dynamics lasted for several sessions. Energetic releases from chest, arms, throat and neck. Within weeks my body changed. It was as if removing a mental armour, an etheric cage of the musculature. Frederic Leboyer, pioneer of 'Birth without Violence' had also been rebirthed and had come to publish his observations of the gentle birthing techniques of water, soft lights and warmth and of not cutting the chord until it had finished pulsating. Normal western births traumatised the chest muscles, the jaw and neck and above all, freezing the breath into a lifelong holding pattern.

49

My shoulders relaxed. I would catch myself sitting or standing in old ways that suddenly were no longer held by tensions but mere mental habits that I could instantly let go and my frame would drop into a more relaxed posture. I began to dance. Wild dance. Where formerly I would have shuffled about self-consciously, I now could let my body flow. I had rhythm! People were enjoying my dance. My clothes changed. I dressed in choicely cut and sensuous fabric. I bought a flute. With women something deep and marvellous had happened. I felt less and less desire and more and more desirable. The merest touch of a hand was a delight. A finger across my chest, a stroke of the head, especially my head, which I had shaved and kept shaved in yogic process for nine months, each touch was complete in itself and no longer unleashed such a desperate hunger for more, or for hands to wander elsewhere. Women friends became casually intimate with an innocence of touching and closeness, especially among the more relaxed gatherings of the rebirthing groups.

All except Sue, who although she took 'knowledge' with Maharaji, and had several rebirthing sessions, still kept her distance. There was an element in her that never surrendered, not just to me, but to the breath itself. She managed to stay at the surface and no one pushed her under.

The meditation techniques given by Maharaji were no instant recipe for bliss. After three weeks of constant practice, two hours each day, nothing had 'happened'. I began to complain. One day, alone in the house around mid-day, I had two hours to myself and I went upstairs to meditate. After the first hour I became frustrated. I wanted something to happen. I bellowed my inward complaint. Suddenly a huge hand planted itself firmly in my back and forced me down to the floor, still cross-legged but bowed down so that my forehead touched the carpet. The pressure ceased and I rose slowly to find myself encircled by shimmering white light in the form of a pyramid and my whole body vibrating with light. My mind remained quite normal with one part saying, 'hey, hey, look at this, look at this!' and another part saying 'piss-off you fool, piss-off or it'll go'. It seemed to last only a few minutes, but in fact a full twenty, when it just as suddenly evaporated and I looked at the clock.

My Zoologist friend Anthony Cheke had been very suspicious of these meditations. He too, had been given the knowledge but found it rapidly dissolved his libido and he just as rapidly gave up meditating. Glad as I was to have anything that dissolved my libido, I too did not persist with the practices. Something in the state I had been shown pulled me away. If that was 'enlightenment' then I could see why enlightened beings did not involve themselves in the political world. In that state it seemed no action was possible. And if it were a question of developing my bodily system to such an extent that I could handle that kind of energy, then such a state would be a long way off.

Whatever, I still enjoyed Maharaji. As I entered the hall in Brighton I was struck by the creamy yellow and deep blue curtains that surrounded the huge chair that was an inevitable feature of his 'talks'. Here again Babaji indicated to me that my teachers were everywhere, from any culture, any friend, any person I might encounter. Maharaji was in riotous form. Joke after joke about how we chase after material things, trying constantly to anchor ourselves to the shifting sands of life's changes. How we try to take so much with us - the image of a trekker with a massive rucksack encountering a very narrow swing-bridge and trying to squeeze on through, even though it was plainly obvious the rucksack had to go. It was an evening of joy and humour, of not taking the spiritual path so seriously, of having fun and doing simple things, about humility, whatever one's work. It would take me a while to get the message.

3

Himalayan Retreat

January 1st saw me carrying a tray of stones, the tray a simple bowl shaped from galvanised metal sheet and stapled, about two feet in diameter and six inches deep. I had piled it high, a game with myself, loading the tray to the limit of what I could swing up from the baked ground to my bare head without overbalancing. I had knotted a long silk shawl to form a pad to protect my newly shaven skin and it required exact balance and timing not to knock this off centre as the heavy weight swung to the top of its arc to rest gently and ready for the tricky descent to the river bed.

We were building an aqueduct from the confluence of a stream upriver to the gardens of the ashram. Even in January the Himalayan sun is hot and here in the valley, away from the mountain winds, working in the heat of mid-day was proving tough. We worked from 10am to 1pm to break for the only meal of the day, and from 4 until 6 in the afternoon. I would learn that when the sun was down behind the hills it was better to work with the small stones on the raised ridges of the riverbed, and when it was high, to be heaving boulders out of the swirling cold waters now emasculated by the dry season and only knee deep. I was up in the baking heat of the ridge alone. I had the tray balanced and commenced my barefoot descent down the narrow footpath between rocks and low thorny bushes, my eyes squinting and focussed on the path.

I looked ahead and there, fifty feet away at the bottom of the path, was Babaji. He was alone and obviously starting up the path. He had a long staff, wore a turban of bright reds and blues and flowing turquoise silk down to his feet. An imp entered somewhere behind my ears and tickled my lazy brain into devilment. 'I' would not step aside, I had the load.

In an instant, the merest blink of an eye, he was in front of me, a flash of humour on his face, and then gone, slipping nimbly past where there was no room to pass, and thwacking me heartily on the backside chuckling as he went on his way.

A moment that the mind could not grasp. Fifty feet in a fraction of a second, as if the movie had jumped a few frames. Life carried on as if nothing had happened. There was work to do.

My mind kept tracking back to the question of why he had called me. An answer to my petition? I had reached the limit of what Tukaram could do to help. My monstrous self importance. Not the conceit of self admiration, but a subtler enemy. I had to be important, famous even, although not for any accolade. It was to have made a contribution but more importantly, not to be anonymous, so that this life had meaning. Fame would work just as well after I was dead.

I had arrived at the ashram in the late morning. The walk up the river bed had taken two hours. The steep wooded valley sides abounded with life, birds and monkeys to delight the naturalist in me. There were no villages en route. Such a welcome relief from the overcrowded towns in the foothills, the shit-ridden streets and constant diesel-fueled noise of the frontier third world.

You can see the ashram buildings shimmering pink and white among the green forest from a mile away. They are perched about two hundred feet above the river bed. Steep white-limed steps lead up to a veranda and a temple. As I had reached the top of those steps his presence had taken me by surprise. I had not expected him to be outside. He was sitting on a wall surrounded by yogis dressed in long black lungis - thin cotton cloth simply wrapped about the waist, naked above, tanned and well muscled, all turning and smiling a welcome. One of them whispered, 'this is Babaji' and turned to where he was sitting. He was swathed in multicoloured cloth and wore a grey woollen mountaineer's hat. His cheeks were chubbier than I recalled from photographs. The black jewels of his eyes were bright and laughing. He looked me up and down with a quizzical, slightly amused air.

'Italiano?', he said, and I knew he knew I was not.

I bowed my head slightly, feeling suddenly shy of him. No thoughts troubled the encounter. They were to come later.

'No, English', I said, knowing again that it was superfluous.

He laughed and there followed a string of guttural Hindi, which had everyone laughing around him. I learned later that he had just ordained that from that moment on, all nations should have their own colour and that they were to choose before the next morning. I had been dressed in black. The compulsion had come a few days before leaving and I had bought a thick black Matinique cotton jacket with a hood, black trousers, singlets, and scarf. I had a set of mala beads made from polished brown lotus seeds. It had served me well on the plane and in the airports. The black protected me. The chaotic energies of milling crowds, unfriendly officialdom, vomiting fat American tourists, did not reach me, as if absorbed by the thick blackness of the cloth.

I was not to know that Babaji had years ago decreed that all his Italian yogis should wear black. They had been dubbed the 'black army', like a Praetorian Guard always at his side. I saw them as fierce, somewhat stern and slightly intimidating. It would be another two years before I would learn a little of what it was to be 'black', yet I knew from the beginning that I was black, albeit an English black.

As I watched others arrive and make that first encounter, I realised how unfeeling I had been. Some would break into tears of joy. All would fall at his feet. Indeed, many did that constantly, at every conceivable opportunity during his daily perambulations. Most of the time he ignored such solicitations. Once I saw him kick someone away as if a fly trying to land on his feet, and to another, jokingly lift his foot and step on the devotee's head, and then once to lean down and touch someone's head with such love and compassion that the world seemed to pause for that one act.

I had felt nothing. I went to the allotted quarters, a cool rectangular room in a long crescent building overlooking a terraced field. There was a small village on the hillside close to the ashram and a local farmer was ploughing the terrace with a wooden plough and a large ox. The gardens and fields were dry, watered now only by the intricate system of channels and aqueducts carrying water from upriver. The forest above and behind the ashram was mostly pine, I presumed an exotic species planted in colonial days and now mature. The forest hummed with insect life. Walks in the wooded hills were sadly forbidden, in order to protect the private lives of the village.

The ashram was basic. The buildings were mud-bricked and whitewashed. On a bed in the corner of my dark dormitory room a large German fellow sweated and heaved through the day in the grip of malaria. Otherwise the cool sheltered room was a welcome haven.

I had settled quickly into the regime. A trumpet would sound at 4.00 am, when it was still dark as pitch. There would follow a semi-conscious descent of the 108 steps to the riverbed. With the low water there was nowhere to plunge and to achieve total immersion I had to lie flat as in a press-up and dunk my supine body under the flow keeping eyes shut to avoid the myriad abrasive particles swept from the gravel bottom. There was always a cold wind from the distant grand Himalaya funnelling down the valley, but the moment my body emerged all cold was banished and it was a joy to stand naked in the dark with the wind drying me. I loved that moment and could not understand the mind's constant refusal to remember that joy and the body's constant reluctance to strip and enter the water. I never carried a torch and hated the single electric bulb the ashram had only that year received from the new power line.

Batheing by the stars brought a rapid return of consciousness. There was then time to meditate before 5am when Babaji would hold a little fire ceremony on his small veranda. He lived in one room, barely enough space for his bed, with a window looking out over the valley. He had no possessions. The constant stream of gifts that flowed to him flowed on, some to the villagers, some back to the devotees.

The moments with him in the early morning were the most precious and I did not miss one day. At that time there were usually only a few of his closest yogis present. We would enter the tiny room and crouch down, forehead tilted toward him, to receive 'chandan', yellow paste of sandalwood and pigment. His touch was deliciously cool. He would then make offerings to the fire. Gee, rice, milk, honey, yoghurt, perfume and incense. The fire-pit represented the mouth of the Divine Mother, the feminine principle that sustained the Earth, indeed, the whole Universe. By this simple act he demonstrated his love, his acknowledgement of the source of all life, all being, every day, without fail, for the fourteen years he had been there in this incarnation.

In those early hours I had seen that his body was racked with pain, his eyes were puffy, and he had a rattling cough. It surprised me. Here was the yogi of yogis, revered as Lord Shiva himself. How could he not be in perfect health, in mastery of his own small physical universe, in bliss at all times?

In the days that followed my self-importance was laid bare. I was back at school. Thirteen years old. He was my old headmaster, hawk-like Idwal Rees, respected and feared, Welsh three-quarter in his time, Captain of Wales and the Barbarians. And I, so keen to be acknowledged, to do the right thing, not to fail, not to look stupid, not to be embarrassed. When the 'head' was about, everything changed. Always the fear of doing the wrong thing, fear of disapproval.

That hunger for acknowledgement and respect, did it come simply through lack of such from my own father, so distant and unreachable, airman, flight engineer, so far from nature, so far from anything I could share? Whatever, between father and school and the watchful eye of Idwal I knew I had to make a contribution. My first contact with history and great literature impacted upon me. Inexorable time. Lives came and went in a great sea of anonymity. There stood out but few real people, the famous. They had contributed and were remembered. They had existence. Not to make a contribution was not to exist.

From then on I had become the only important person to me, and worse, as the average person about me displayed their obvious destinies in every mundane concern and habit, I became more important than they. In such barren fields no love could grow. Each person who had come into my life had become a foil in the pursuit of my need. And so it was with Sue, now lost to me. It hurt still. A hell of my own making. When Babaji offered us a wish, it was that I would have her back.

Every time he came near, I would be projected back into that consciousness of early schooldays. The same feelings arose, the fear of failure, of disapproval, of not doing things right. Others had it to. All around the work would rise to fever pitch, backs would straighten. Once he walked by and some semi-conscious over-devoted Italian trod down a seedling tree newly planted. I bent down behind them and patted and firmed it back into place. He had turned as if seeing before he turned and patted me on the shoulder, saying simply, 'Mr Gentle'.

Each day at Herakhan was a lifetime. The world could have ceased to spin. Heaven could have offered nothing more. The huge grey rocks warmed by the sun, the dark forest and swirling waters. Air, fire, water, earth, all felt bitingly real. The hard work sweated out generations of puerile thoughts, attitudes, past decisions and stances, holding and hoarding, grievance, resentment, petty angers and jealousies, out from the pores and into the earth, carried by the waters of the Gautama Ganga, vapourised by fire, transmuted by the constantly repeated mantra Om Namaha Shivaya....and the soul refilled with sweet singing in Sanskrit, of love and light and hunger for divine harmonies. So many words for the divine, so many facets of the Goddess, so many aspects of love.

I spent my quiet moments in the afternoons by a turn of the river where there were big white boulders. There was often a kingfisher there, the same species as in England. And once, a spectacular wallcreeper, such a dingy name for a bird more like a butterfly in shape, crimson wings, black above and the palest grey head, and one I had seen before high on the highest 'wall' of an alpine peak.

There were few English people there. One woman I had met in rebirthing groups, then called Poppet Clegg, had metamorphosed into Suma, rebirther, singer, and follower of Native American teachings. She had produced exquisite recordings of American Indian and Himalayan Yogic chanting in a group she called Prana, the Sanskrit word for divine breath. One John Chaney arrived, whom I did not know then, but we quickly realised I knew his new wife, Chrissie, a 'premie' from the Oxford rebirthing group. Neil Oram, philosopher, playwright, poet, was also with the English contingent, but kept much to himself. He never joined any of the mens' work and was obviously blessed by Babaji who would have given any other man short shrift for hanging around the women's realm of the gardens.

I attracted the attention of a short sallow-skinned New York Jewish lady with the classic Brooklyn accent. She had stopped me, held my face, told me she knew me from past lives in Egypt. We talked often and I divulged my work, my dilemmas and questions. At one point she looked again at my face and insisted I must keep it in the public arena, any publicity was valuable, that just seeing it would remind people, trigger memories of their past. She was a 'light worker'. I had by then come across such cosmically industrious beings. My entry into the New Age with Leonard Orr, rebirthing, the Glastonbury camps, emerging Green Party and the women of Greenham, had left me with ambiguous feelings. I would not dismiss it, neither could I embrace it. They were harmless enough, meditating, burying their crystals, beaming the colours of the rainbow, energising the ley lines, the 'stones', the sacred sites, Shasta, Iona, Findhorn or wherever. My outer world was the political and the scientific, and my inner world the emotional, the power of thought, the necessity of cleansing and the opening of the heart to ordinary human love. Enough of a task.

My new found friend was called Bhavani, a Sanskrit name for the motherly aspect of the Divine Feminine. I was not unopen to her perceptions of past lives. In the second year of the rebirthing process gateways had begun to open. In the first month I must have had about ten two-hour breathing sessions. After the first blissful state, they had been marked by physical and emotional releases, memories of childhood, the birth canal, even a discarnate argument about not wanting to come back to this emotion-ridden planet. Leonard dubbed the latter, 'conception trauma'! After a year I had done close to fifty sessions. The physical effects had ceased. I could move tremendous amounts of energy through my system without cramps, tingling, tetany or any obvious disturbances. There had been medical controversies in the press about rebirthing's 'hyperventilation' and its dangers, but all cramps and pain could be released by simply carrying on breathing, whereas, of course, a doctor's first instinct when pain is encountered is to stop the process. Without fail the body-mind would reach a peaceful energised state, a cycle would complete of its own accord with a definite beginning and an end, and it usually did not last longer than two hours.

I had concluded from observation of my own process and sitting with perhaps a further one hundred such sessions, that it was not the pace of the breathing, but the 'connection' of the in-breath and out-breath in one smooth unbroken movement, that did the work. In that simple technique lay enormous power.

At the end of the first year a large group of us had gathered at a country house, Gilthallion, in Sussex. Four of Leonard's students had set up to lead the group of perhaps fifty people. I had gone with various 'goals'. There had been a wave of American 'goal-orientated' spirituality. To be spiritual you had to be powerful. Powerful people did not live on the dole or drive rusty old cars, or like me, work hard for a pittance and experience all manner of relationship hassles. However, my goals reflected my consciousness at the time: to experience really free orgasm, and its opposite, the mystic stillness of Tantra. I wasn't sure I had ever experienced either, having never felt free and out of control, and not having had a suitable partner who could instruct me in the quieter kind of energy exchange.

I cannot say I feel these manifested out of any reality-bending mindwaves of my own. More like Babaji's little play, 'if that's what you want, here, see, it's no big deal'. Both had come my way in the first two days, although the second in dance rather than bed. Sex was not the only thing that needed sorting out, but perhaps because everybody was sorting it out, the results came quicker. My lists of affirmations and goals read embarrassingly now. I quickly doubled my income from its former precarious level and now commanded half-decent fees for my international work on treaties and conventions. That had a lot to do with concepts of self-worth, self-esteem, fear of disapproval from others, and hence a willingness to receive. I had bought a car, an old, white, Volvo saloon. I wore decent clothes that drew constant approval from the women in my life. I had come, slowly, to like and appreciate my body to the point, at least, where I enjoyed being in it.

In those first two years of rebirthing group work, I was surrounded by seekers and teachers who seemed to focus upon effort of will, the discipline of constant affirmation aimed at bending reality. Mostly, the reality to be bent related to money, jobs or perfect sex partners. I had a certain lack of discipline in these endeavours, to be sure, but there was another factor at work. The Universe would constantly surprise me with its mystery and humour. Sometimes small, as when calling Sue in mid-workshop, having had some insight about my egoic forms of control and wanting to talk at length, only to find one ten pence coin for the long distance public call, but shoving it in anyway with the thought that the 'cut-off' might fail, which it did and gave me a full twenty minutes. And sometimes rather humblingly big, as when catching the bus to London one morning I had been musing on 'the perfect woman'. Americans were strong and assertive, but not mysterious, Australians sensitive but lost, French erotic but unreachable, English perfect for bringing up children but so reserved....then it had to be Japanese, though taller would be nice, they were so well dressed, so elegant, ancient mystery, skilled in arousing the flame...she would be a painter, interested in wildlife, academic, beautiful, excellent cook....I caught the crowded bus and then just before it left the city, an exotically beautiful Japanese woman got on. There were several spare seats, including the one I rapidly removed my briefcase from. She sat next to me and for half the journey I rehearsed every opening.

Eventually, sheer humiliation at the prospect of getting off without saying anything forced an opener. She was a student of art. She loved nature. Did I know anyone in the University who could take her to Wytham Woods? The woods belonged to the Zoology Department. She was studying for her PhD, researching the influence of Japanese painters on modern European art, loved to cook....how much more, I would never know, because, although I took her phone number and promised to ring, I knew I had no space in my life for such a person.

Sometime after the first few introductory days at Gilthallion, I was, I thought, about to come out of a strong hour-long breathing session. There had been no marked feelings or visions, when suddenly an image of childhood surfaced clear as day. I was in a small caravan parked in the school quadrangle, it was around the age of 12, and the caravan was that of a mobile dentist. The space was small, crowded by swing-trays of instruments, drill, dentist and female assistant. Gleaming stainless steel all around. I was at that senseless end-point where the mouth is full of pink mouthwash, bits of tooth, blood and burnt filling, when, cheeks bulging, I heard the distinct order to spit.

I splattered the lot directly at the dentist, his assistant, and the gleaming instruments, to a shocked and ineffective chorus of 'no, no, in the bowl, in the bowl...'

At that point in the breathing session I went into uncontrollable laughter. Great rolls of infectious mirth that took over the whole room of breathing bodies. It was a large room and people were rebirthing in pairs. At some point I flung my arms wide. Suddenly there was a blue sky above, a wind, heather underneath, and a figure standing above me, sword raised and driving into my stomach. I cried out a long wail of pain and sorrow. The kilted figure raised the sword high and drove it into his own chest. I began to howl in grief, great sobbing waves engulfed me. For ages I could not speak. My inexperienced rebirther was replaced by Cara (later known as Kamalu, a devotee of Babaji), who began to tease out of me the scene. My mind had instantly known the full story. The assailant was my brother in that lifetime. I had let him win the fight. It had been about women. I had slept with his woman. All I could say was, 'I've killed my brother' repeated and repeated between the sobs.

The poor rebirthers assumed at first I was confessing some dark secret from this lifetime. Gradually Cara gained access to the story and had me say, 'It is now safe to love'. That brought more waves of grief that consumed me for a full three hours.

That had been my first 'past-life-recall'. It followed an episode the previous week. Firstly, a massage by a friend, the yoga teacher, Johanna

O'Connor, in which she had 'seen' a scar in my solar plexus. Then, whilst rushing to a public meeting at Leiston in Suffolk my cheap hire car had spun off the road after hitting mud and a lamp-post had carved its way through the middle of the unworthy Morris Ital just behind my seat. Rather dazed I had tried to proceed with half the car hanging off, then ran to a roundabout and thumbed a lift the rest of the way, delivered my talk on nuclear reactor safety, before collapsing on Leonie Caldecot's bed (she had a cottage in the vicinity) and suffering my wilfully delayed shocks. As she administered to the fevered brow, my loins wanted rather more intimate contact with my married friend and these unsafe longings triggered horrific spasms in my stomach muscles out of all proportion to any such dangers.

Triangles of love and their emotional dangers thus featured rather strongly in the karma I was carrying. I had had other glimpses of countries and cultures. I felt a deep empathy with old Japan. I had had a feeling for Japanese art since a child and tried to emulate it in my own paintings of birds. I could readily judge the quality of Japanese artistic works, the use of space and line and colour. Since University days I had cultivated Bonzai trees. My deep love of nature connected me to Zen, its painting and poetry. It was not hard to see generations of Japanese monk in my facial features. On my visit during 1982, Manami Suzuki and I became brief lovers, and in that intimate space realised a long historical bond through many different kinds of relationship. She had still some of the old Japan in her, whereas all around the Mickey Mouse culture of modern Japan paralysed my feelings. I had gone alone at her bidding to Kyoto for time to rest. There were over forty monasteries with their gardens to choose from and I had the fortune to stay in small non-touristic Bhuddist retreat. Early in the morning I had set out for the nearest temple gardens-the famous cathedral of Myoshin-ji. In the cathedral grounds were 40 branch temples, with Taizo-in one of the oldest.

As I walked between two high hedges, an energy descended upon me that brought floods of tears, and I came out into a zen space of gravel and boulders which I instantly recognised. For several minutes I knelt transfixed, watching a mortal combat on the gravel between a huge hairy spider and an equally big wasp. The wasp won. In a temporarily altered state I sat beside my garden's arrangement of pond and rocks, with frogs and dragonflies and singing crickets. After two hours of stillness I found a small kiosk selling postcards of the monk Motonobu Kano's work. He had been a famous painter as well as a gardener in 15th century Japan. It was then I looked with shock and horror at the picture of my pond and its twentieth century concrete jetty for tourists to walk out on. I had sat on it without perceiving, as if protected for those two hours from the assassination of form and harmony created all those years ago. I let out an angry yell at what they had done to 'my' garden, and then a grateful sigh for those protected hours of peaceful reunion.

Japan's former glorious art, its martial combat, the Shakuhachi flute....all felt so close to me, I had a constant sense of bewilderment and irritation that I could not now paint, fight and play like a master. Less accessible were other lives. I felt a clear link to Tibet. However, close to the surface now were feelings for Germany. I had learned the language whilst hospitalised from a road accident just before my entrance to Oxford when the examiners then insisted on two languages at 'O' level and I had only French. I passed the oral despite never having heard the language spoken. I could not have sounded anything like a real German. There had been my work in both South and North Germany in the 70s and whenever hitch-hiking during my teenage wanderings, I had instantly felt at home when I crossed the border and could speak a little of the language.

At Herakhan it was possible to inquire into past lives. Babaji was accompanied most times by an old and revered scholar by the name of Shastraji. The elder was also an astrologer and diviner of past and future life histories. Visitors to the ashram would book sessions and queue outside his little room. He was a lovely man with a silver handle-bar moustache, never without his prayer-book from which he constantly recited hymns and poems to the Divine Mother. I booked a session. I had little interest in the past, however, for what had come so far from rebirthing sessions had come at times and with such energy that I saw it simply as part of the overall healing process, and for me, that was best left to the intelligence that took over in that surrendered state. I didn't need anything for my inquisitive mind to feed upon. Unfortunately, this wisdom did not stretch to my desires for future knowledge.

I wanted to know about my work. About my future with Sue and the children. The old man had a little ritual. You thought of a number. He then twiddled what looked like a dial on his wrist and then began to speak through a translator.

'Your work will be very successful. You say three brothers, but two brothers is good, three is bad, one brother is harm to you. Of your wife, this is in the hands of Baba, she will come to you, but for how long, only he can know. You must take care of her. If you take care of her, all will be well. Ah, I see you in prison, twice. You will be beaten.'

There was some more about having two or three sons and a daughter and how I would be blessed if I took no meat and no alcohol. I was thankful. For some, Babaji had asked that they become yogis, which meant total celibacy. He added that when I was 55 I would be a great yogi.

I was disturbed at the material relating to my brothers. Later I ran up to him and asked, how can I work with that, with prayer, would it do any good...? He had kept walking and only muttered, yes, maybe, prayer would help.

Bhavani began sending me people to rebirth. I did the sessions in Babaji's small cave by the river, the place he had first manifested. Nobody disturbed me on this holy ground and I took that as a sign that the work was approved. I found that I could 'see' energies at play around the rebirthee's body. I had access to information of past lives. A New Zealander, once a German general, still psychically rigid with the years of discipline and lack of feeling, cut off from the feminine, alone and with waves of grief descending as he broke through the layers of memory. Another, a mutilated prostitute, reliving the pain as the psychic scar tissue released its energies. I felt privileged and humble in my brief role as agent in their healing.

Toward the end of my stay I caught an infection in my eyes. Probably from the river gravel. They hurt immensely and I was as good as blind. At one point an old German-made army truck had made its way upriver to deliver supplies and a number of us hitched a lift on some errand to Haldwani, the nearest town. As the truck jogged and jolted its way, the tarpaulin flapping loose, the engine revving, seated bodies swaying either side, a sudden vision unfolded. I was in a room facing German officers, held by two soldiers. With a massive effort I broke free and ran from the room and down a maze of corridors with the sound of the soldiers running in pursuit. I burst out of the building and into the night. The pursuers drew closer and I knew I would be caught, and more, killed on the spot. I became desperate in my desire to live, to get away and be free, yet certain in my knowledge I was going to die. The movie did not show the end. I was left with a feeling of deep shame. A kind of spiritual recrimination. It was a desperate and unseemly way to die. I should have stood my ground. Stood for my truth.

That truth was clear to me. I had been a soldier. More, a model soldier and an athlete. I had totally immersed myself in the ethos of the male, in performance, I am sure I had been a runner, my fancy stretching to the Berlin Olympics just before the war, a time that always held a poignancy and branded on my memory in the photographs of Leni Riefenstahl. Then the war had come and I was lost. The first encounter with 'enemy', rifle levelled at the human forms struggling across a snow-covered landscape, I had simply stilled and then walked away in a daze of confusion as to where I was and what I was doing.

There had been no self knowledge. No clear realisation. I was charged with cowardice in the face of the enemy. I would be shot. The circumstances were clear, but what had stayed in the memory was that headlong rush for life and freedom, the desperation and lostness and the dark pursuit that followed. For as long as I could remember I had been pursued in dreams by armed or otherwise dangerous males, police or soldiers. Never had I turned to meet them.

The past life dream sparked a recollection from this lifetime. At school I had started out in the Army Cadet Force, the CCF. I was a model cadet. My closest school-friend, Christopher Bult, of whom I will talk more, was best cadet, and I came second. We were the ace-shots of the school, gaining our 'marksman' badge with the old 303 rifle. Up until then we had only used the normal bulls-eye targets and I could put a round on the decal at four hundred yards. Then came drill with the modern Self Loading Rifle, or SLR. I didn't like it as much, too light, the trigger too feathery. The first day on the range we had to shoot at cut-out metal figures that popped up randomly at various distances, but much closer than I was used to. The figures simulated advancing troops and we had to use rapid fire. They had coal-scuttle helmets and German uniforms. I left the CCF shortly after. I never knew why. I stopped feeling right at that point and there was no shame in it, and I went bird-watching on the allotted afternoons.

Bhavani explained, how the lifetimes of Buddhist training had cut through the unconscious at those points, both in this lifetime and the last. Now there was work to be done. We had to become fully conscious. There were dark times ahead and a new kind of fighting would be required.

Babaji had drawn many people to him from many different religions. There were Sikhs, Sufis, Christians, Buddhists, Jews, eclectic 'New Agers'....and of many countries. Most were contacted telepathically. Some took years to find out where the call had come from. He did not give discourses. He very seldom taught anyone yogic techniques. His occasional utterances were in the guttural local dialect. He sounded like an uneducated mountain man. His appearance varied enormously. He could have been any race, his skin a pale yellowish brown, his features full, reminiscent at times of a South American Indian as much as an Himalayan Hindu. He lived simply, ate seldom, rarely left the Ashram and then only to visit a few of the holy places of Northern India, the remote temples or at times, ashrams in the cities. His following was not great in numbers. He had said often, he did not require large numbers, only one good student would be enough, one with the courage of Jesus, or Buddha, Krishna or Ram. What little he had said was faithfully recorded and printed in little booklets.

His general instructions were simple. All past yoga was no longer relevant. True meditation and the path of the yogi in this chaotic age was all but impossible. Very few had the required discipline and dedication. He did not ask for it. He asked of his followers that they dedicate their lives to Truth, Simplicity and Love. In this age, only work would prosper the soul. In work for humanity was true salvation. The ancient yogic 'religion' of the Sanatana Dharma was the oldest religion and the seed of all true religions and was the best foundation for this life. He demonstrated that every day, from morning bath, simple ceremonies in honour of the divine, and hard daily work. Ashram food was basic, vegetarian and prepared once a day at lunchtime.

He had spoken of a great 'turning point' in history, the 'kranti', a time of immense destruction that was approaching. We could not expect to know its time. We should be constantly alert. At one time he had said, 'where there are mountains there will be sea, where there is sea, there will be mountains'. This had resonated with other messages from the Hopi, from Sun Bear, and from readings of Edgar Cayce that I had immersed myself in over the past two years. Cayce had prophesied of earth changes, cataclysms and earthquakes. I had studied geological treatises, particularly on the structure of the oceans. At that time, catastrophists were still out of fashion in the earth sciences, whereas within ten years, geologists and evolutionary biologists were to come full circle and re-embrace the theories of their founding fathers and align themselves with much of the mythology of flood, earthquake and 'fire from the sky' that is a mark of all the ancient civilisations.

Babaji urged his 'devotees' not to be afraid, that there would come a time when they would have to let go of this body, it was just a vehicle, a time to leap into the fire or the water. Most of humanity would be destroyed by the calamity. Thereafter, a new golden age would dawn.

He taught on a personal level but directly. He had said, 'do not ask questions. As the questions arise in your mind, they will be answered. I will speak to you inside.' Everyone had their own personal discourse with him. This 'being' could speak telepathically to any or all of the fifty or so people in the ashram simultaneously. People would experience his physical presence, as I had done that first day moving the stones, when in all probability, he would be sitting somewhere else surrounded by other people in another part of the ashram, or the river bed, or in the temples or gardens. The yogis who attended him knew it was a show, a theatre, and could tell when 'he' was more or less in the body they were relating to. Those who had the extended sight, who could see at vibrations of light beyond the visible range of ordinary sight, would talk of a constant stream of visitors come to pay their respects.

On the normal visible planes to which I was limited, I witnessed a delegation of Sikhs arrive and pay homage. The previous year, Lamas had arrived from Tibet. The Governor of Uttar Pradesh arrived by helicopter and with military escort. Yet, Babaji was no widely known personage. He had arrived in 1970 at the cave across the river from the ashram. Local villagers were well-used to wandering Saddhus and the young boys had been taking offerings to what they saw as a beautiful youth of perhaps eighteen years. When the old men arrived and saw the old Herakhan Baba, the word had gone out of the return of the reputedly immortal yogi, 'Babaji', of Yogananda's autobiography.

The cave is at the same spot where as Herakhan Baba he had disappeared into a ball of light while bathing in 1922. The young saddhu presented the older men with the vision of his previous incarnation and then after a few days, all could see only the new body. He then climbed the Indian mountain with the name Kailash that dominates the valley, (there is a much larger mountain with that name in Tibet, sacred to three religions). At its grassy dry summit there is a small temple, with little shelter from the wind, and a fire pit. He sat there in deep meditation without moving and without taking food or water for forty days. That had convinced the locals that he was the old yogi and could take title to the ashram and small temple in the valley. It transpired that a yogi-holy man, now revered as a 'saint', Mahendra Baba, had spent his whole life in prayer that Babaji would return to the physical plane. Just before his death in 1969, Babaji had appeared to him in a locked room at a mountain ashram, and told him his pleas had been heeded and he would soon return.

At first, westerners were few. Leonard Orr had arrived at the ashram in 1978 and through the spread of 'rebirthing' several hundred foreigners came to him for guidance. Some did not need to make the journey. He would appear to them or talk to them 'inside'. So it had been with me, although he had not appeared in any form, he had given me internal guidance, sent his colour-coded messengers, and I knew, provided me with levels of psychic protection that I could not of my own accord manufacture.

The time for leaving drew close. There was a sadness in the air. Twice every day the devotees would gather in line and take him offerings. Gifts ranged from simple bundles of incense, cloth, a mala, a few pieces of fruit, to all manner of expensive items. On one occasion I was in the line when a rich westerner gave him a gold and diamond ring. The next in line was a poor villager and Babaji simply handed the valuable on, as was his custom. The constant give and take of the universe was played out by this simple rite. He always had something to give. It was a source of pain to me that I would go unconscious in this process. I was constantly missing the opening times of the little shop, and would scrabble to find items to take. How disorganised I was at simply giving!

Someone urged me to go and ask Baba to safeguard my family, that it was a normal request when far from home. Unthinking, I asked. There was a brief translation, and then he answered, quickly and annoyed, that I should know better, that when anyone comes to him, they should know that there family is under his protection.

Toward the end of these brief assemblies, there arose a sad and mournful chant, an aire that filled the valleys, Sita-Ram, Sita-Ram Bolo Pwa-ray (the last word I have spelt phonetically). Babaji was wrapped against the morning cold with an assortment of western woollies, including, for a brief spell, a thick Arran sweater I had bought for him in England. He felt vulnerable, at times like a frail grandmother. There were dark tones to the puffy skin under and around his eyes. The early sun would glance down through the huge trees that grew from the rocky cliff out of which his simple quarters and the veranda upon which we gathered had been hewn. The dappled shade was constantly alive with birds of every kind. Something of the timeless would descend upon the simple ritual, on chants that were thousands of years old, sung when Jesus came here, and before that, before the Buddha.

I returned to England on January 15th. Still unable to see properly. Head freshly shaven. Dressed in black. Clear in my purpose.

4

Work in the World

Upon return to Oxford I rested in my room for several days. My eyes were still sore and I did not attempt to approach the mountain of work. 1984 stretched before me in the schedules of my diary: meetings with Trades Union officials, TV companies, House of Commons Committees, officials at the Department of the Environment, trips to Dublin, Washington, Isle of Man, the Scientific Group of the London Dumping Convention in London. The work related entirely to nuclear issues: reactor safety, emergency planning, comparisons of health risks between coal and nuclear fuel, the agricultural consequences of a nuclear meltdown. These were in connection with the Sizewell Inquiry. Then there was the ocean dumping of radioactive waste. The National Union of Seamen had forced the government to comply with the moratorium under the London Dumping Convention until such time as certain scientific issues could be resolved. Not only was the scientific review work going to be demanding, there was a punishing schedule of media interviews, briefings with the NUS, Parliament committees and the Minister for the Environment.

Susan was now ensconced in a pleasant two-bedroom house in West Oxford. I felt accepting of that separation, but it was hardly conducive to the work ahead. My emotional swings of anger and grief might not be over, and there was absolutely no leeway in the schedule for any disturbances in my focus. I had to find some distance, however difficult that would be for Matthew and Owen. I had become firm friends with Ian Fairlie, who worked as a research officer in Transport House, and had been instrumental in pulling support of the Unions behind the anti-dumping campaign. Moreover, he had a sound knowledge of radiation safety issues. There was a spare room in his house in Islington, which he shared with three or four others. It would make an excellent London base for working and sleeping over, and provide me with a welcome respite from Oxford. I called and he immediately agreed.

Once organised, I met with Sue in a restaurant in town. She remarked on my peacefulness, and how it was obvious I had spent time with a 'holy man'. She was softer, but weary. Her skin was very pale against her dark coat. Such a distant wintry beauty. My heart longed for the closeness we once shared. I had approached our meeting with a new sense of peace. It did not last the length of our interaction. A sharpness descended upon me. I wanted to know where the relationship was going with Stephen, her lover. She could not say more than that it felt right to her and they had no plans. I told her that whatever she was avoiding in me, she would eventually have to face. That what she was doing was wrong. She stiffened, closed up and we parted. I was left to dwell in my self-righteousness.

I was annoyed at myself and annoyed at Babaji. Why had he not bestowed upon me a little more wisdom and compassion and humility? All those mornings with the coolness of his hand across my forehead, to so little effect? I decided not to visit the children until I could feel a stronger change.

I phoned Robert. He was relieved I was back. In his slightly overdone serious voice he said he needed to see me immediately, he'd come to Oxford, he couldn't talk over the phone. We agreed to meet at Maida (pronounced M'eye-tha) Suarez's house in Juxon Street, West Oxford, a block away from Sue's. I regretted it afterwards. I hadn't seen the children in three weeks, and they would be just around the corner. I imagined them having supper, having their baths and their stories, and the pang of longing hit me.

What is it that so disturbs the psyches of two people, once in love, for so many years entwined and interpenetrated, with children so needing of their combined presence, that they cannot come close, as if a distant switch has been thrown and magnetic polarities reversed? In ten years I have had some insights, but then I had none, then it was a struggle to accept, a raging, a desperate wishing and a petitioning of the powers.

As I left to meet Robert I met Bruno Tollentino. He was then a don at Oxford. He had come to visit my colleague Roger Kayes. They had struck up a friendship around Roger's newly discovered curiosity with the paranormal. Bruno was a somewhat infamous character. Bisexual, extrovert, utterly charming and likeable, a talented astrologer, and a devoted practitioner of a Yoruba-derived religion, a Brazilian combination of Voodoo and Catholicism the name of which continues to escape me. Roger, the Capricornian sceptic of all things unscientific, was strangely captivated.

I always enjoyed interactions with Bruno. He had a close liaison with one of Sue's friends, knew the children, and I know was genuinely interested in their welfare. But he unsettled me. His was a religion of magical offerings, appeasements, and spells. He communed with ancient African river gods and goddesses. My problem was not with the plethora of Gods but that this supplication of powers actually worked. It was not clear then how he financed his rather flamboyant lifestyle, but he had talked with Roger of influencing various contracts and deals by intervention of the spirits, (doubtless he had some legitimate means, but many years later he was jailed for trafficking in cocaine). More, I think, by force of Bruno's personality, than by any evidence of paranormal successes, Roger was showing signs of becoming a supplicant himself. I had elected not to interfere.

Maida Suarez. Round-faced Spanish beauty. Constantly bright and effervescent. I had often retreated to her flat after interactions with Sue. She never consoled by sympathy. Always she would penetrate to the heart of where love lay. The road out of my emotional turmoil would become clear again. She had a purity of spirit and insight that I will always honour. She also had a lovely athletic body. Waist and hips kept trim by a total paranoia of growing fat like all her relatives from the Basque country. Her youth had been wayward, involved in ETA, escape through France, and now a marriage of convenience to the strange guy in the flat above, a sad character, never out of faded black clothes, long hair, unemployed, who for all I could gather, spent his time collecting pieces of broken motorcycles. This 'husband' had several times attempted to move the marriage toward a physical consummation, which Maida had resisted, leaving a tension between them.

It had been good for me to be close with Maida. Occasionally I had stayed over and shared her bed. She would always guide my wandering hands with good humour away from anything approaching an erogenous zone. Sex for her had to involve another dimension, and although Robert now regarded her as 'his' girlfriend, Maida would always tell me she was not 'in love' with him. Maida was in love with someone we never met called Nick, an admirable fellow devoted to the dispossessed of the Third World, who seemed constantly to be in Africa. She lived for his return and never ceased to affirm they would marry. She would ask me...'do you think Nick and I will get married', to be instantly followed with 'I'll kill you if you say no'. The relationship had brought much needed humour and friendly intimacy.

Maida had also been with us on the 1983 Big Ben 'action', baptised in Cannon Row jail, and was now fully trained by Ron in the art of chimney-climbing. Robert had that to discuss with her. And with me, developments with the astral 'warriors'. For the latter we retreated to a public house in Jericho rather than let Maida in on developments at this stage.

Robert looked tired, much thinner in the face since the time before Christmas. He had the capacity to change physique enormously, at times very heavy in the gut to the point where middle age appeared to have exerted its grip, and then, either through strain, or in better times, intense physical work-outs, usually in the form of karate training, he could look lithe and graceful. As it happened, both influences were at work, he had been training and he had gone through a difficult emotional time with Kim over Christmas.

There had been a further meeting with John Taylor while I was away. John was exasperated by inaction on the part of Greenpeace. The chemical waste drums were still being dumped. They had 'seen' stacks of the drums in a warehouse in the midlands. Whilst Robert was there, Charmayne had 'gone out' and watched some cylinders being dumped. They had radioactive markers on them. Charmayne could not help her rising anger and, apparently, when emotional energy is coupled with the psychic effort required to astrally project, the physical body may manifest. In this case, she half-manifested in the form of a wraith in the galley. The crew panicked, spilling bowls of soup everywhere. Charmayne was catapulted back and felt decidedly ill for the experience. John had been told by Pan that the waste came from the navy yards at Plymouth. He was also told that what Charmayne had witnessed had yet to happen. In other words, she had projected into the future, and moreover, had affected it. They had been reprimanded. John had impressed upon Robert that the 'warriors' were beginners, they did not know the rules, and they could get hurt.

The 'warriors' had also begun to encounter 'opposition' on the other side, and Charlie had been physically hurt. Damage on the astral level could carry over, and they were unsure of the rules governing the interactions of one level of reality with the other. John had described one opposition character very clearly, a tall thin aristocratic man with a beaked face, 'Very unpleasant piece of work. Quite high up. Obviously an adept.' And he had been told the opposition was coming from Masonic lodges in London.

As Robert talked I had a clear image of a character I had met only a few months previously. He was tall, aristocratic and of a decidedly 'beaked' visage. Being unsure of the laws of libel in these matters, and bearing in mind that my little vision during these paranoid times could be a gross injustice to the man, I will not refer to him by the name. He had been on a key international tribunal to which I had given evidence. My evidence had been a damning indictment of the British nuclear industry, specifically, the history of radioactive waste discharges at Windscale. BNFL, the operating company, had broken international guidelines on waste disposal in the most cavalier fashion by discharging massive amounts of radioactive Plutonium into the Irish Sea. Despite the public outcry in Britain, this was still not widely known on the Continent, and the international jury of environmental experts had been horrified by the evidence. They found BNFL 'guilty', but of course, there could be no legal redress, since the UK government had legitimised the discharges and the international legal framework had no way of punishing those who offended against the guidelines of international customary law. Our beaky character had been one of the experts. He did not appear at all friendly and I had assumed that being 'old school' he just hated his beloved Britain being made to look so bad.

Robert rapidly concurred. He too had reason to suspect the man, despite his environmental credentials. He had chaired many key committees and had great influence in Whitehall. Earlier he had played a key role on a committee that reviewed evidence relating to pollution of the North Sea and the activities of Tioxide in particular. Robert suspected him of letting Tioxide off the hook. If this man were indeed an operator for industry, then he was a very clever operator, even without astral aptitudes.

'So, how much do you know about the Freemasons', I asked Robert.

'Only that they were responsible for Grandad's death! Do you remember Mum telling us that? That he had crossed them by not joining in some corrupt practice and they bankrupted him.'

I had long forgotten. Our grandfather had been a photographer, and all I knew about him was that he had been gassed in the Great War, and eventually died in the depression, when he could not find work. His not finding work had much to do with having crossed the local Freemasonry.

Whatever, it was important that we did a little research. Neither of us knew anything about modern Freemasonry. I had snippets from Christopher, my long-time school friend, who had joined the Metropolitan force after school and since emigrated to police Australia, and also from one of Sue's brothers in the Leicester Constabulary, but nothing more than that the Masons were a secret society the non-membership of which could seriously hinder promotion prospects. We both knew they had rather petty rituals.

Our knowledge of the astral dimension and its rules was also limited. Robert re-iterated what we both knew from martial arts training, meditation and yoga, which was that with advanced training it was possible to project the 'astral body', create a double, and even de-materialise and re-materialise the physical body. In such a world, the normal reality of time and distance would not operate. It was apparent that bilocation occurred at the speed of thought. Telepathy we were familiar with. Astral surveillance was something we had not given much thought to and we obviously needed to know more about its potential.

Robert admitted he was spooked by the whole thing. He did not sleep well. Sometimes he felt a presence in his room. The lights behaved strangely. Bulbs seemed to blow more frequently, and they would flicker and crackle. John Taylor had erupted in a diatribe of complaint about Greenpeace and that 'fat slob' Babaji, about how the true warriors were taking all the risks, and how Robert and I could so easily be 'used' by the other side unless we were really centred. Our women were our weakness. They were not beside us. How could you be a warrior if your woman was not totally with you! 'Three brothers', he had said, 'Pan says there is power in this'. Pan had told him we had important work to do, but that we were vulnerable and must be careful.

Neither of us knew much of Pan, or Arthur, or any other element of the western mystery tradition. Robert's spiritual life was traditionally Buddhist, mine also eastern, through Yoga, and recent reading, of the 'Aquarian Gospel', courtesy of Dave Wilmott. The latter book had led me back to an appreciation of Jesus as an Essene Yogi, and was another strand to the general supposition in India that Jesus had gone there to learn and to teach. We had both made contact with rather vague karmic roots in North American medicine paths. But of our own country's traditions, we knew virtually nothing.

On the practical front, the 'astrals' had reconnoitred the scaffolding around the base of the Ben and considerably helped Ron with the planning. Apparently that was when they had first encountered the opposition. With regard to the dumping operation we were stuck. Neither of us could afford time away from our other work to travel down to Devon and Cornwall. Robert had corresponded with the naturalist, Trevor Beer and we now had formal evidence of the waste drums in as much as Beer had described them in letters to MAFF. However, without Greenpeace's resources, we could not mount an operation to intercept the ships, and Robert did not feel able to approach the Board. He suggested that I come down for another meeting with John Taylor.

I told him of my plan to move my office to North London and outlined my programme of work. The move would take a week to complete, after which we could meet with Taylor. We shared a little of our respective difficulties with our women, feeling our vulnerabilities in this regard. I related Shastraji's prophetic 'two brothers good, three brothers bad' and 'one brother is harm to you' and then wished I had kept it to myself. It obviously disturbed and annoyed Robert and he urged me to dismiss it as an unhelpfully negative influence. We parted, with Robert heading back to Maida's and I to walk back through town to East Oxford. I kept wide of Juxon Street despite the strong desire to visit.

I walked through the city centre. Busy people leading normal lives. Despite the crisp winter day, I recalled a summer poem written years before.

Slowed sweated thoughtless,
unobserved, random purposeless,
fleshy
avoiding
        looking down holding hands
gathering food and distractions
leaving the sparrowed streets
humanity on a hot day

I had always felt this separation from mundane lives. How different this world would be if everyone sought a greater purpose! Yet they had something I had not. Homes to go to, human warmth, simple faithful love. Predictable futures.

Not so! My righteous other-half cut in, 'look at the divorce rate, the numbers of children without fathers, sixty percent of whom lose complete contact with their children, and this security, you know it is an illusion, collapse is inevitable, if not a nuclear holocaust, then a slow and steady degradation of planetary ecosystems.....Gaia herself will intervene, did not Babaji prophesy, and in so many of the other traditions, the Hopis, Sun Bear, Edgar Cayce....and this is 1984, Orwell's year..... Pluto in Scorpio.... Pluto is Shiva, Lord of Destruction.... Pluto rules the underworld, hidden powers, and *is* that destructive force necessary to break through the illusions of separateness, the dwelling in dualities. Scorpionic sign of a cleansing death....the death before rebirth and regeneration.....'

My haunted self disposed of a pizza in one of the sanitized parlours, watched bemused at a party of well-dressed women, out for an evening of gossip, and made its way to an early bed. Those women remained. White synthetic blouses, pale skins, lipstick, nylon-coated legs and that imagined erotic sound as thigh meets thigh in the ritual crossing and uncrossing....why did bared knees have such an effect? Bone-whitened flesh, desire to touch, yet just a knee the touch of which never fulfilled that promise of a magic pulse. And blouses awaiting their unbuttoning, the gate to sacred ground, nipple temples and aureole of darkened oily skin. They could still exert their pull, these women without person, with obvious emptiness, desiring so little from life, having sold out, if ever they knew, content at the deal, saving for the house, the car, the suite, the children, once the beloved was netted. I had overheard the gabble. Not one word of Thatcher. Of Cruise missiles. Of the web of real women spinning their love under the stars. Yet still I could be pulled. It did not take much. Simple proportions, with which one of them had been well blessed. Why was the game so rigged? How many Greenham women had such appeal, with their cropped heads, ringed noses, baggy-trousered big bums and tattooed arms. Thoughts of all those beauty contests on television, joining in with the assessments, always preferring the longer legs, the essential 'gap', the fullest lips and that power of pronounced cheek bone. Then the goddess of the Pizza parlour would speak and the spell would be broken. From another planet - an ordinary world, Birmingham accent.

I dispelled the reverie with mantra. Om Namaha Shivaya. I surrender to God. Sleep came slowly. I dreamt of a shadowy pursuit and half-awake I turned to face my pursuers, ready for combat. Four men advancing, menacing, armed with handguns. I could roll to the left. Down a bank, into the river. Force the dream to counter my reality of never being able to dive, to stay beneath the surface, never having mastered underwater swimming. Then I was awake to the moon. Such resistance to simply dying. Always the same response, fight or flee, and in the fighting I am never competent enough, always outnumbered and outgunned.

I wasted no time in the move to Islington. Ian's house provided the light of regeneration, the antidote to Oxford. He had stripped all the wood on doorframes and skirting boards and it caught the pale winter sun through huge south-facing windows. The kitchen was communal, and there I met Merrilyn Julian recently moved from Australia. She was tall, dark-haired, elegant and attractive, but in those first few weeks I was thankfully free of sexual impulse. Merrilyn became a source of wisdom, healing waters to return to at night, to talk of poetry and literature and wild places where driftwood washed white in the sun. She was a literary editor at a large publishers. There began a slow rejuvenation of those parts of me so divorced from western culture, a re-opening to heritage, to sensitivities I had long presumed dead.

The effects of my relocation were instant. Suddenly evenings were full of conversation around warm food home cooked, bottles of wine, possibilities of an evening out. Ian and I had always been close. Although professionally we had limited contact at campaign meetings, we had an instant trust and shared our stories of love and sex and the struggle to relate successfully to women. He would listen with concern as I related interactions with Sue, and would gently shake his head with a conviction that she was truly lost to me. One part of me denied what I knew to be a more finely honed knowing of woman, and another part registered the knowledge and fear that he was right, that there were natural laws, as when a leaf has fallen.

Shortly after the move to Islington I received a letter from William Waldegrave, then environment minister. The government was to set up a Commission to review its policy of radioactive waste dumping in the North East Atlantic. I was invited to join a four-man committee to be chaired by Fred Holliday, professor of Geology at Durham. Other members of the team were to be Brian Funnell, professor of Biology at East Anglia and Bob Clarke, professor of Zoology at Newcastle. The secretariat would be based at the Ministry of Agriculture, Fisheries and Food (MAFF) laboratories at Lowestoft.

I had met Waldegrave some time ago when brother Robert and I had gone to see him to talk over various environmental matters. We had been conducting our own private survey of Britain's trees and were convinced of acid rain damage. We also discussed Tioxide and radwaste discharges and dumping, both issues with which he was genuinely concerned. He had been the first, and perhaps the last, Conservative Party politician with which I could discern any feeling of genuine concern for the environment. However, that was not the reason I was invited to the Holliday Committee. The Trades Union Council had been asked for a nominee and they had insisted upon myself as an informed critic. The professorial appointees had no specific knowledge of the issue.

Further to this appointment, the Department of the Environment also set up a Research Advisory Group, to which I was also appointed. This, initially at least, was because they wanted to hear what I had to say. I think there was a discernable shift within government and Whitehall away from its hitherto unquestioning support of the nuclear industry. The Yorkshire TV programme had made by far the biggest dent in the establishment's confidence and it was now rapidly re-aligning itself, at least as far as the 'back-end' of the fuel cycle was concerned. Following James Cutler's programme early in November 1983, itself co-incident with a radioactive spill from the site at Sellafield which forced the closure of 25 miles of beaches, the Department had moved onto the offensive. The new advisory group would examine the government's current research programmes in the light of criticisms of its inadequate performance as the industry's watchdog.

In addition to this, the government had also set up another independent review under Sir Douglas Black to examine the statistical claims of excess childhood leukaemias uncovered by Yorkshire TV's research. This review would also require detailed inputs of critical material.

These new developments were to come on top of a heavy workload already well developed. The Sizewell Inquiry into the building of a Pressurised Water Reactor, of American design, the first to be commissioned in this country, which was to last over a year, was now under way and we were scheduled to give evidence over the spring and summer of 1984. We had negotiated contracts with the National Union of Mineworkers for a critique of the nuclear industry's approach to comparative health data. The industry had published work attempting to show that, watt for watt, uranium mining and nuclear reactor operation produced less health damage than coal mining and subsequent burning of the fuel in power stations. Another consortium of unions, including the Fire Brigades Union and National Union of Public Employees (mainly on behalf of the ambulance workers) had agreed to commission a report on the implications for emergency personnel of a major nuclear melt-down. Finally, the Agricultural Workers Union had requested a report on the implications for agricultural production of such a massive contamination incident.

Furthermore, Gordon Thompson, who, after our work at Windscale, and following the West German government's Gorleben Review, had been offered a post at Princeton, and was now firmly ensconced in Cambridge, Massachusetts, had now been taken on by the Town & Country Planning Association to critique the arguments on probabilities of a meltdown. It was to our great advantage as critical scientists that the reactor was of a standard American design. The UK establishment could not maintain the fiction, so assiduously held with regard to British designs such as Magnox and AGR, that the reactor core could not melt. We had ample American 'safety' studies which elaborated the failure mechanisms and their consequences, whereas all such British material was classified and unavailable to the public.

Meanwhile, the moratorium on nuclear waste dumping won at the London Convention in 1983 had to be followed by attendance at Scientific Group meetings where a special Inter-Governmental Panel was set up to review the basis for the decision. Greenpeace had 'observer' status, and I was to participate as their nominated scientific expert. There was a real danger that experts drawn from the nuclear industry and nominated by the 'pro-dumping' states, (Britain, Japan, USSR, France, and South Africa), would dominate the discussions. Somewhat unusually, the UN had given me complete access to working group meetings and the freedom to contribute to the scientific debate.

This represented a formidable workload. Fortunately, Roger Kayes was now working full-time on the Sizewell issues, collaborating on the emergency planning and health review reports. He was to fly to the US and gather information on their much stricter requirements. Charlie Arden-Clarke was also free to work with me on scientific issues relating to the ocean ecosystem and modelling of dispersal.

However, there were problems with accepting the government's invitation to the Holliday Committee. Firstly, it was typical of all government 'independent reviews' for a group of 'experts' to be appointed, the majority of whom had little knowledge of the main issue, and who would needs rely upon expert support from the very departments they had been set up to review. In this case, MAFF would be providing not only expert advice, but also secretarial support. This invariably means a key drafting role in the production of the report. MAFF, of course, had been licensing the dumping since it first began.

Furthermore, the literature relating to the dumping issue was vast. As the licensing authority, MAFF had developed sophisticated computer models attempting to predict the fate of radioactive contaminants released on the ocean floor. Such models integrated knowledge from several disciplines: physical and biological oceanography, sediment chemistry, radioecology and radiobiology, in all of which the frontiers were continually advancing. Our main criticism of the current modelling attempt was that it could not deal adequately with a huge range of uncertainty, and a major way of displaying the truth of that uncertainty (it being harder to elaborate upon what is not known than upon what is known) would be to demonstrate how quickly knowledge was changing and how in only a few years previous assumptions about oceanic processes had been demonstrably wrong or naive. The new assessment would therefore require a thorough critical review of oceanographic sciences as well as radiobiology and this would require major financial resources.

Waldegrave was offering £70 per day, and I was informed I would need to reckon with at least six one-day meetings! I called to see him and pointed out that on an expected £420 I could not possibly participate, nor could I agree to MAFF as a secretarial base. I would need to employ research and secretarial assistance to do the job properly.

Fred Holliday was quick to support the point about MAFF and the secretariat was changed for the Institute of Oceanographic Sciences at Wormley, an organisation with little obvious vested interest in the current modelling programme. Waldegrave agreed to pay £1500/month for six months and I engaged Charlie and Roger within PERG and an outside consultant from the Open University, Dr Steve Cousins, a specialist in biological models and complex systems. We had an effective science review team.

I now needed 'secretarial support'. In truth, I needed more than a secretary. The task ahead would involve site visits to MAFF at Lowestoft, to Harwell where the waste was stored, and the committee meetings themselves. Whilst such meetings could be cordial, the environments were draining of my spirit. I would need someone who understood the subtler pressures and with whom I could have a close personal rapport. The psychic phenomena had begun to worry me. Whoever worked with me could expect trouble and would have to be psychically strong. Elaine Lawrence came to mind. We were good friends and having a sociology degree she could easily handle some of the research tasks. I called her and she immediately agreed to pose as my secretary.

When she came round a few days later, I cautiously broached the subject of the kind of 'trouble' we could expect. She needed no elaboration. After my call she had some indication that forces were at work. She was then living in a basement flat in Highbury with Alan Thornton (one of the founders of Greenpeace in the UK, who then moved on to create the Environmental Investigation Agency). The night of my call she had retired early. The next morning Alan could not wake her, and found her still asleep at 2pm in the afternoon. With much difficulty he revived her from a drowsy state. She did not tell him that late in the night she had woken, gone to the medicine cabinet and downed a whole bottle of his sleeping pills. She recalled only a constant repeated thought, 'I must kill myself'. Fortunately, Alan used only homeopathic medicines. The next day, when alone, she had felt a presence in the room. Her way of dealing with such things was simple and effective. It was to conjure up a vituperous anger and unleash it with verbal power in the direction of the psychic interloper. As far as she was concerned she was now on her guard and quite confident in handling anything that came at her. I was greatly strengthened in the knowledge that I would have someone with me whose sensitivities allowed free discussion of the trials we would doubtless now encounter.

I reflected upon Shastraji's assurance, 'Your work will be successful'. This had seemed impossible only two months ago. Now, after seven years as an outside critic, I was to sit on a high-level government-appointed review, and to be employed as a consultant by the Department of the Environment. There was constant press, radio and television interest in Sizewell, in Sellafield's discharges, the childhood leukaemias, and in the radioactive waste dumping at sea. We had adequate finances for the first time.

It was a point to reflect upon the long haul since the foundation of PERG in 1976. I shall dwell a little on the science, because it is central to an appreciation of the dark events that evolved in the course of that benighted year of 1984.

As I have indicated, nuclear power had become our main focus of work not simply because of the very real physical risks that it presented, and not simply because I, personally, did not like the buildings intruding into my favourite landscapes, however much that was the initial impulse, but because it represented the powerful symbolic centre, I will not say 'heart', of modern man's drive for control and exploitation of the earth's resources. The earth's last secret, the mineral uranium's hidden powers, had been unlocked. Mankind had stood upon a threshold and science had led him to it. It is not recorded, as far as I know, for I am no scholar of the history of science, whether any of those earlier scientists were cautioned by conscience to turn away, to leave the uranium in the ground, or if they did, whether their paymasters listened for one moment. Certainly, the Hopi

Indian elders cautioned the first uranium miners to arrive in the South West. The mineral was sacred, it must stay in the ground, its task to balance the earth and sky.

To the technologists that unlocked its secrets, uranium offered the ultimate weapon for the control of enemies and the winning of wars. Hitler's technicians had been at work on a bomb, and no doubt the good guys felt humanity's need to get there first. After the war, the slow fission reaction offered limitless control of man's other enemies, the vagaries of nature. There would be electricity 'too cheap to meter'.

There had developed a priesthood of technicians in white coats, for whom control of nature and ever more sophisticated and powerful weapons to control threats to 'freedom', had become a religion. In debate, the emotional content showed itself despite their claims to rationality. If we did not progress nuclear power, then we would move back into the 'dark ages', the 'lights would go out', and a primitive third-world future would await us.

In the early years of the policy debates, I believed that nuclear corporations and the huge sums of money they spent, were such a large part of the overall industrial economy that they were central to 'economic growth', especially since the oil-price hike had diverted large amounts of cash to other economies. Events in the USA following the scaling down of the industry after Three Mile Island showed this to be a false assumption. Not that I was any advocate of 'economic growth' with its mindless index whereby any exchange of money, or measure of 'increased production' was automatically regarded as a measure of progress. Within that index, anything that caused money to be spent had equal value: the biggest motorway pile-up increased growth, likewise any other disaster as long as it didn't bankrupt the insurance industry; and, of course, every tonne of oil and coal produced and burnt was 'good' and nobody could price the losses, the costs of carbon dioxide build-up, global warming, acid rain, asthmatic children or dying forests. Later, there would be attempts to price the destruction in Cost-Benefit Analyses, but of course, that which could not be measured could not be priced and would simply be left out of the equation. Even today, after two decades of debate, governments are only beginning to develop, let alone use, better indices of 'growth' in terms of real progress.

In the mid-1970s there was a developing critique of this mindless economic growth and progress. There were mass protests against the motorway construction programme, the AGR reactor at Torness, and the siting of a huge gas and chemical works close to housing estates at Canvey Island. On the continent, there were hundreds of thousands on the streets in Spain, France, Austria and Germany, protesting against nuclear power stations. Within the more obvious 'green' camps, there were critiques of a farming policy that was engulfing huge areas of marginal wildlife-rich land and producing mountains of unmarketable produce. There was opposition to the ineluctable march of 'economic' forestry that invaded semi-natural wilderness areas in the flow country of Scotland and the quiet corners of Portugal and Spain, and left monocultures of spruce or eucalyptus beneath which nothing would grow.

In 1979 I had a chapter published in a book edited by the economist Colin Sweet on the risks and costs of developing the Fast Breeder Reactor. I was then asked to write a piece for the respected scientific journal 'Nature' on how the odds were stacked against the nuclear opponents in the technological debates. These arguments could be transposed to almost any area of technology and science. Firstly, the industry held on to any information the release of which would jeopardise its image of control, but readily released huge masses of publicity material and claimed credit for openness. Crucial 'event reports' (accounts of near-misses in reactor operation) were not available for independent scrutiny. That material went to the regulators in Her Majesty's Inspectorate with a 'confidential' tag. Anyone outside of that rather cosy relationship simply had to take things on trust.

We had discovered small amounts of engineering detail on major faults in the AGRs, and I made these public in the article. In addition, with the help of Gordon Thompson, we critiqued the presentation of 'consequence' studies - supposedly 'worst case' accidents where leaks of 'Chernobyl' proportions were possible (noting that Chernobyl in 1984, Chernobyl was two years in the future). Even when the industry came clean and admitted the potential, the data were presented in obscure 'probabilistic' terms, whereby the catastrophe was ascribed a remote probability of occurrence, such as once in 100 million years. This small factor was multiplied by other probabilities, such as of the wind blowing toward cities instead of out to sea, and of different weather conditions which affect dispersal, and finally multiplied by the chances of those exposed by such a cloud getting a cancer as a result. By multiplying their best guesses at frequency of failure with solid statistics on weather and cancer risk per unit of dose, the guesses took on an aura of science rather than engineering judgement. The final results were presented in indecipherable tables of figures showing miniscule individual risks of death at varying distance from the reactor.

There were at that time no simple maps of expected land contamination, areas of evacuation, areas of agricultural restrictions, or the *total* number of people who would suffer death or disease. We criticised the whole approach to 'probabilities' upon which the siting policy and justification for nuclear power stations was based. It was necessarily a technical argument that, at that stage, only professionals could engage with. As it would later trespass, our approach was vindicated by changes in the way the US, Swedish and German authorities presented their data, and of course, the major impact of contaminated land, produce and evacuated people in the aftermath of Chernobyl.

'Nature' published two letters in response to the article, both from the nuclear industry picking me up on what they supposed were inaccuracies but which did not address the fundamental argument on availability of the right kind of information both to outside scientists and for parliamentary scrutiny. There was no response from the sleeping mass of engineers, physicists or chemists, professionals or students, that had marked the open debates in the USA. Nuclear reactor safety had remained an unopened issue, to which we would return at the Sizewell Inquiry.

The significance of 'Windscale' in all of this was multifarious. Certainly, it posed and continues to pose, huge physical risks on a scale that was, until 1986, unimaginable. In that year the world saw at Chernobyl just what potential for disaster lay in the uncontrolled aerial release of radioactivity. I will not dwell on the lessons of that event, having committed myself to as little post-1984 wisdom as I can consciously achieve, except to remark that in our expert testimony to the Sizewell Inquiry in 1983, we accurately predicted the wide-scale problems of the contamination of land and restrictions of agriculture as being far more devastating in their immediate effects than the hidden long term increase of cancers, or for that matter, the thirty or so 'early deaths' from radiation exposure in the emergency personnel who fought to contain the fire. Before our testimony, emergency workers had no idea of what to expect in a full-scale melt-down, having been drilled to deal only with the slightest of aerial releases.

In 1977 we had attempted to persuade Justice Parker that the industry's estimated consequences should one of Sellafield's liquid nuclear waste tanks lose its cooling and boil - of a small risk of a few cancers over fifty years - were totally inadequate. There had been a determined effort to conceal the fact that even one such waste tank had ten-times the potential for aerial release as any nuclear reactor. There were ten such tanks and if one failed, they could all fail. We had evidence of this from detailed calculations done at a German government institute of a possible 'loss of cooling incident'. The industry's witnesses had managed to conceal this fact by refusing to carry their own analysis beyond the initial boiling phase on the grounds that it was unrealistic to expect that they could not repair any fault in the system. Parker unfortunately agreed with them and chose not to represent the German material to parliament for debate.

We had one more card to play. Making much of the secrecy, we petitioned for the complex computer model that calculated the consequences to be released to us. Parker, surprisingly, agreed, although I am sure that nobody expected us to be able to make use of the boxes of punched cards delivered to us by a reluctant United Kingdom Atomic Energy Authority. Firstly, we had to find a computer large enough. Even then, it would take many hours of computer time and prove hugely expensive. An old Zoology colleague, busy modelling populations of voles on a certain northern University's computer agreed to help. Gordon managed to get results, but they appeared too high! We were stuck. Time on University computers could no longer be guaranteed and we needed help in debugging the programme. Somehow the word had got out and I had a call from 'someone close to the UKAEA'. Alan Francis, a computer wizard at the Atlas Rutherford laboratory, offered to help.

Alan discovered what he was convinced was a deliberately introduced bug in the programme, and we were spared the inevitable humiliation and waste of time delivering false results to the inquiry. However, time was running out and we could no longer use University resources. Alan hacked into the only other computer he knew could handle the size of the programme. From his small attic room in Abingdon, at God-forsaken hours before dawn, he made good use of the UKAEA's own computers at Harwell - he was, in any case, about to resign from the industry.

On delivery of the results to the inquiry, results that predicted six-figure casualties in unfavourable weather and assuming just one tank had failed, Parker ordered an in-camera session with BNFL's engineers. They did not dispute the consequences, merely re-iterated with rising emotion, that it was inconceivable the system could lose all power for 2-3 days. They insisted the boiling phase that they had modelled was adequate, because cooling could easily be restored.

This was nonsense, and they knew it. In order for a tank to boil, the cooling, venting and agitation systems had to fail for 8-12 hours. That, in itself, was the initiating event. It could occur through electrical fire, sabotage, earthquake, aircraft impact, or terrorist attack. These were admittedly going to be rare events, but of their nature not capable of having exact probabilities ascribed to them. Once that had happened, and boiling had begun to vent highly active radio-caesium into the working environment, access and repair could not be guaranteed. If they were willing to take the events that far, they should carry them to conclusion. After 2 days the water would have boiled off leaving a 2000 degree molten mass of salt which would melt stainless steel and vaporise the concrete. Ninety per cent of the radioactivity would escape to form a cloud across the landscape. Within half-a-day the cloud could reach Manchester, or Liverpool, Glasgow or Dublin, depending on the wind direction. To save thousands of lives, these cities would face the decision of evacuation.

Tempers rose. BNFL and the UKAEA argued we would unnecessarily alarm the public. We were regarded as security risks, the information of use to terrorists. Gordon, went extremely red under the collar at this and argued that secrecy was no guarantee of safety from terrorist attack and the public had a right to know the risks they were running. In the end Parker agreed with the industry, and shamelessly extracted from Gordon a statement, later used to dismiss the work we had done, in that 'the analyses were admitted by Thompson, not to be assessments of risk under realistic circumstances'. Gordon had meant that we could not attempt a 'realistic' assessment when denied crucial engineering information on the design of the system.

We were not to return to this issue in Britain for another 17 years. In 1994, I am currently engaged on a return match, with several of the northern cities sponsoring a campaign to have the tanks made safe. But the issue itself did not go away. In 1979 an identical installation at Cap la Hague in France lost all power to the tanks, actually to the whole site itself when an electrical fire destroyed key parts of the safety system. Only the electric fence was working. The engineers, sweating by all accounts, brought a duplicate system from the nearby submarine dockyard at Cherbourg. Reports that had to be made to the European Commission showed they had taken four hours to effect the repairs.

In that year, Gordon was retained by the Government of Lower Saxony, a West German State with its own regional parliament, to head a critical review of the KEWA Corporation's proposals for an identical THORP at Gorleben, of which I earlier made mention. Here PERG was given every assistance, from engineering drawings to a proper consultants budget to do the job. Gordon brought in experts from France, the USA and Sweden. I made an unofficial visit to Hannover, where I was still remembered from Gorleben days, and unofficially allowed a few quiet moments with access to the photocopier and among all the engineering drawings submitted for planning approval – we now had the realistic data we needed. In the final report of the regional government, the minister stated, 'we will under no circumstances license the production of liquid high level waste to be stored in non-fail-safe tanks'. The industry was told to develop fail-safe options because however small the probability of a complete failure, the consequences were so great as to be totally unacceptable.

Despite detailed representations to Her Majesty's Government, Parker's judgements stood. On this issue, at least we were to have negligible effect in Britain. I am sure, however, that the high cost and delay inflicted on the Germans killed 'reprocessing' in that country (attempts to license a site were finally abandoned in 1990), and as a by-product, made sure Sweden did not embark on the technology. Unfortunately for Britain, or the public and taxpayers, at least, this created more business for BNFL!

There were some successes, however. We had opened up the controversy over discharging large quantities of exceptionally dangerous radionuclides into the Irish Sea. In particular, the special license issued in 1970 for the discharge of plutonium from the refurbishing of atomic warheads. By 1980 these discharges were curtailed and by 1985, several hundred million pounds had been spent on effluent treatment plant (more jobs for the boys!). The plutonium still resides on the bottom of the Irish Sea. About half a metric tonne of it, where one millionth of a gram ingested would be a lethal dose. We made public the fact that original estimates of its eventual fate overlooked sea-to-shore transport mechanisms such as sea-spray and sediment remobilisation. Our research and provocations led to sampling of house dust and court cases for contamination and putting children at risk- unsuccessful in the end, and eventually to the indications of excess childhood leukaemia, to be later confirmed by the Yorkshire TV team and subject to the government's inquiry under Douglas Black. Now, in 1984, we were about to give evidence to Black's committee.

In our investigations of Cumbrian health data we also discovered evidence of older people dying of multiple myeloma, another radiation-linked disease, but neither the Yorkshire TV crew, the press, or the government showed interest in an old people's disease. Even when, in 1980, the statistically significant excess was confirmed by the County's own epidemiological consultant, Peter Tiplady, the issue never arose again.

In all of these scientific debates on nuclear risks, there stood in the background a steadily shifting perception of the physical risk of low levels of radiation itself. When the nuclear-electrical power programmes had begun in the late 1950s, levels of exposure below those which could cause immediate and observable changes in the blood, were thought virtually harmless. There had been evidence of excess cancers in radium workers, and of excess leukaemia a few years after Hiroshima, but these were from relatively high doses. It was thought prudent to keep workers at 'safe' doses below 5 rem (an old measure) per year. Public limits were arbitrarily set at one-tenth this figure. After two decades of epidemiology, largely on survivors of the atom bomb blasts, there was considerable pressure from scientists in that field to change the limits. Low level radiation had long-term cancer risks that had been underestimated.

The problem with changing the limits was that large investments in plant and technology had been made which exposed many thousands of workers in the reprocessing industry to levels just below the 'safety limit'. There was little room to reduce that limit. These workers, not to mention the public, had assumed that safe meant safe, that is, no risk, when in fact, to the scientists, it meant 'relatively safe' compared to other risks of contracting cancer or falling off a ladder in the building industry (which happens rather often).

We believed then that if the standards of exposure were altered even by a factor of two, the reprocessing industry, and all dreams of a plutonium economy based on Fast Breeder Reactors, would founder. The cost of protecting workers to double the standard by halving exposure, would be too high. In the 1970s the reprocessing operations and attendant research into plutonium-fuelled fast-breeder reactors supported a multi-billion dollar industry in Europe, Germany and Japan. Added to that was an even greater industrial commitment to a nuclear weapons programme totally dependent upon plutonium production and the machining of the metal into ever smaller warheads. It was not stretching things by any means to say that there were industrial, military and banking interests that felt the whole future potential of civilisation was at stake. Plutonium was not only the key to nuclear weapon developments such as the neutron bomb, the Fast Reactors were supposed to breed their own plutonium fuel from waste uranium and thus, with reprocessing to extract the 'plute', would go on forever and unlock vast reserves of energy to last long after the world's oil or coal stocks were exhausted.

Into this world of scientific debate had stepped in 1976, a diminutive, bespectacled old lady from Oxford University, Dr Alice Stewart. She was, however, no stranger to controversy. In the late 1950s and 60s, as an epidemiologist specialising in child cancer statistics, and with the help of a speech-impedimented, typically nutty-looking but nevertheless genius statistician, George Kneale, she had proven that X-ray programmes for pregnant women, hailed as a medical advance, were leading to leukaemia in significant numbers of the children born to those mothers. Her work was contested doggedly for years. Just like any other industry, for example, the long fight against lead in petrol, the radiological profession deployed its own experts to cast doubt on the results.

The industrial sectors of the industry had set up the ICRP, International Commission for Radiological Protection, to oversee standards. Although it sounded authoritative and independent, it consisted entirely of self-selected experts from the industry, and its main role was to defend the old standards and resist change. Alice had a long battle against the ICRP and the industry's goliath, one Edward Pochin, who, after 20 years of effective rearguard actions eventually conceded defeat on the X-ray hazards.

Due to this pioneering work, Alice was contracted by the US Government to examine the records of US radiation workers in the reprocessing operations at Hanford. She reported in 1976, claiming to show that low-level radiation was at least ten times more carcinogenic than previously thought. Her employers, having expected her to find no effects at all, immediately fired her. She had no funds at Oxford to continue and now resided at Birmingham Children's Cancer Registry, where she and George carried on with a much smaller budget. Pochin, on the other hand, whose main academic work was to collate spurious comparisons of nuclear risks with probabilities of getting struck by lightning, swallowed by a dam failure, or falling off a ladder in the shoe industry, was awarded a knighthood for his services to radiological protection. He was also appointed as Justice Parker's technical 'assessor', along with Frederick Warner, chemical engineer and chief consultant to the nuclear industry, also later to be knighted for services rendered.

The small group of us working at the Windscale Inquiry in 1977 had helped Alice give evidence, and she would also report again to the 1983 Sizewell Inquiry. As I write this, I can tell you that her estimates of risk were finally accepted in 1990, but she has yet to receive any honours.

Whilst Sir Edward Pochin had been busy on his epic works, the mundane task of shadowing Alice's almost impenetrable statistical analyses, always written up and accepted by the most reputable of journals, had fallen to a hapless John Reissland, chief statistician at the National Radiological Protection Board and well out of his depth with the likes of George Kneale.

Thus, in 1984, we had a culmination of many strands in a mounting psychological battle between technocratic conservatives and the emerging green consciousness. Nuclear power had ground to a halt in the USA, was to be phased out in Sweden, ceased its expansion in France and Germany, was banned in Denmark, Ireland and Austria (where they had moth-balled a spanking-new reactor), and of questionable future in Holland, Italy and Spain. The Fast Reactor programme was experiencing solid opposition. At Kalkar in Germany, court actions had withheld licenses for the final commissioning, only in France and Japan were FBR programmes progressing, whereas in Britain, the industry would have to go to another inquiry in 1986 on the FBR and reprocessing at Dounreay.

However, 'alternative' low-energy paths were not exactly winning the day. Only in Scandinavia could it be said that 'softer' technological solutions were being sought. In Britain, oil, coal and gas were in such abundance that no amount of lobbying could deflect the business to be made in expanding their sales. Except, that is for coal. Here would be displayed the true nature of the Conservative government's relationship to technology. Nuclear stations were dependable, their unions generally right-wing. The electricity then generated, however, relied on coal for 70% of output and left the coal miners in a powerful political position. This was also true of some other European countries.

In 1982 we had produced an energy policy review for the Group of Independents in the European Parliament. In the prologue we noted prophetically that by 1985 enough new nuclear power would come on stream to displace what were now whole communities and regions dependent on coal production. Areas of Belgium, France, Wales and Scotland would cease their historic production, even though there were large reserves still underground. Once nuclear stations had been built, they would have to be deployed to provide base-load electricity. The stations had been six to ten years in the building, commissioned in times when electricity use had been expected to increase at far greater rates than recession-torn Europe had actually experienced. Each station had thus accrued huge capital debts and these could only be recouped by displacing coal.

In the light of these findings, certainly not limited to our small research group, we had endeavoured to bring the coal miners into the anti-nuclear cause. They had enough political influence and, if needed, obstructive power, to make a major difference. Unfortunately, history is dogged by personalities, and the coal miners' gladiator, Arthur Scargill, sank most of those possibilities of alliance. We had not hitherto encountered 'socialist worker' methodologies in the British green movement. I, personally, being politically rather ill-educated, was shocked at the lack of democratic feeling, the carefully disguised tactics of delaying and blocking important committee decisions until late, when less aware members had left and Scargill's men could be sure of a majority. A major anti-nuclear alliance could not come about under these circumstances, and Scargill was left with a rump Anti-Nuclear Campaign which had very little connection with grass roots support outside of its Sheffield base.

I played some role in that limitation, and it is a pity there was no real meeting, for we were not opposed to direct action of the kind Scargill later directed. Had it focused upon nuclear power stations, perhaps it would have gained greater public support. As it was, we were to see, in 1984, the demise of the miners as their General Custer confronted Thatcher's vastly greater powers. I cannot help feel that the conservatives eagerly awaited the confrontation as a perfect smokescreen for closures of productive pits that would have competed in the 'free market' now underpinned by the heavily subsidised nuclear base-load generators. In those years, the nuclear industry was able to produce data that purported to show a competitive edge on costs. Critics were not given access to the information on which these claims were based. Only much later, when the government tried to privatise the industry, was it clearly admitted that coal was cheaper.

In addition to the energy policy show-down, the West was gearing up for its other great work, that of the defeat of Communism. The avowed strategy, claimed in hindsight following the events of the late 80s, was to bankrupt the Soviet Union and its allies by forcing the pace of weapons technology. To this end, cruise missiles were being deployed to Orwell's 'Airstrip One'. Britain was engaged upon a test programme of new smaller atomic warheads, France was developing its neutron-bomb, and enraging the whole of the South Pacific with its tests at Mururoa. Britain and the US were to commission a new generation of nuclear 'Trident' submarines, bristling with increased numbers of missiles and multiple warheads. Reagan was also intent upon the Star Wars programme of missile defences.

To anyone in the East, it must have looked like Armageddon was just around the corner. With a former 'B' movie actor holding a finger over the buttons, and a sycophantic Margaret Thatcher appearing less rational and human with each year of office, my own bet is that the Russians reformed out of a plain and simple instinct of common sense and a common future on the planet.

The last nuclear strand to the knotted ropes of 1984 was that of ocean dumping. In a way, compared to the other strands, it was hardly significant. The dumping operations only handled 'low' level waste. That is to say, the concentration of activity per unit volume was low, for it was the same nuclides, the same toxicities, but mixed with large volumes of filler, drummed and dropped over the side. It was waste too active to find a cheap option for landfill and not worth the expense of storing in the sites reserved for higher activities (and for which no disposal option has yet been agreed). The volumes, however, were large, at up to 100,000 tonnes per annum, and so, the total integrated activity was not insignificant.

The dumping programme was now led by Britain, which accounted for 98% of the radio-activity. Belgium, Switzerland and Holland contributed bulky but much less active material, and the Paris-based Nuclear Energy Agency (NEA) oversaw the 'international' programme. All other states, most notably, France, Italy, and the USA had long ceased dumping radioactive waste at sea. The International Atomic Energy Agency (IAEA) had issued 'guidelines' and standards of exposure for sea-dumping. In the UK the Ministry of Agriculture, Fisheries and Food had responsibility for the licensing of the operations and they had to consider the effects on fisheries and human health.

In all of these august bodies of science and regulation there ought to have resided some safeguards. But here is where Brian Wynne's writings about pluralism in science are most relevant. To model the effects of ocean dispersal demands a very large investment of resources in computers, mathematical models, monitoring and collection of relevant data from laboratory studies of sediment behaviour, food chain accumulation and final absorption in humans. In the whole of Europe such detailed studies had then only been undertaken by MAFF. Their experts sat on all the important scientific review committees of the NEA and IAEA, neither of which had undertaken much relevant primary research themselves.

Actually, for all the investments in 'assessment' of the NEA site there had been no published Environmental Impact Assessment during the whole dumping programme from 1958 to 1982. Clear guidelines for these assessments had been made by the IAEA in 1970, with particular reference to comparison of alternatives to dumping. Our first criticism was that the dumping had contravened international law by ignoring the recommendations for impact assessment and comparison with alternative land-based options. The IAEA had never made any representations to the NEA about the absence of such studies. Our second criticism related to the IAEA's assumption that the appropriate measure of environmental impact was the individual dose, and hence individual risk of death that would accrue to a member of the public sometime hence who might eat contaminated fish. This dose limit was the same as that adopted for any other nuclear site in the world (except Britain, which was five-times laxer), but of course, in situations where those at risk had some say in the debate about risks and benefits.

The IAEA regulations themselves would only limit the ocean dumping to about 10 separate sites where dumping at each site could reach 10 times the current dumping rate until such time as the world's population faced the dose-limit (for the oceanic mixing tendencies would lead very largely to an homogenous dose). Apart from the fact that 'individual' dose limits at nuclear stations represent a trade-off of risks and benefits within the society that used the nuclear energy, and these doses would accrue to billions of people who received no such benefits and could not be involved in negotiation of that trade-off, no one had calculated the 'collective dose' from these operations. This figure, sometimes called the 'collective detriment', is the sum of all the small doses worldwide divided by the risk per unit dose. It gives a simple number of human casualties in the form of cancer cases.

We had called for such assessments to be performed, and MAFF was busy adding these calculations to its oceanic model of dispersal. I should add that there was considerable scientific debate as to the meaningfulness of these measures. Individual doses from the one dumping operation were always going to be extremely small, and the collective dose, when integrated over the life of the more persistent and dispersive nuclides,(ten thousand years or more), even if producing thousands of 'casualties', relates to statistical deaths which would be invisible against a backdrop of hundreds of millions of natural cancer deaths.

However, in scientific terms, the absolute numbers were not the point. International legal frameworks required that the collective detriment from one 'option' be compared with that from others, such as landfill or deep disposal. This had not been done. This point alone, (plus Greenpeace's buzzing Zodiacs) guaranteed our moratorium would continue until the work had been done. Even when calculated, we would highlight the thorny problem of how to compare units of 'detriment' at a British landfill with units spread among Pacific islanders gaining no obvious benefits and no say in the decision to dump. The weighting of 'local' versus 'distant', 'worker' versus 'public', 'immediate' versus 'long term' detriments, when all measured in the same unit, would become another thorn for those intent on comparative assessments.

There was also the question of non-quantifiable impacts. The oceans were viewed as sacred by many cultures, and dumping barrels of industrial wastes was an insult to their values. The social meaning and value of these impacts could hardly be accorded a unit and factored into simple equations. No sociologists were employed on NEA or IAEA assessment panels. Indeed, when the only psychologists funded by the IAEA to research public perceptions of nuclear risks, had warned that such installations and activities may 'represent a public threat of death, sufficient to undermine the very creativity of youth', the team was immediately sacked and the reports buried. I had unearthed these papers (grey literature from the Royal Society) and presented them in my own submission for Justice Parker's benefit, but he simply skated over it in his report, saying he did not know how to assess such evidence.

The fact that the London Convention had voted for a moratorium had sent shockwaves not so much through the industry, which could doubtless cope and would have no problems absorbing the small extra costs, but through the scientific regulatory establishment. This establishment had a network of laboratories engaged in a multi-million dollar modelling exercise of the oceans and their capacity for absorbing radioactive wastes. The ocean floor, or beneath it, was now the preferred final resting ground for the much more concentrated high level wastes. Geologists had identified the abyssal plains of the world's oceans as the least disturbed most stable place on the planet. The modellers were now engaged upon designs of 'penetrometers', rather like missiles, which would be dropped from the surface and bury themselves, with their cargo of waste, into the accumulated ooze of the ocean floor. The high level radioactivity would be contained in borosilicate glass and encased in stainless steel, the argument being, that although there was a lot of it, it would leak out only slowly and much of it get locked in the sediments. The annual release to the 'biosphere' would not be much greater than that currently 'accepted' for the low level waste dumping operations (in which no containment is assumed because the barrels are ruptured on impact).

One can thus see that the apparently unnecessary business of dumping relatively innocuous waste that could easily be stored on land had another motivation, that of setting a precedent in the use of the oceans as a legitimate sink for the more problematic vastly greater amounts of high-level wastes.

Given the IAEA's weakness over standards, and the simplistic modelling, if the NEA programme were legitimised, there would then be no barriers for the oceans becoming the final dumping ground for all of the world's accumulated nuclear waste. For this reason, the USA, USSR, China, France, South Africa and Japan, all of which had no overt dumping programmes of their own (the Russians had a covert operation which we did not then know about), supported Britain in the Convention vote. And for this reason also, we were prepared to turn any stone in the hunt for scientific evidence that oceanic modelling was inadequate to predict consequences, even of an apparently innocuous amount of waste dissolved in the vastness of the North East Atlantic.

In this endeavour I had been joined by Professor W. Jackson Davis, a marine biologist from the University of California at Santa Cruz. 'Jackson' and I rapidly became friends. He had been a veritable acacia in the side of the American establishment, then funding its own large research programmes to parallel the 'self cleaning' ocean model of our own dear MAFF.

One of the most persistent thorns related to an old US dumpsite off the Farallon Islands some distance out from the Californian coast. Jackson had reviewed data gathered from monitoring operations in submersibles and calculated prospective doses via food chains to Californian consumers. The links were rather tenuous, but photographs of leaking drums were made public and a wave of protest propelled Jackson from his lab studies on the nerve endings of sea-cucumbers (a kind of marine slugs), to the international fora of the UN's oceanic protection conventions.

For his troubles, Jackson found his research budgets cut, even though he was a well-published scientific leader in a field that had no relation whatsoever to the political issues. He lost his laboratory for PhD students and the all-important 'summer salary' that constantly threatened his liquidity. Fortunately, he had tenure. And as a consequence of championing the oceans, he was befriended by the president of the Republic of Nauru, a ridiculously small island state founded on trading its phosphate-rich soil for money. Jackson became their unpaid (at his own insistence) legal representative at the UN. That was another thorn for the US State Department, as Jackson had as many votes at the UN as they had! He and I had now embarked on a collaborative strategy for undermining the models of the ocean ecosystem.

It may appear that my work was rather 'nuclear-dominated' and to a great degree it had been. However, through the network of PERG I had also embarked upon other work, often indirectly through design and management of projects, rather than writing myself. Chief of these were small surveys of tree die-back and reviews of the burgeoning scientific theories to explain it. Up until the mid-1980s, the general public had little overt evidence of an awaiting environmental catastrophe. Little of the ecological debate had penetrated the public psyche. I believe the rapid die-back of forest trees in central Europe between 1981 and 1984 was the greatest single influence on a sea-change in attitudes and perceptions, most of which did not impinge so greatly on a Britain which had little forest left to lose. The other major impacts were the widespread deaths of seals and small cetaceans, especially in the North Sea, the rapidly thinning ozone hole, and increasingly unpredictable weather as a harbinger of global warming.

By 1984 the public had become sensitised to the potential for rapid environmental change. The scientific world also underwent a major shift, almost to the level of a change of paradigm. Although some of the mechanisms of the observed environmental degradation had been known and the processes predicted, the exact time of onset, the threshold as it were, and the rate of change, had proven beyond the capacity of environmental science to predict. All of pollution regulation had, until then, been built upon a supposed ability to predict the 'limiting capacity' of the environment to absorb pollutants. Acceptable levels of safety to humans (from doses of poisons) or of damage to wildlife such as trees, fish, birds, whales, dolphins, seals, or whatever was perceived as 'valuable', depended upon science's ability to predict the fate of pollutants and the degrees of damage they would cause.

We were now witnessing widespread 'ecotoxic' effects due to levels of acid in soil, oxides of nitrogen in air, increased low-level ozone, and high level chlorine stripping of ozone in the atmosphere, as well as the ever present rise of carbon dioxide. These were not complex molecules, but basic chemicals which were now far in excess of their normal global fluxes as a result of the fossil fuel use that underpins industrial growth.

Environmental science had proven inadequate in predicting these effects. In 1984 the first rumblings of dissent within the establishment had begun. German fisheries scientists were correlating fish disease with metals pollution, and the first of the North Sea Forums began talking of the 'Precautionary Principle' whereby action should be taken to curb potential pollutants without necessarily waiting for science to prove their damaging effects. This principle was to become the main plank of our future arguments. Now, in 1994, it has been accepted in all major international legal treaties and conventions on the protection of the oceans, but then, it clashed headlong with what I began to see as an 'Assimilative Capacity' mafia, a group of scientists whose lifelong career had been predicated on the prediction of environmental limits for assimilating poisons, and more insidiously, that levels of 'acceptable' damage could be defined. The latter computations were carried out, very largely, by small committees of which they were key members.

Such psychological commitment to the old paradigm of predicting effects was also underpinned by vested interests in monitoring and modelling programmes. Large numbers of marine biologists, chemists and oceanographers were employed on these programmes and many research labs were dependent upon government funding linked to dumping and discharging of wastes or potential repositories under the sea floor.

Whether nuclear or chemical risk, energy policy or agriculture, oceans or forests, the work of my small research group over the seven years from 1976 to 1983 had been entirely negative. That is to say, we were critics. Our job had been to block, to slow-down, and possibly to divert the various courses of the industrial rush to ecological catastrophe. Each of us dreamt of a positive science, the constructive answer, of being part of the solution. Each of us believed in the role of science in providing answers to the dilemmas of energy and food shortages, materials scarcity, and stability in a global run-up to the next ice-age.

By 1984 we had made little headway in this regard. I had sought unsuccessfully for funding from the Government for comparative field studies of organic agriculture. We had wanted to review data on soil chemistry and stability under different agricultural regimes, of resultant biodiversity, nutrient cycling (pollution from nitrates was already evident in Germany at that time) and carbon fixation. Charlie Arden-Clarke had progressed a proposal in which several of the government's leading field research laboratories had agreed not only to participate, but to accept PERG's lead role in co-ordinating a project that would involve themselves and other institutions in Universities and the private sector. It took us until 1989 to complete our own academic reviews, carried out by Charlie, and funded by small grants from charities and the World Wide Fund for Nature.

Although we were not funded to carry out the field projects, I know that we had some effect in instigating the funding of others. These attempts at positive contributions may be the subject of another and later book! At this point I wish only to say that the imbalance had not escaped me, indeed, it weighed heavily upon my spirit.

5

The Quest

On the evening of February 14th I was back in Oxford to confer with Roger and Charlie on the work ahead. I was alone in my room. The telephone rang and Kamalu informed me that our beloved guru had died that day, apparently of a heart attack. She told me the devotees in Britain were devastated and would soon be gathering to sing and chant in mourning. I was curiously unmoved by this news. Despite having spent time with Babaji in the flesh, his teachings had been largely telepathic. I simply found myself wondering why he had left, as if he had suddenly taken an unannounced vacation. It would be made clear soon enough. I had a date with Maida Suarez.

Maida had cooked supper and we sat on her floor, legs out-stretched and interlocked, facing each other, hands held, serious and formal compared to the usual giggling snuggle-heap that was our joint delight. Her face began to change before my eyes, like the pages of a photograph album flickering rapidly, until one page fell open, a vision of a handsome man with long flowing locks, a Cavalier, a Royalist.

Maida said, 'we were lovers once, do you see that?'.

'Yes', and as if some antennae were now tuned to ancient records and available as memory, I knew we were both men. I was a cleric of some kind, not royalist, not gay and free, a serious student of theology, Cambridge, some scandal and....

'You killed me didn't you', she said, as I too saw, and felt the betrayal of a knife thrust deep in a trusting moment of intimacy. Tears welled in her eyes.

'What more do you see?'

More faces. The last a brown and slightly mongoloid youth. 'Bolivia, I think, you died young.'

She told me she'd had a long love affair with South America and its Indian culture.

There was more, like a film unfolding of this lifetime. She knew, as if watching the same screen.

94

'You see me with Robert, don't you. That cannot be. I love Nick. I am not in love with Robert'.

'Nevertheless, you will be together for a short time,' I said seriously.

There was more, but a curtain fell, as if the director of a play had suddenly decided the audience had seen more than it should.

'I am not allowed to see any more'.

For the next twenty four hours I had abilities, 'siddhis' in yogic terms, that I had not experienced before. It was as if Babaji had liberated a pulse of energy through my system.

The next day I was talking with friends, among them Martin Jackson, part-time follower of the Buddha, sometime climber in Ron's team, who had also been out to spend time with Babaji in Herakhan, and who worked as a bicycle mechanic in the locally famous bike shop known as 'Walton Street Cycles'. As we talked I saw a beautiful display of emerald green energy, denser than light, like a fluid, dancing mask-like about his forehead and eyes. I asked if his eyes were alright, and he told me he had been having some healing for eye-strain.

Later in the day I had supper with Gabriella Hock, the acupuncturist, and some of her friends and colleagues. As we sat together and I looked around at their faces, they changed and I knew the past lives of each, and the common bond once established in the mountain retreats of Tibet. Gaby had also taken Babaji as her guide and teacher. She, like so many other 'devotees' in Britain, looked to him more as a God than a Guru. For her he was without doubt the great Lord Shiva, and she had built a small temple in a spare room, with a large photograph above an altar, and pictures of Krishna and Hanuman with little bronze statuettes of the monkey-god and his elephant side-kick Ganesh. I felt uncomfortable around such shows of traditional religious practice, but the temple room had a sweet purity, a heart-space borne of humility and innocent supplication. Much as I felt a superiority, a rightness in progression from ornaments and images to a space beyond representation, I could not accord my mentality a beneficence and slightly hungered, therefore, for this devotional simplicity.

Gaby, as with most of the devotees, was confused by the reports of the death in Herakhan. Babaji was a 'maha-avatar', an immortal, who as Lord Shiva, had mastery over physical death. Had he not manifested without birth? Did he not dematerialise in a ball of light at Herakhan in 1922? How could he then die? I felt we would learn soon enough. Maybe it was time we emancipated ourselves from 'guru'? What was he anyway, but a light-show, a theatre, a divine play to teach, to show us how to be? Maybe this was his way of telling us, time to embody this wisdom, time to embody the energy of Shiva ourselves? I mused to myself that John Taylor had not been impressed by Babaji. On several occasions Pan had been rude about the 'fat slob'.

Later that week, Robert, Ron and I met at Delafield Road for the next encounter with our astral friends. They were not in good shape.

John had lost patience with the lack of action from Greenpeace. They had taken matters into their own hands. Having located the store of barrels, they would now fly them to Parliament Square and stack them in a giant pyramid. Nothing like it had been attempted 'since Merlin flew the standing stones'. They had been focusing all of their psychic power, but the opposition had been fierce, and they were visibly drained.

Robert and I could get little word in. The monologues were hard to follow. Pan was evidently less than impressed and was full of trickery. He made pointed reference to our women, how they were still the weak points in the chain. The warriors had given up on us and nothing more could be done with the dumping. They would try again with the barrels. We would know soon enough if they were successful. Just make sure the press were there when they succeeded! He asked me about Oxford, about the people around me.

When I got to Bruno, he broke into an un-interruptible tirade.

'Call a spade a spade, he's a queer, a bum bandit. You are surrounded by weak links. How can you guys expect to do anything if you can't even get the support of your women? You are out of balance. All this shaven-head stuff, meditation, Buddhas, mantras, yogis, 'all-is-love'. Well not all is love. We need to fight and to fight you need to be strong. You need to be centred, otherwise you are lost'.

For all our weaknesses, it emerged that Pan had set us a quest. The three brothers were to find the Chapel of the White Lady. It was a power centre, and that was all we could be told.

John broke off to take Ron into an adjoining room where Charlie was preparing to go out and once more reconnoitre the aethers around the Ben. Ron had brought maps and drawings and indicated a 'grey area' at the foot of the tower, behind the security fence and not visible from any angles. There was evidently a lift that travelled up through the scaffolding and he needed to know whether you could get a man in the space above it. The climbers would not use the lift as doubtless the power would not be on at that time, and if it were, they could get stranded if it were switched off. The lift had to be disabled and the best way would be to get a man chained to it, but out of reach of the first wave of security guards. If the lift were not disabled, the guards could get to the top before the climbers.

Charlie lay down and closed his eyes. John guided him out of his body, asking him to focus his attention on some familiar place outside of the room, and then he was there, in front of the Ben, with no interference. He was relieved there were no more encounters with the opposition. He began to describe the base of the scaffolding and pace out the distance between the security wall and the lift. Ron took notes. He asked if there was space on top of the lift for a man. Charlie affirmed this, and said if someone was there the lift could not be moved without crushing him.

'That's it', said Ron, 'that's what we need to know.'

In the car afterwards I recounted to Robert and Ron an incident I had passed whilst travelling from Birmingham to Oxford, close to the large army munitions depot at Gaydon which lies half way between the two cities on the old 'A' road north of Warwick. For the first time that I had noticed, the entrance had been guarded by armed soldiers in combat fatigues, and I had passed an unmarked white van parked off the road close to a bridge. Armed soldiers were clambering down the bank checking the underpass. There was no obvious link, just a feeling that this depot was where the waste was stored, and that they were clearly getting jumpy.

Chapel of the White Lady. It made no immediate sense. How did they both feel about this stuff? Pan and Albion? Could we trust any of it? What were we supposed to do when we got to the Chapel? Ron chuckled. What did it matter. There was no other way we could get this kind of information on the Ben. Robert was excited about the quest. He felt the chapel was located on Humberside. He had been up there several times in the last month on the campaign against the Tioxide plant. Somehow I didn't think so. The whole thing began to feel so tenuous and far from the real work, that I decided I would leave finding the chapel to him. I had enough on my plate.

Between Reading and Oxford the train passes by water meadows and paddocks. The flat plain is bounded by slight wooded rises. The houses are old and the landscape cannot have changed much since Tudor times. It was always at this point that I'd put down whatever I was reading, lean my head back and take in the view. My table was now covered with scientific papers on ocean ecosystems. It was late afternoon and mist was forming across the fields. The carriage was half-empty. Everyone else had their heads in papers. It was an odd feeling, to look out at a landscape of peace and tranquillity that hurtled by and would be gone within the minute, and I, trapped in this metal box, insulated from that reality, a voyeur on another world full of different meanings, of feeding horses, and mending tack, slow worlds with tasks that repeated with generations. There was a fleeting moment, a sensation of one-ness as if taut wires stretched across time as well as space, holding us all together, spirit-bound, farmer and paper-readers, yet nameless and faceless to each other.

I shuffled the papers into my case. I had two books with me. Stephen Knight's 'The Brotherhood', which I was half-way through. And Sri Yukteswar's 'the Holy Science'. The latter was a battered copy, read several times in the early years of reconnecting with yoga and breathing techniques. I had picked it up because of the growing doubts over Babaji and the disjunction between the eastern teachings and this strange western 'new age' concoction we were faced with. Sri Yukteswar had been Yogananda's guru. He was an absolutely traditional yogic master with an ashram in Calcutta at the turn of the century. Yukteswar's guru had been the legendary Lahiri Mahasaya, a yogi-saint credited with the same level of miracle-working and healing as Jesus himself, and a bane to the British infantry that hounded him from mountain to mountain in the hills and caves of Almora. Lahiri Mahasaya's guru was the immortal Babaji who appeared to him in disembodied form.

Babaji had also appeared to Yukteswar and set him the task of writing a book that would bridge the gap between western and eastern religions. 'The Holy Science' took the great Sutras of yogic lore and compared them with the teachings of John's gospel. The book also arose out of Yukteswar's heartfelt plea to Babaji that the intellectually advanced souls of the west be given access to the ancient yogic sciences, a system of understanding that encompassed God and the material world, in contrast to western science that had no concept of such a continuum.

In yogic understanding, God is both physical energy and love. The Solar System revolves about a deep source of 'attraction' that is the seat of Brahma, the universal magnetism. The sun's journey around this source takes 24,000 years and it comes closest when the autumnal equinox comes to the first point of Aries. It is furthest from this source when the autumnal equinox is on the first point of Libra. Within this astronomical reality there are forces of attraction and repulsion. What we understand as the physical reality of atoms - all the material world - the yogi terms 'maya', that which reflects the light.

Maya is constituted from the energy of repulsion or resistance to the fine power of attraction that is the 'light' of Brahma. This structural world of atoms is both real and illusory. It is real in as much as the Universe is constructed of elements which have attributes that are positive, neutralising and negative, and that the balance of these holds the physical world in place. The planets revolve in utterly predictable ways. Elements have characteristic behaviours. Western science has discovered some of the laws of electricity and magnetism and the properties of light and radiation.

But for the yogi, the physical world is also a 'conscious' world. All matter is spiritualised by the energy from the deep source. This energy has consciousness, and that consciousness is love. The difference between our individual consciousness and that all encompassing consciousness is that the divine source is purely love and vibrates at a higher rate, whereas ours is baser, contaminated by other energies similar to those that cause the atoms to maintain their resistance to the great attractor. All matter is thus spiritualised, under constant attraction, always in a sense, at-one with God. But, of course, it is only matter. The 'human', though constituted of matter, also has an individual consciousness and for some reason this is separate from God.

The yogic master has raised his own vibration so that he or she resonates with the divine vibrations of the source. The master becomes 'at-one-with-God', or 'realises' God. God becomes a tangible living reality of the master's consciousness.

In Sutra 5, Yukteswar writes,

'The Omnipresent Love aspect of Param Brahma is Kutastha Chaitanya. The individual Self, being its manifestation, is one with It'

Thus, the attractor, Brahma, emanates an energy that is life force and love itself, which Yukteswar equates to the Holy Spirit or the Holy Ghost. This shines upon the Darkness, Maya, and its individual parts and present in every man, to attract every portion of it toward the source, the Divinity. But the Darkness, Maya, or its individual parts, Avidya, the Ignorance, being repulsion itself, cannot receive or comprehend the Spiritual Light, but reflects it.

'The Holy Ghost being the manifestation of the Omniscient, is no other substance than God himself, and so these reflections of spiritual rays are called the Sons of God - Abhasa Chaitanya'. Yukteswar quoted from John 1:4,5 and 11:

'In him was life; and the life was the light of men.

'And the light shineth in darkness; and the darkness comprehended it not.

'He came unto his own, and his own received him not.'

So, the game was rigged. We are all sons of God. But being in a state of ignorance we cannot do other than reflect the light. When our world of atoms and planets is furthest from its source, the spiritual vibration is at its weakest. The yogis called this Kali Yuga, and I had thought that was now, but Yukteswar's book has a calendar and it was evident that the sages of his lineage held that we had long past the Kali Yuga and were now into the ascending arc of the Dwapara Yuga - 194 years into it when he finished the book in 1894. Thus in 1984 we were in the Hindu year 284 Dwapara and moving once more into the 'light', having gone through the descending arc of the previous 13,484 years. The dark period in this calendar is a mere 2400 years, but good to have behind us anyway. Curiously, its nadir was AD 500, the 'dark ages' of Europe.

Another correlation relates to the position of the 'vernal equinox'. On Yukteswar's 24,000 year calendar, it is now on the cusp of Pisces/Aquarius which accords with western astrological tradition.

Unfortunately, until the sun gets back into the upper quarter of its cycle, the vast majority of people are simply not going to be able to raise their vibrations to align with the divine. The 'golden age' or Satya Yuga is 4800 years away! So much for all the prophecies of a Cataclysm any day now, to be followed by the Age of Enlightenment. Until that age, only 'advanced souls' or those with considerable discipline would be able to reach God.

Thus, the journey into the light for the yogic disciple. 'The Atom, under the influence of Chit (universal knowledge) forms the Chitta or the calm state of mind, which when spiritualised is called Buddhi, Intelligence. Its opposite is Manas, Mind, in which lives the Jiva: the self with Ahamkara, Ego, the idea of separate existence.'

The mind is not separate from physical reality, but the Ego is the idea of separation. Under this illusion, amply supported by Mayan 'realities' at every step, the individual chooses to keep his back turned on God. The yogic path starts with the first deliberate turning to that light.

Yukteswar describes 'twenty four basic principles of creation': five forms of gross matter - solids, liquids, fire, gas and aether; fifteen 'attributes' of these when polarised by the divine magnetism into the three states of negative, positive and neutral, all fifteen of which have corollaries in the organs of senses, the activities of organs, and the objects of the senses. The fifteen together with the Mind, the Intelligence, the Heart and the Ego are the same twenty four principles or Elders of Revelation 4:4,

> 'And round about the throne were four and twenty seats; and upon the seats I saw four and twenty elders'

Yukteswar states,

'The aforesaid twenty-four principles, which completed the creation of Darkness, Maya, are nothing more that the development of Ignorance, Avidya; and as this Ignorance is composed only of ideas as mentioned above, creation has in reality no substantial existence, but is a mere play of ideas on the Eternal Substance, God the Father.'

How can I forgive these bloody sages their sexism!

There are then seven spheres.

'This universe thus described, commencing from the Eternal Substance, God, down to the gross material creation, has been distinguished into seven different spheres, Swargas or Lokas.

> 7th Sphere, Satyaloka. The foremost of these, the sphere of God - the only real substance, Sat, in the universe. No name can describe it, nor can anything in the creation of Darkness or Light designate it. This sphere is therefore called Anama, the Nameless.
>
> 6th Sphere, Tapoloka, the sphere of the Holy Spirit, which is the Eternal Patience as it remains forever undisturbed by any limited idea. Because it is not approachable even by the Sons of God as such, it is called Agama, the Inaccessible.
>
> 5th Sphere, Janaloka, sphere of spiritual reflection, the Sons of God, wherein the idea of separate existence of Self originates. As this sphere is above the comprehension of anyone in the creation of Darkness, Maya, it is called Alakshya, the Incomprehensible.
>
> 4th Sphere, Mahaloka, the sphere of the atom, the beginning of the creation of Darkness, Maya, upon which spirit is reflected. This is also the connecting link, the only way between the spiritual and the material creation and is called the Door, Dasamadwara.

3rd Sphere, Swarloka, the sphere of the magnetic aura, the electricities, and characterised by the absence of all creation - Mahasunya, the Great Vacuum.

2nd Sphere, Bhuvarloka, the sphere of electric attributes, characterised by the absence of the gross matters of creation and hence called Ordinary Vacuum or Sunya.

1st Sphere, Bhuloka, the sphere of gross material creation, which is always visible to everyone'

Oh, well, on that last point, I see what I see and where I am! However, all is not lost, for Yukteswar goes on to outline the 'seven churches' where 'the material body of man has seven vital places within called Patalas, because he is created in the image of God, 'so is the body of man like unto the image of this universe'. And quoting from Revelations,

'And being turned, I saw seven golden candlesticks, and in the midst of the seven candlesticks one like unto the son of man....'

'And he had in his right hand seven stars...'

'The seven stars are the angels of the seven churches; and the seven candlesticks which thou sawest are the seven churches'

The Universe thus consists of fourteen distinguishable stages, the seven spheres or lokas and the seven patalas. The patalas are what the New Agers call the 'chakras'.
The human body, or Son of God, is also screened in five sheaths of reality, with the spiritualised 'atom', Chitta, or Heart, at its core, then an aura which is a manifestation of Buddhi, the intelligence, then the Mind, or Manas, then Prana or life force, and the fifth is the gross matter, the atom's outer coating which supports the visible world.

This world is thus ever under the influence of Omniscient Love and Omnipresent Repulsion. The inanimate world is at the level of the 5th sheath, the plant kingdom at the fourth and animals at the third. Mankind has evolved to the second sheath, the seat of knowledge, known as Jnanamaya kosha, and has acquired the intelligence of determining right and wrong. When the intelligent being cultivates the divine spirit within his heart, then the innermost sheath, Chitta, becomes manifest. Man is then called Devata, or Angel in the creation, and when this heart is withdrawn into itself, man becomes Sannyasi, free, the Son of God, and enters into the creation of Light.

I read on through the pages of this ancient yogic knowledge. In places, Yukteswar's urge to equate the yogic categories with those of modern science jarred. Atoms, electricities, magnetisms. But when it came to the parallels with John's gospel, so much fell into place.

> 'These things saith the Amen, the faithful and true witness, the beginning of the creation of God....Behold, I stand at the door, and knock; if any man hear my voice and open the door, I will come to him and sup with him, and he with me' John 1:6

Yukteswar described the yogic practices of turning the senses inward, this, the secret knowledge that Guru Maharaji had given me. He talked of the experience of the energy sheath of light, and of hearing the divine vibration, the 'word' that John exalts as the beginning of creation, the divine sound 'aum', the 'amen' into which the adept immerses himself, and curiously, that in the inner journey, the listening, there is heard a 'knocking sound' before the 'aum' is heard.

Okay, so I had backed-off from all that. I had been shown the sheath. I had felt the presence. I was in no doubt the Divine Source was Love. I had even felt it in me, as me. Theoretically, I had no difficulty with being a Son of God. Given time, I could get to where Jesus was, heal the sick, walk on water, dematerialise at will. And get 'offed' by the Patriarchy. Richard Bach's little story came to mind, Donald Shimoda's death. He knew it was coming. Something willed, something contrary. He invited it. Was that Jesus's own karma. Did he blow it? Did he really know the whole of it? Or did the hidden vestiges of his own ego get magnified by that one pivotal act of martyrdom upon which the Catholic terror would feed? Nine million wise women would wish he'd never been born.

The yogic path was to turn the senses inward, withdraw the consciousness and energise the spiritual centres. The energy of the base chakra, the kundalini, at first resonant with the darkness, begins this serpent journey up the spine. In 'rebirthing' the connected breathing begins to energise the centres. In more advanced practice the pranic sheath is drawn inwards and integrated. The electric body is washed and purified and begins to vibrate on ever higher levels until it resonates as pure heart. When that stage is reached, the material body no longer reflects the light, it is one with the light and shines forth itself with love. Yukteswar writes,

'Emancipation (Kaivalya) is obtained when one realizes the oneness of his Self with the Universal Self, the Supreme Reality.'

and quotes again from the Bible,

'To him that overcometh will I grant to sit with me in my throne, even as I also overcame, and am set down with my Father in his throne' Revelation 3:21

'But as many as received him, to them gave he the power to become Sons of God, even to them that believe on his name' John 1:12

This had always been my understanding. I could remember way back to my first prolonged encounter with the figure of Christ on the Cross, which was not until I spent two years of the sixth form in boarding school, when each Sunday we would all have to go to church. I'd look at that figure of pathos and know there was something inherently wrong, blasphemous even, in the whole set up. I could not articulate it then, but know it now to be in the energetic relationship between congregation, icon and priest. Jesus had tried to show the way for anyone to become like him.

'Jesus answered them, Is it not written in your law, I said, Ye are Gods?' John 10:34

Verily, verily, I say unto you, he that believeth on me, the works that I do shall he do also; and greater works than these shall he do; because I go unto my Father.' John 14:12

And maybe Jesus as Yogi did not die on the cross, but suffered willingly and in final death-like trance was brought back to life and spirited away by the woman healers around him. Some say he lived to a ripe old age in Kashmir. For such an adept it would have been a simple matter to appear as solid and real, or ghostly and wraithe-like, whether dead and gone, or live and well, or any stage in-between. I recall putting this to one of Susan's Methodist brothers shortly after our marriage, only to back off at the obvious charge on the issue. Jesus had to have died. It was an article of faith. I could not discern whether that was simply because it had said so in the bible, or because there was an underlying primary need for it to be so.

In my last year at University I had written,

You shall continue to believe
blood and water flowed from a corpse
that the heart of the man broke
under the pain and suffering of his world
You say he had to die
it was written
it had to be.

But is it not there
beneath that earnest brow
a knowledge
a nervous pang of knowing
that had he not died
had there been that slow and rhythmic twitch within
a pulse of ordinary life
then he shared with you
more than you can bear to know.

Toward the back of Yukteswar's book there is a list of the 'powers' that come when 'Being thus victorious over the powers of Darkness and Ignorance, man becomes one with God', they include the power to make the body as small or as large as one will, as light or as heavy, of obtaining anything or bringing anything under control - in short, the act of will having power over the physical universe. This included power over physical death itself, the choice to be immortal.

The latter was a reminder. I had grown disenchanted with that part of Leonard's teaching. There were people going around believing they were already immortal after only a year of rebirthing. It was no longer a mantra to use to bring up all the hidden negative thought patterns that sure as anything would manifest in an untimely death, but had become an actual belief. I could not fault it, after all, without faith it could never be done. But something was wrong. Was there not a fear of death, of growing old, grey and wrinkled? It smacked of eternal California. It had become a goal, an end in itself.

Why would a yogi choose to keep his body? Yukteswar said it offered the opportunity to work out all the heart's desires in one 'lifetime'! Thereafter, I suppose, the soul is freed from the bonds of this existence and can make the journey through the seven spheres back to God. But what then? Why the fuck are we separated off in the first place? All us lost souls caught in Ignorance. So the calendar spins, the sun comes close to Brahma again and lo, we all realise who we are! Then pendulum swings, we lose it over the next 4800 years, enter another Kali Yuga when everyone gets lost in Maya, more rape and pillage and no one gives a fuck for anyone else until the sun turns the circle again. And in the midst of the darkness, a few hard-working souls, avatars and bhoddisattvas risk getting nailed to a tree for showing where the truth lies.

M'Raji had said we got lost so that we'd know what it was like to come home! What a wank. Here's God, Omnipresent, shining out there at the start of it all. No separation. Then there is a huge bang. Bits of Him get blown at light speed, or faster, who knows, all over the Universe. Then He waits four and a half billion years for evolution to build him a body that mirrors that Universe and gets to choose consciously to re-unite with him. Except in Sri Yukteswar's calendar, we get to do that without effort every 24,000 years anyway. And what were we all doing in the last great Golden Age? That was 13,500 years ago. Oh yes, Atlantis. Conveniently lost beneath the waves. And before that? Scrubbed out by the last Ice Age?

How many rounds had we done? Mankind was a monkey only a million years ago. That's forty turns of the wheel. Not much to show for it. So what's the game, Babaji? Get off the Wheel? By the looks of my fellow man, it could take a long time to get them all off. Has everyone got a soul? Is everyone a potential Jesus but just sleeping? What did M'raji say once, that for every soul that makes it, God gives him (or her) a Galaxy to play in. Is that it? We are all potential stars? For each enlightened soul a star is born! Then they get to play God, birth their own ideas. I'd like to meet the God that thought up this little solar system.

And the adepts. Yukteswar assumes they are all heartfully devoted souls. The siddhis are made out to come as the soul advances. But what about these damn magicians telepathising all over the place, exiting their bodies, fighting it out on the aethers. To whom do they owe their allegiance? Some mish-mash 'Jabulon' according to Stephen Knight. If they are so off-track how come they get the powers? And they've got the whole damn material world sewn up anyway.

It was now dark, the train pulling in to Oxford station the Isis reflecting the lights of the town. One thing for sure, I was not going to make it as a yogi in this lifetime. Something didn't add up. Where was woman's wisdom? All this God the Father, God the Light. All I know is that Love is real. And I know what I value and I know who is destroying it. And I have a brain, a mind as sharp as any sword and I'll fight for what I love. It's the only reality I can trust. Yukteswar, your gospel was for another time. When the oceans were still clean, the forests uncut, no acid rain, no plutonium warheads. Like Babaji said, all that matters now is work. Work and Love. Keeping the heart open. Enough of a task.

6

Darkness Visible

I returned to the tasks in hand. Sifting through references on sea currents, upwellings, abyssal storms, sediment transport, particle flux from surface to ocean bottom. The marine ecosystem was a fascinating world of which I had hitherto only a basic knowledge. I enjoyed the intellectual demands of new material. Ocean waters when they reach depths of several kilometres are not homogenous, but consist of layers, stratified plates of different salinities, temperatures, and crucially, current directions. Whereas the surface waters of the eastern Atlantic move South, the deep abyssal waters four thousand meters beneath, move North. It can take several hundred years for these waters to resurface in zones of upwelling. These zones are in the Antarctic seas, which are reached after a long circuit of the North Atlantic basin, after which the bottom waters then head south down the western Atlantic seaboard past the Americas.

Close to Iceland there is a massive conveyor belt taking dense cold polar water down to join these waters as they turn and head south past the coasts of Canada and the USA, not to surface again for several hundred years. The behaviour of the different layers of stratified water is poorly understood. In their long-term circulations they apparently maintain their integrity and do not mix with adjacent water. However, where each layer meets, there is a kind of sheer-zone and in these interfaces, the behaviour of material dissolved in the water, or caught on particles, may be less easily predicted. Contaminants might travel more rapidly through the sheer zones, and even against the direction of flow.

Thus, where one body of water is sinking, as it sheers against the upper layers, it could provide a rapid route to the surface, a 'short circuit' for any contaminants dissolved in the deeper water. This knowledge was just beginning to seep into the literature on ocean ecosystems. It was not yet in any models of contaminant circulation.

The radioactive waste dumping programmes had deposited several million tonnes of waste in mid-Atlantic, at 4000m depth, on the assumption that the waste would dissolve in the abyssal water but not surface for several hundred years when most of the shorter-lived radioactivity would have decayed virtually to nothing. Furthermore, the long-lived activity, in the form of plutonium, neptunium and americium, was particle-reactive, and would adhere to the clay sediments at the bottom. The ocean was, when modelled thus, and with respect to the most dangerous of the long-lived nuclides, effectively self-cleansing.

Into this neat world of the MAFF model ocean, we began to intrude our intimations that all was not as it had been assumed. We reviewed the latest scientific papers on the transfer of kinetic energy from surface storms to the abyssal deep. Scientists at Woods Hole Oceanographic Institute had begun to map the effects of severe abyssal storms in the western Atlantic, storms capable of removing massive banks of sediment off Massachusetts and depositing them as far away as Bermuda. Moreover, vertical eddies would appear several miles across, which maintained their integrity to great depth and wandered across the ocean for hundreds of miles. Within these vortices, like a twister in air, currents spiralled through several layers of otherwise stratified water. Could these be routes to the surface? How could a computer model based upon a non-mixing stratified system be adapted to accommodate them? How frequent were they? What was the largest size observed? Few of these questions could be answered, because the research was at such an early stage.

Another paper painted the intriguing picture of a mobile carpet of sediment on the ocean floor. Sediment cores, the usual method of gathering data, only sampled consolidated sediment, and it had been assumed that fresh sediment simply dropped down onto the surface to await consolidation. The surface of the sediment, however, was stirred by the constant motion of the bottom stratified dense cold water, creating little eddies and vortices as it moved over the uneven abyssal floor. For several metres above the seabed this material formed a mobile mist of particles driven along and aloft by the current. This moving carpet could be dated, and the latest research showed that material might not settle for hundreds of years. Whereas the North-Eastern Atlantic had deep sediments millions of years old and undisturbed by abyssal storms, the sediment interface was far more complex than the model assumed.

Biological oceanography was also throwing up surprises. The dark cold depths had been presumed all-but-lifeless only a decade ago. But the picture all depends on the sampling methods. Random grabs and trawls had shown little, but when baited traps were set, all manner of scavenging curiosities of nature showed up for the feast. Little was known of their capacities for vertical movement, but certainly, the strange rat-tailed scavenging fish had also been caught in mid-waters where they could themselves meet predators moving down from the surface. Pathways were opening up.

On the other research fronts we were making good headway. We could show that the comparative health indices used by the nuclear industry to assert that nuclear power production was cleaner than coal were seriously flawed. The industry-sponsored researchers had compounded so many different kinds of impact into one measure that the single index had little effective meaning. The death of a child from leukaemia had been equated to so many man-years lost from disease, and was not differentiated in quality from the man-years lost when a paid worker got cancer. There were ample sociological works to show that deaths in the public sector should not be equated with deaths in a workforce, let alone deaths of adult males in paid employment with those of children. Where risks were compensated for by monetary reward, and could be consciously reduced or avoided by appropriate actions, different indices should be used.

When these studies were disaggregated and like compared to like, and per unit of electric power produced, the amount of disease and deaths in coal mining was not that different to uranium mining, and likewise, in the other parts of the fuel cycle, such as power station construction, transport, and waste disposal.

Public deaths were harder to estimate. Should one use Britain's appalling record of leaky reprocessing plant and out-moded reactors as a guide for the future, in which case there were many more public 'deaths' to consider, or the American experience with no reprocessing and advanced reactors? Should one consider the consequences of one disastrous 'melt-down' every 10,000 years with 10,000 casualties as equating to one-death-per-year, and compare it on the same scale as routine annual emissions, (as the industry would have it done), or did such an event merit separate treatment, in which case, it was certainly not comparable to coal-fired emissions.

We were confident of demolishing any simple statements that the industry could make on the comparisons of coal and nuclear health risks. We would present scenarios which would graphically illustrate for the first time in the public arena the devastating consequences of contaminated land, of towns and villages uninhabitable for decades, of millions requiring evacuation and relocation, and of the billions of pounds in lost production, sterilised agriculture and ghost towns. Coal, to be sure, produced acid rain, killed lakes and forests, and caused asthma. And there was global warming with its unpredictable consequences. We would make plain to our paymasters, the Mineworkers' Union, that we would speak freely of these risks. Our job was to make sure the other side could not score undeserved points with their naive comparisons.

We would also make clear for the first time the total impracticality of current emergency planning for a nuclear melt-down. The fire and ambulance services had never been told what to expect. They had been led to assume that the worst could not happen to British-designed reactors and thus all emergency drill in Britain related only to small leaks producing radiation fields far below the lethal threshold. We had exposed this fiction several years previously with work on the Torness reactor when Lothian Regional Council had contemplated legal action to prevent its construction, but that had made no inroad into the standard emergency plans for all the other reactor sites. With Sizewell, there could be no excuse. It was of an American design, and the Americans had published studies of fault sequences leading to melt-down (known euphemistically as 'degraded core analyses'). Three Mile Island, although a core-melt that had been 'contained' (in 1979), had served to counter any complacency on the credibility of such scenarios.

The authorities, however, were still insisting that UK emergency plans were adequate and that for the worst accident it was simply a matter of scaling-up the response. We would argue that such simple adaptation would unnecessarily expose dozens of emergency personnel to lethal fields of radiation. A key element in the work was detailed reports of Dutch, German, Swedish and US emergency drills, and Roger would visit all of these countries to talk with their planning authorities.

There was an intellectual satisfaction in ferreting out the science, searching for controversy and disagreement, bringing to bear our own assessment of likely truths, stepping back from the game, and deciding where to place that movable pointer of objectivity. We were at once critical scientists engaged on finding that picture of the world that rang truest, and snouted sharks of the legal waters scenting our prey and building our case. We both knew that no scientist was ever free from bias, whether political, psychological, or monetarily induced, and that yet some such endeavour toward objectivity was science's noble quest. In this case, it did not matter who was 'right', what mattered was that there was a fair debate. What was accepted truth would shift as the sands of knowledge shifted, or with fashion and prejudice, but the game must be honourably played.

Around this time I learned of the death of John Reissland. I was informed over the phone by George Pritchard, Greenpeace's nuclear campaigns director. As Harwell's chief statistician in the field of cancer risks, I had met him several times. He was a decent and thoroughly self-effacing man who had been given the unenviable task of leading the intellectual critique of Alice Stewart's work. As I mentioned before, he was not up to the complex epidemiology, and his criticisms, which I had only seen in the un-refereed grey literature of the industry's in-house publications, had little impact on the scientific debate. However, once made, they were adequate enough for the industry's public relations teams to use the term 'criticised' or 'not yet accepted' for Alice's controversial work.

Reissland had died whilst investigating smoke in the roof-space of his home. He had suffocated. The inquest had found 'death by misadventure'. George had grounds for suspicion and did not believe it. Alice Stewart had told him Reissland had contacted her only a few days before and said he was coming round to believing she was right after all. Such an event would have been momentous. Reissland was the establishment's highest profile critic of her work. It could have meant the end of reprocessing, even the end of the nuclear fuel chain. At a minimum, two and one half billion pounds of investment would be at stake at Sellafield alone. George informed me that Stewart believed Reissland had been murdered before he could go public.

Reissland's death caused me to turn again to research on the Freemasons. I read Stephen Knight's book at one sitting. It documented the growth and spread of Freemasonry throughout the police, judiciary, lesser legal professions, military, parliament and among the royals. An estimated six hundred thousand men, largely professionals, belonged to the secret society. Knight's researches also uncovered several levels within the society, of which the majority of its members were unaware. It could readily be conceded that those members of the three ordinary levels or 'degrees' were indeed little more than a Rotary Club bent on good deeds and a little back-scratching, although there were widespread reports of bad feeling among non-members in the police force. However, Knight identified thirty more degrees. Top Masons were of the 33rd Degree, of which there were very few. This elite met internationally and consisted of men in some of the most powerful positions in their respective countries.

What interested me in Knight's revelations was less the standard issues of accountability, nepotism and shady deals, but his documenting of the rites. What to a journalist was clearly irrelevant hokum, had the impression of extremely formalised and exact magical rites, derived from a mixture of ancient Egyptian ceremony and modern romances of the Kabbala and quasi-Christian, even Arthurian mysticism. It was the Egyptian stuff that concerned me most, although I had no particular understanding or reason. An intuition that therein lay real psychic power and age-old agendas.

I followed the reading of Knight's book with Larry Gurwin's 'The Calvi Affair', a chilling account of the murky background to Roberto Calvi's apparent suicide on Blackfriar's Bridge in 1982. Calvi had been a banker to the Masonic underworld. It was alleged he had supplied hundreds of millions of Vatican dollars for arms deals with South American dictators. The implications for the Vatican concerned me less than the pictures of Calvi's boss, Licio Gelli, a man with a mesmeric and haunted look, whom I immediately supposed to be an adept.

Gelli was then on the run. His hold on the most powerful Masonic lodge in Italy, P2, had been exposed. Indeed, the whole Masonic power-structure of a modern industrial state had been laid bare. Membership of Gelli's lodge included admirals, generals, heads of the secret services, industrialists and bankers, judges and chiefs of police. I reasoned that anywhere outside of Italy such a structure would be inviolable. Italy was different because of its 'magistrates', a courageous elite that had been empowered to bring down the Mafia. Only men of such unimpeachable qualities and determination could break open such a power structure. In the wake of the P2 scandal the Italian government had issued a warning to all fellow West European states, that it had evidence of collusion between P2 and all of their 'secret services'.

I had also collected one or two papers on astral projection techniques. The literature had seemed initially to consist of a few dubious paperbacks on how to have an out-of-the-body experience. However, I quickly learned that serious research had been conducted as early as 1940 and that after initial publication, research laboratories had been set up at Stanford in the US, and in Russia. The respected journal 'New Scientist' carried a news piece on the Stanford Research Institute's programme, funded by the US navy, when one of its top researchers resigned, charging the Navy with intentions of using the research for military purposes. The scientist, obviously a politically rather naive fellow, had stopped off in London on his way to Russia to confer with other experts in the field about misuse of the research findings.

I gathered the following. In the 1940s a small group of psychics had designed experiments to demonstrate the potential of 'remote surveillance' techniques. The experiment involved setting up trials in New York and Boston. Reputable doctoral level scientists confirmed the results. Firstly, the 'sender', located in New York, zeroed in on the laboratory of the 'receiver' in Boston. The receiver then took a book at random from the shelf, opened it and read silently to himself, a random line from the random page. The sender was able to accurately read aloud the line, duly recorded by those present.

The SRI programme had taken the research further. Firstly, adepts had demonstrated they could locate and read documents, even underwater. Secondly, a training programme had begun to see how successfully ordinary people, or those with whatever identifiable aptitudes, could be trained to carry out such surveillance. Most researchers felt the Soviets were leagues ahead of the West with several dedicated institutes.

The implications were not, however, limited to surveillance. People could be followed and their thoughts read from any distance, but they could also be subjected to projected thoughts. Experiments with telepathy had shown an adept's ability to communicate thoughts directly to the mind of the receiver. People could not only be placed under 'surveillance' but also influenced.

Orwell's world began to take shape. Big Brother was not now a network of cameras and televisions, not dependent upon electronic surveillance, but upon a spider's web of thought patterns that could be astrally scanned. Would this be possible? Could an adept or a network of adepts tune in to any wayward thoughts, any movement in the aether that began to challenge the ascendant order?

Calvi, Knight's book, and the astral surveillance data, presented another possibility. Suppose that the higher orders of Masonry, kept secret from the masses in the first three orders, did contain adepts capable of thought scanning and projection? The vast number of initiates from the professions, wholly untutored in these arts, would be potentially controllable or at the very least, monitored for their loyalties. But loyalties to what?

Their agenda escaped me. Why the involvement in nuclear power? And why nuclear waste? And if nuclear power generation and the inevitable waste production had some deeper purpose, then why dump in the sea? Masons are well enough established in the USA and France, and they had no ocean dumping programmes. Why bring so much public opprobrium? Perhaps it had nothing to do with esoteric meanings and was simply an ignorant mafiosa of business and power, caught now by a rising public indignation and hell bent on not losing face. Or money. We could still cost them dearly on a business level.

I reflected on Roberto Calvi, 'God's banker', as he had been dubbed by the media. Here was a respectable family man, entrusted with hundreds of millions of dollars of the Vatican's money. He was a Mason, yet the Vatican was the sworn enemy of Freemasonry. His boss is a gangster, Licio Gelli, well-known in Mafia circles, and friend of Michel Sindona, a mafia boss languishing in a US jail. The money trail led to some of the most notorious regimes in South America. Gelli was friend to an Admiral Rega, an Argentinian known locally as 'El Brujo', the magician, with a reported taste for personal involvement in the torture chambers and 'disappearances' of that dark period in Argentina's history. I was to learn later that some of Gelli's friends were well-placed in more acceptable circles - George Bush becoming President of the USA, and Silvio Berlusconi prime minister of Italy!

Calvi would have known little of this. At some point he must have crossed them, perhaps beginning to realise what was going on, and the frightened man ran to London. The inquest made little of the impossibilities of his death on the bridge from his own unaided hand, hanging from scaffolding, a middle-aged, portly and unfit man venturing out over swirling waters in the black of night.

I met with George Pritchard. He had gone to visit Reissland's widow and taken with him a chemist, a friend from the veterans' association (he was working with veterans claiming compensation for radiation exposure during the atomic weapons testing). They had gone over the incident in the house. Reissland and family had arrived home to the smell of something burning and located the source in the loft. He had gone up via a ladder and crawled into the roof space. There had been a muffled explosion and a lot of smoke and he was asphyxiated. The inquest held that the insulation in the loft had caught fire. George's companion inspected the loft and was convinced that it was not flammable.

I left the matter with George and did not return to it. I would shortly have enough of my own problems. To my knowledge, George took things no further. I had a welcome trip to Ireland scheduled. For the past year I had been working with that small organisation in West Cork, calling itself HOPE (Help Organise Peaceful Energy), and despite the quaint title, and unpretentiously rustic approach to life, they were remarkably effective politically. The main purpose of the visit was to deliver a paper to a technical meeting of the Paris Commission in Dublin. The Commission was an inter-governmental body with oversight of the North East Atlantic, from Iceland to Portugal, and charged with protecting the oceans from pollution from land-based sources such as Sellafield. The paper would show how the Sellafield management had consistently failed to adopt the 'Best Available Technology', as they were required to do under international guidelines.

Either side of the meeting would be public talks in Dublin and Skibbereen, and I would have time with my newly found friends in the far west. There would also be informal talks with Irish government ministers as part of a major Greenpeace campaign against Sellafield and to solidify Irish support for the moratorium on sea-dumping.

The last time I had been in Dublin, in June 1983, was the occasion of my first beginnings of a strained relationship with my Greenpeace friends, but a cementing of bonds with the west of Ireland that deeply nurtured my spirit. That month I had had a strong message from Babaji to begin a programme of purification. I had taken 'mundan', that is, shaving my head, and out of an intuitive sense, wore only white clothes for a month. I had not expected to leave the confines of my quiet work in Oxford, but Greenpeace had wound its campaign against Sellafield to fever pitch, with threats to block the waste pipeline. I had also prepared material for the Paris Commission meeting in Berlin. Normally, we could only submit

114

papers, but Greenpeace had lobbied for the opportunity to address the Commission in person and I was the only person who could deliver the paper effectively.

There are many perceptions and prejudices held about Greenpeace and its personnel. Firstly, many environmentalists then presumed them a commando of ex-hippies spiritually driven to their heroic acts. I very seldom encountered anyone with a specific spiritual practice, and my closest associates in the radwaste campaigns had a positive aversion to it. They were no hippies either. Hans Guyt, normal apparel tea-shirt and jeans, whichever ambassador he was meeting, was an ex-radio operator and skilled seaman from the Netherlands merchant navy. His relaxed manner, balding head and long wispy hair, belied a quick temper and abrasive action should anyone show the least aggression. For all his external and feigned uncouthness, he was a brilliant political campaign manager, marshalling the Greenpeace lobby teams at international conventions and making sure that the right material got into the right hands.

Remi Parmentier was altogether different. Hounded out of France, he lived in Madrid, where he ran the Greenpeace office. Friend of the new regime, of writers and poets, an educated man who would seldom discuss anything intellectual, small as Napoleon and equally pugnacious, he respected all protocols, dressed smartly, but never exuded anything other than a totally superior and disdainful air. Remi was a veteran of the whaling campaigns, of the escape of the Rainbow Warrior from Corunna harbour, when Spain harboured the illegal whaling fleet, and there in Vigo for the tumultuous welcome of the Warrior when the circle turned full and Greenpeace were defending Spanish fishing grounds from the dreadful English dumpers.

And then finally, Pete Wilkinson, ex-telephone engineer, masterly campaigner for Friends of the Earth in the days of their recycled bottle campaigns, recruited by David MacTaggart shortly after his encounter with French marines off the island of Mururoa, when he sought out the 'meanest son-of-a-bitch' in the UK green movement. Actually, Pete, though tough, was far from mean, and after five years of working together from Workington to Barrow, we had a warm rapport and he a bemused tolerance of my spiritual quirks.

I have described in academic and legal papers the abilities of NGOs such as Greenpeace to turn UN conventions and treaties, through the power of lobbying, the securing of votes, the provision of essential briefings for diplomats, and the support of quality scientific work. This side of the organisation received no press coverage. Indeed, it would have been counter-productive. Yet without it, the gains of the 'warriors' in the high speed Zodiacs, risking their necks in front of waste ships, incinerators, sludge dumpers or nuclear submarines, would have been lost. The power of international law was brought to bear in many areas of the campaigns: firstly, against the dumping of radioactive waste, then ocean incineration of toxic chemicals, sewage and industrial waste dumping. In 1983 these campaigns were beginning to get geared up. It would take ten years to win them all and have watertight legal conventions restricting or banning them outright.

Thus, my immediate colleagues were not so well disposed to the spiritual brown-bread-and-sandals image and had long since distanced themselves from the mystical birth of Greenpeace under the guidance of Canadian Indians. On agreeing to give a speech to the Paris Commission I had neglected to mention my own new apparel. The first they saw was when I arrived at the meeting, a roundtable of dark-suited diplomats, the Nordics, the French, the Brits, the Germans and Spanish, all indistinguishable by outward appearances. As I walked in, all heads spun round and in a stunned silence I delivered the telling indictments on Sellafield, urging them to take action, and left with everyone still staring and silent. The material was good. The delivery was fine. I am sure the Paris Commission did not know what to make of the white garb and the bald head. But from then on, my Greenpeace friends had a somewhat guarded attitude.

A few days later I was in Dublin for meetings with ministers. At least the children at the docks found expression for the apparition. They came running in gaggles, 'Serr, serr, are yer from this planet, or what?'

I made my first contact with Mary O'Donnel and Jeremy Wates from HOPE, (later renamed 'Earthwatch') and at last, environmentally committed people who could understand my struggles of consciousness on a spiritual path.

We had repaired to a bar on the waterfront, where an Irish labourer, well-holding his liquor, approached with 'Sure, I can see yer'a highly evolved being', and proceeded to tell me his story. I had just invited several of the HOPE members to a session of yogic teachings and rebirthing. There was Jeremy, HOPE's organiser; Phil Kearney, a psychologist and family therapist; Richard Hardwicke, an Oxford Human Sciences drop-out and blow-in to the west coast, and a couple of other members, all male, and I invited our labourer, by name of Michael, though doubting he would show up.

We had our meeting and Michael did show up. I took everyone through a rebirthing session. Each was deeply moved by the experience. Michael, however, went completely out of his body and I could not get him to stay in it. That was how he had learned to cope with a violent childhood and hidden his sensitivities to other worlds. He could not ground his powers, not own them, not make use of them.

When he eventually came back, he smiled, and said, 'they're waiting for you, Peter, they'd like you to visit' and described a monastery in China where he'd been welcomed by black-dressed monks practising marshal arts. I could see in my mind's eye a little group of happy smiling Chinese frantically waving from the other side of the planet. None of us saw Michael again.

The white-clothes episode was at least a year behind me. I had done a considerable amount of scientific and political work for it not to have put too much of a dent in the relationship with Remi, Hans and Pete. Hans had cautiously asked about clothes and was re-assured that I was back to normal, but groaned when I informed him I was once more with 'mundan'.

He joked, 'Just so long as there's no beads. Please, Peter, no beads or you're fired'.

When had I ever worn beads? Oh, yes, and all-black clothes. A North Sea Forum Conference in Bremen, got mistaken for a some-kind-of-priester by the Germans. Someone must have told him.

I love Dublin. Once it could have been called beautiful. Now there were just patches of that former elegance, the Georgian terraces, Parliament and Trinity College, and pocked in between, new brutalist banks and shoddy offices. There is nothing about the city as structure, except that the scale is handlable, and perhaps that is it, it fosters feeling, a centre, a community that bubbles about the shops, alleyways, pubs and cafes.

I had lunch with Robert Blackith, professor of Zoology at Trinity. He is a statistician of some renown and we discussed Alice Stewart's work and the latest data from the Sellafield cancer statistics. Robert had presented evidence at the Windscale Inquiry in 1977 and had become an implacable opponent of nuclear power, taking a key role in the eventual prohibition on its development in Ireland. He was pained to hear of Reissland's death. I did not share with him the darker suspicions of Masonic involvement, but he was not slow to see the implications. I envied him his life in a non-nuclear country where there was no massive and competent army to strike out and reclaim parts of a jaded empire, as Thatcher had done only two years previously. Where factories did not churn out nuclear submarines bristling with missiles and multiple warheads, where their airbases were not now forward deployment zones for the even more self-righteous and massive army across the Atlantic.

Robert Blackith was never in the best of health and looked frail. He should, by rights, have enjoyed his later years as the world's leading expert on small grasshoppers, the identification of which requires a Doctor of Science degree in Biometrics. Instead he had exhausted himself in the fight against Sellafield and in keeping Ireland non-nuclear. I recalled, when first arriving in Ireland and staying at his house, how I had asked for a hot shower and been told the sun had not shone for long enough that day. The whole house ran on minimal energy, had white-painted one inch thick cork tiles on the walls, biogas cookers, solar panels and a thriving forest garden.

This time I was staying in the Royal Marine Hotel and in guilty appreciation of a hot deep bath. After lunch with Robert I reflected that he was the only environmentalist I knew who had translated his concern into a personal lifestyle. In PERG we drove ten-year old cars, but more out of poverty than choice. Likewise, no pensions, no insurance, no savings, so that at least we were contributing minimally to the financing of the planet's destruction. We jetted about, all the same, and added one more kilo of carbon dioxide to global warming. Maybe, in older age, we could retire to a forest garden and eco-friendly house and tell our kids we did our bit, however ineffectual, to save the oceans and forests.

And what of nuclear power? Would our children understand why it had been such a threatening monster? Every week one of the quality newspapers would carry a full page advertisement for cheap, clean and everlasting power. White-coated guardians of the future, surrounded by dials and facias, stainless steel and stainless faces. Images of control in a world of enemies, uncertainties and natural chaos. It had seemed so much more powerful an image of monstrosity in the 70's, symbolic of a centralised society run by technocrats, a thin democratic veneer, but in reality, technology had itself become dictator and the white-coats its priest-like servants, 'slaves of the white skeletal monster, blind to the history they recreate'.

Where would history place our endeavours? Neo-luddites, or visionaries knowing what was to come? It was 1984. Britain was Airstrip One. Our leader a parody of womanhood. My father who fought for this freedom winces at her every utterance, her appearance, and saddest of all, the sycophancy she elicits in so many foreigners. Iron Lady. What is it they admire? Some distant matron of their old boys' school, the longed-for certainties of authority, single mindedness, a mother to stand up for them, swing her handbag and clobber the school bullies, whilst Dad was away.....

at night you wake
urinating the poison from your body
and not sleeping not thinking
hate

By 1984 the hate had gone. I no longer cared about Thatcher. But then, I never watched television and seldom got to visit my ageing father. I hoped he'd survive her reign. Cruise missiles. I was glad of the womens' camps at the gates, the dances on the bunkers, how they sneaked past, undermining the aura of powers, simple symbols, spiders webs and childrens' dolls on the fence. Forever recorded, whatever happens.

That is where Orwell's vision failed. He did not see the magic in the face of oppression, nor the pathetic posturing of the mighty men, how it never seemed to work quite like it should. The reality of nuclear power had shifted. Cracks and leaks and molten messes. Leukaemic children. Ordinary ten gallon drums going over the side. The mystique had gone. On once beautiful rivers in France, and once beautifully desolate coasts in Britain, the concrete mausoleums would remain for an hundred years and more.

That was what hurt. The despoliation of beauty. In truth that had always been my motivation. Had I not used the peoples' fears of genetic disorder, cancerous children, contaminated seas and livelihoods? I, their champion, with my own hidden agenda. Yet I do know that in feelings we are the same, oppressed by that which we fear and hate, caught in injustice, an ethnic minority about to be condemned to a reservation for unprogressives, and not able to speak our caring, our language of love long dead in the land.

The public meeting in Skibbereen was uproarious. Another wave of indignation against the dumping to reach Dublin and force the ministers on. Ireland being such a small place, and its population for the most part busy in agriculture, even the smallest pebble makes waves. Pity the ministers, caught in a vice between the economic bullying power of Britain and the rage of concern in their land.

After the meeting, a small group of us retreated to a remote converted school house in the forests of Glengarrif on Bantry Bay. I had hastily put together a poster-poem and it had drawn twelve people. Phil Kearney had travelled with us from Dublin, and Jeremy and Mary came from the HOPE office in Bantry harbour. It would be too embarrassing to repeat all of that ragbag of words and thoughts, portents and pretentious knowings. They are a forgiving lot in West Cork. But parts reflect my changing,

Take thought, all you who would protect the planet,
what shall it profit you if you gain this world?
Only to lose something more precious.

So you would reclaim the Earth, who is your Mother! You would
restore her! Out of fear you come. Time is running out. Fear of
lack, of food, of space, of peace. And in your fear and unpeace
you would create Peace! You are the Green preachers of
harmony, yet you are not in harmony.

Listen to your Earth. She is not sick. You do not see deeply.
Beneath the surface she is moving. She will be whole again. You
are young. She is old and moves slowly. She does not die, any
more than the Earth that is within you can die. She renews
herself. Her Rebirth is so grand. She trembles, she floods herself
with tears. Her face is cleansed and becomes young again. In her
winter she takes the unconnected unto herself, the withered of the
vine she restores to the Mother. Look not to reclaim Her, for she
is already reclaiming you. It is you who are sick.

In those three days of retreat I gave of myself, of everything I had been
given, the secrets of the breath, the unlocking of past traumas and negative
thoughts and expectations, of the simple cleansing of ritual batheing, of
the offerings of fire to the divine, the polarities of God and Goddess, the
unfolding of the heart in love. I had not seen myself as spiritual guide or
teacher. What wisdom I might have, never seemed to make it through to
the interminable mess of my relationships. Babaji had whispered gently,
'go to Ireland, start rebirthing'.

I had objected, 'I have no intuition. I would only want to work with that,
free from form, working with what comes in the moment'.

He had replied, 'put yourself there in the middle, your willingness will be
enough'.

In that place of leadership there was always an inner voice, as if intuition
were a function not of some faculty of the mind, but simply a willingness
to occupy the position. It was at once humbling and nourishing. I planned
little. My friends organised everything, from rooms, sleeping spaces, food
and payments. People paid if they had money, or gave something of use if
they had not. As is often the case in Ireland, from people with very little,
flowed great amounts. We had several hundred pounds left over from
which I created a small fund for furthering the spiritual work.

Not that such a term does justice to our explorations. What is this 'spiritual'
work, but the spiritualising of work itself? We had no fixed ideology of

religion. Anyone of any creed was welcome. To spiritualise work was to unlock the energies of the heart, so that work could become, in Kahil Gibran's words, 'love made manifest'. To unlock the heart entailed a long slog of cleansing the mind and body of its past resentments and fears. The 'rebirthing' breath was the first step in a dynamic process. It began with the surfacing of personal experience, childhood patterns, parents and siblings, and might move to involve flashes of past lives. And then the ever present 'collective mind' of symbol and archetype. In this we were supported by the rich heritage of western teachings. In our new yoga, east and west were meeting. In my own psyche, bridges were forming between the ecological and political worlds, and the inner world of psychology.

I returned to England at the end of March much refreshed. It was then I learned of the death of Hilda Murrell. She was an elderly rose-grower who had apparently surprised a burglar, been stabbed, dumped in a hedgerow and left to die. She had been found several days later by someone walking their dog. At the time there was speculation that the burglary was not a simple matter. Her nephew had been a signals officer at Navy headquarters during the encounter between HMS Conqueror, the submarine that sank the cruiser Belgrano, with great loss of life, during the war between Britain and Argentina. There had been intense debate surrounding the orders to sink the cruiser, with the Argentinians claiming the vessel was already heading away from the conflict zone during frantic attempts to negotiate a peace, and that Thatcher had ordered the sinking in the full knowledge that it did not pose an immediate threat and with some intent on maintaining the conflict.

The issue had raged in parliament and there were rumours that the submarine's log, which was reported as 'missing', would confirm the suspicions of Thatcher's critics (it was later revealed that it had been shipped to the US Defence Department as part of a deal on wartime information from the submarine). It was suggested that Murrell's nephew, Commander Robert Green, had come under surveillance by the security forces, and that MI5 itself had bungled the operation when searching his aunt's bungalow for the missing log. Whatever the status of the log itself, it was certainly the case that an MP, Tam Dalyell, had access to signal data from the submarine and this contradicted Thatcher's interpretation of the events and that a flap was on to locate the source of that information.

It was also reported in the newspapers that Hilda Murrell had been working on evidence for the Sizewell Inquiry. Up until that point I had taken no more than passing interest and had not matched her name with that of a request we had received many months previously for an array of highly technical PERG reports on nuclear risks. The correspondent was the same lady rose-grower. Attached to the letter requesting documents was a critique she had written of the Government's White Paper 8607 on

Radioactive Waste Management. I had glanced through what she had written at the time, enough to note that it was a masterly assessment of the issues by a layperson, in particular, laying out the respective roles of civil servants and industrialists in the political morass that then surrounded the science and politics of future land disposal options for nuclear waste. I had thought then, if every concerned citizen could make such an intelligent and articulate response to a public inquiry, the battle would be quickly won.

I initially dismissed the possibility that her death could have had anything to do with the Sizewell Inquiry. There was nothing in her material that was not already public knowledge. Could she in the meantime have unearthed something of significance? Inquiries to friends quickly revealed that one Gerard Morgan-Grenville, whom I knew personally to be an extremely level-headed rather straight member of the 'greens' and not given to paranoia about the state, had reported Hilda's last contact with regard to her Sizewell work, when she had phoned saying she would send him copies of her material 'In case they get me first'. She obviously felt she was under surveillance.

There were a number of strange circumstances to the killing. Firstly, the police reported the phone line had been pulled out. Secondly, nothing of value had been taken, although the rooms had been searched. Further, her assailant had taken her from the house, in her own car, and driven through Shrewsbury town centre out to the other side where the body was dumped in a hedgerow on a nearby hill. She had been alive when her body was dumped but died of exposure and shock from a series of stab wounds.

Writing this now in 1994, if I am to stay with what I knew ten years ago, there would be little more to say. However, I am overcome now with a sense of shame that in all this time I have taken no more than a passing interest despite numerous books and television documentaries and a recent police investigation into the handling of the affair by the Shrewsbury detectives. The police still maintain the killing was perpetrated by a lone burglar without political motive, and that having interviewed the Security Service, they have been assured there was no official file and she was not under surveillance.

In this one case I will, however, comment in the light of recent information on what is still an unsolved murder. I will begin with an extract from Hilda's letter of 27th April 1983,

'Since talking to you I have received Professor Lindop's paper which of course is absolutely splendid, but does not say that a nuclear bomb on the HAW tanks at Windscale would devastate the whole northern hemisphere. She gives a map of the area that would be affected by such an attack in a N.W. wind -it cuts a great swathe down the country, taking in

Liverpool, Birmingham and London and penetrating a good way into Europe. Incidently, she says that this would be the effect of a hit on 'a tank'. It would hardly be possible to hit one without breaching and so dispersing all the others, would it?

'Please don't bother to answer all this unless there are howlers that need correcting. You will find my remarks quite naive - but this is rather the intention. I am trying to speak for the dumb mass of humanity who are unaware in any way of what goes on over their heads. But I do think it is a really serious matter when a Government Department puts out such stuff as occurs in Paragraph 7. I was greatly surprised that the same idea comes in a Radioactive Waste Management Advisory Committee report which I found in the Public Library, so it is deliberate.

With so many thanks for all you are doing.....'

In twelve pages of referenced critique of the Government White Paper, there were no howlers. I will quote from just one section, the one she refers to above,

'Para. 7 and graph on page 6. "One basic characteristic of radioactivity, which actually assists in waste management, is that it decays over time."

'BUT - it is precisely the 'decay' of unstable elements which is the radioactive event, and which therefore poses all the ensuing problems. To say that decay actually 'assists with waste management' is to stand the whole situation on its head, and is unbelievably fatuous.

'Most of these very dangerous elements or their isotopes would never have existed at all but for man's meddling with the very building-blocks of the Universe. Nor do they disappear to nothingness, as the word 'decay' might imply. They form decay-products (not even mentioned here) which are also radioactive, and often work through a whole series of them before reaching a state of stability. Some of them are more dangerous, or alternatively, longer lived, than the elements from which they started. For the same reason, the graph is meaningless; no elements are named on it. A rough average must be represented, but a rough average is no way to present facts as serious and as complicated as these.

'That bright and cheery thought is as pure an example of newspeak as could be found. Windscale into Sellafield is another. The deep mental dishonesty they betray is terrifying.'

There is one thing I feel sure about, and that is had Hilda Murrell discovered anything we did not know, she had the intelligence and wit to use it with powerful effect. In recent discussion with my friend Palden Jenkins, I re-iterated my thoughts that is was unlikely she would have discovered anything the Industry or Government would have feared. His response was that Government had as much, if not more, to fear from one ordinary person who could articulate an opposition from the masses. This Hilda Murrell could certainly do and Government would have known this well in advance of the Sizewell Inquiry because she would have sent in her response to the White Paper. Furthermore, by raising the issue of the security of the waste tanks she would have given them all the more reason to watch her.

There is however, one further twist in the story and one not so far reported in any of the articles, books and films. Hilda was in contact with a nuclear physicist called Dr Don Arnot as far back as April 1983 (there is a footnote in her letter to the effect that she had talked with him). I vaguely remember meeting Don during public debates around that time. He had become an active critic of the Government's nuclear waste management programme, particularly its attempts to find sites for disposal underground. Two years ago from when I now write, Don was asked by my local council, Meirionnydd, to contribute to a seminar on the risks of restarting the Trawsfynydd Nuclear Reactor, not six miles from where I live. Although I had been relatively inactive in the nuclear debate, they had also contacted me and asked for a presentation on the state of the lake and problems of decommissioning. Accompanying Don on his journey to Wales was Commander Robert Green, whom I had not met. Robert made contact after the seminar and stayed over. We talked about Hilda. He told me something of great import to the case.

In Don Arnot's researches on the PWR reactor, he had uncovered a weakness in the design relating to the fuel assemblies, which he believed would have great consequence for the Inquiry. He prepared his evidence but never got to the Inquiry. Shortly before it convened, he suffered heart failure and very nearly died. Robert told me Don is convinced he was poisoned to prevent him testifying. With regard to Hilda, his feeling is that the security services (or whichever freelancers were operating on their behalf) were checking to see whether Don had passed information to her. She died because of what they thought she might know.

These elements certainly alter the view that I had then, which was that Hilda's death could have had nothing to do with information as such, but was likely a bungled job of routine surveillance, mixed with whatever psychopathic tendencies surfaced in the not-so-intelligent operatives. I can well imagine that had she been conscious, she would have been hard to intimidate and her oppressors would have felt the lash of her disparaging wit.

As it happens, in this year of writing, 1994, the police enquiry under Stalker has re-iterated the earlier untenable explanation of the lone burglar, and a new book is published this October by Judith Cook, entitled 'Unlawful Killing' in which she presents her analysis that three sub-contracting operatives to MI5 (accompanied by a girlfriend) bungled the job of searching for documents (which she assumes are related to the Belgrano affair). One of the operatives committed suicide, something we had known in 1984. What was new, however, was that another of the alleged operatives in the story had been killed in 1987 in suspicious circumstances whilst trying to evade a police stake-out. Cook maintains that he had been appalled at the killing, and thus, implicitly a security risk.

The outfit subcontracted to put the Sizewell objectors under surveillance was a company called 'Zeus Securities', and its head a man called Vic Norris, who according to Cook was a convicted child sex-abuser and known Nazi sympathiser. Cook traces the story whereby the job was further contracted out to a shadowy north of England organisation called 'Ceres' under a liaison officer with links to MI5 and MI6 calling himself 'Demeter'. Once again there is a curious surfacing of 'gods' and 'goddesses' as if in mockery of the divine.

7

Return of the Ninja

On a bright day in the first week of April, in the midst of the heavy work schedules, a change of venue found me unexpectedly in Oxford. I called Sue but the phone was engaged. I decided to visit unannounced. She answered the door, looking pleased to see me, which translated, as ever, into 'do you want to come in?'

'Is that an invitation?' I said, wearily. I knew it was, but could never quite accept the implication that it was I who was pushing at some boundary and she who would submit.

'Let's be friends, Peter. The children haven't seen you in weeks'.

I could see their bright faces pushing through the banisters upstairs. Owen was now three and Matthew seven. Matthew was home because we had not yet sent him to school, having decided to educate him ourselves. This had fallen largely to Susan, with an input from me of bedtime stories in the calmer days of our interactions. As he turned seven Matthew had taken the story book one evening and simply read it back to me with hardly a falter. No attempts had been made to 'teach' him. He had learned to read simply by watching and listening. They came bundling down and jumped upon me. They were beautiful children. Their hair, which would later darken non-descriptly, was blond and thick. Bright blue eyes, my side of the genetics. They seemed happy and well.

Sue called through from the kitchen, as if amused, 'By the way, did you come round here the other night?'

'No. I've been in London. Why?'

'Strange. Thought it must have been you. Someone had been in the garden. The washing line had been hitched-up out of the way.'

I remembered talking with Robert in his car after seeing John Taylor, sharing our unease, having momentarily a vision of Sue's backyard and a feeling of concern. Was someone now snooping around here?

She asked how the work was going and automatically put a kettle on the gas stove. I recounted the breakthrough of the Holliday Commission, but did not mention Reissland or Hilda Murrell. She did not read newspapers and would not have heard from her circle of friends. She was growing closer to the Catholic church and of late would engage me in theological discussion, which I afterwards always regretted. There seemed to be no meeting ground. After one emotional bout some months previously she had begun divorce proceedings and I had received a solicitor's letter muttering on about 'unreasonable behaviour'. I had replied with an exaltation of unreason. Love and passion, were they not also 'unreasonable behaviour'? I had heard no more of it. Sue now informed me she had dropped the proceedings.

I did not want to get drawn into talk of our marriage. She was certain that what she was doing was right but whenever pressed only ever referenced it to 'feelings'. I had by then learned to separate, semantically at least, feeling from intuition, and had often tried to discern whether her 'feeling' of rightness was more of a resistance lodged in the body, in which case I had some hope it could be 'released' by appropriate work, or whether it was a deep and certain knowledge, an intuition of a rightness and therefore to be accepted and respected.

There had been many times when we could talk and feel close, but this was not one. Sue was friendly but distant, matter-of-fact, as if I were hardly known to her, like a visiting official. She asked how long I intended to be working in London and how much the children would see of me. She could not disguise her disapproval, although clearly on their behalf. I felt caught in rising feelings I did not want to let out. I did not attempt further explanations. I could hear the sound of fun and games upstairs and a sudden sadness lumped my throat.

I got up, turning to leave, not looking at her. My thoughts flooded out, despite my moving to leave.

'What you are doing is wrong. You will see it one day. You guard your boundaries, but you don't let anyone in. You and your little rubber cap. Bloody Catholic hypocrite. All you are learning to do is to feel safe outside of any real relationship with a man. You've said you want equality, but you don't, you want control. That's what you teach them. How to get by without a man, without compromise, mother without father, that's your example, that's what you are teaching them...'

She was shocked. Asked me not to raise my voice, but the children had already stopped playing and were at the top of the stairs as I went out through the hallway. I got out before the tears came, of sadness or rage, rage and recrimination at my self, anger at her, grief at the impossibility of just stopping, lying peacefully close, being there in the mornings when they woke.

I had at least got out without a rage, but that was little consolation to the knowledge that they were there, the two boys, left with their bewilderment, the impossibility of their understanding and the wish that it could be otherwise, Mum and Dad together again. How much we had failed them, short-changed them, all for what? Neurotic concepts of growth and space and equality. I hungered for those boys, remembered their births, the darkened rooms, Matthew's quiet entrance and peaceful smile. Owen with the chord about his neck and the midwife labouring unruffled to get him out safely, little Buddha, perfect round face. Who needs karma when you've got fucked-up parents?

I walked across the Parks and the long way around St Catherine's, my old college, past the church where we had married, down Longwall Street and headed across Magdalen Bridge. There, for no good reason, I paused and watched the river.

'You will be beaten' said Shastraji's voice.

I watched the water swirling in the pale spring light. There were daffodils on the banks of the Isis. The sky was clear and blue. I reflected on his message. 'You will go to prison, twice'. Once I had already notched-up.

'They will try to frame you', said an inner voice. 'Be careful'.
At this I stopped musing and became attentive. Frame me? What? How?

Immediately a startling vision flashed before me and I staggered, looking for a place to sit down. Sue and the children were lying on the floor of their house, blood everywhere, hacked apart. Shocked, I made my way into the Botanic Gardens to a bench by the river.

My thoughts reeled. Of course it would work. They could kill the children and easily lay the blame upon me. Crazed husband. History of violent rows, emotionally upset, pressure of work. It happens that way, a man kills his own children because he can't be with them. They have enough control of the police, the courts, easy to frame me. That would knock me out of the game.

But not so easy. They'd have to be sure of the timing. Alibis. They couldn't risk it so easily. I was forewarned. I must have an alibi for every minute, every day and every night.

I abandoned thoughts of working in the libraries, hastily packed the documents I needed and caught the bus into London. Roger had been away. The thought of staying over in Oxford was too much. There was nobody I could tell apart from him. My friends Dave and Cathy had moved the previous year. Maida was with Ron on a trip to reconnoitre chimneys somewhere in Yorkshire. Ian and Merrilyn would be good company.

On the bus I reflected on the vision. If they were to stage such a frame-up they would require a skilled assassin, and knowledge of my every move. Could they monitor that astrally? Were they right now tuned in to my whereabouts, even my thoughts? Whatever, I had a bit of time to get organised.

I had grown close to Merrilyn in the three months of living in Northchurch Road. Once, we had been alone in the house and she was cooking. For the first time I allowed myself to see the sexual woman in her, and I shamelessly watched her tight-jeaned figure as she moved about the kitchen. I crossed that unmarked line between friendly hug and sensual invitation and she had been waiting for that. It was not a smart move. Sex I did not need. Closeness yes. I was wary of how it would be interpreted. I was not free. I had little time to give. And then, even with time, what then? She gave a great deal and a genuine love had developed in me for her immense qualities. She had written when away, exquisite cards, usually photographs of leaves or rocks, and her writing, evocative, composed, masterly, reflecting her soul, the depth of her education and deep sensitivity to nature, to the spiritual quest for harmony and balance, and a commitment to fight, for the women at Greenham as much as for the breakthrough of women in the circles of politics, science and art.

Our closeness served us that night. I related the vision. For London nights, at least, I would have my alibi. But I could see the sadness it brought her. For all her strengths, she yearned for the times she had known as a child. She had taken me to the statue of Peter Pan in Kensington Park, where she had been as a child with her father. There she had cried for the loss of innocence. She cried for me that night. I was not comfortable with tears. For all my rebirthings, for all the crying I had done, I still felt unable to place myself, like a bird of the air unable to dwell long on the surface of water.

Once back in London, my rational mind re-asserted itself. I was becoming paranoid. Murrell's death could have been simple burglary. She knew nothing of consequence. Reissland an unhappy accident. Elaine's dream and her sleepwalking a coincidence. I went to the movies with Merrilyn and saw Blade Runner for the third time. Then she took me to see 'Les Enfants du Paradis'. Opposite masterpieces. I worked all hours on the ocean dumping briefs for Greenpeace's international lawyers, had meetings with the Department of Environment officials, in particular, David Lewis, one of the Whitehall faceless for whom I developed an immediate liking and some faith in the process returned.

At this time we were propositioned. The first concerned a large oil exploration company called Cluff Oil. One of their executives, Alex Copson, somewhat of an inventor in rig design, wished to employ PERG as 'independent' assessors of a scheme for drilling holes in the ocean floor into which would be dropped Britain's problematic store of nuclear waste canisters. Roger and I had a meeting to which he had flown in many of their top people from the US. I had consistently outlined why it would never get a license in international waters, and Copson had now formulated a plan for a site off the north coast of Scotland. He offered a huge sum, by our standards, £100,000, for us to independently compare his option with all the others. Whitehall had been less than enthusiastic, and he had in mind that inviting us would somehow show that Cluff had considered all the environmentalist objections.

We backed off. It was clear that whatever our findings, and there could not, in all honest science, ever be a cut-and-dried answer to the comparative risks of all the options, underground-on-land, as opposed to underground-at-sea, above-ground-storage as opposed to below ground disposal, walk-away or monitored, sealed or accessible, clays or granites.... Copson would gain credibility for his option by our involvement. Whatever we said, it could be ignored in spirit, even if listened to in practice.

The second proposition was a good deal more sinister. Robert phoned and asked me to join him for lunch. We were to meet Paul Bijou, who also had some ideas regarding nuclear waste. We met in a smart hotel for a lunch on Bijou. Robert had invited Marek Mayer, a respected environmental journalist who ran a data service for professionals. Robert had warned me in no uncertain terms of Bijou's 'vibes'. He had the air of a successful business man with expensive tastes. His company had the rights to a certain select portion of Mauritania, a region of worked-out iron ore mines at the end of a long railway line into the western Sahara. What an ideal place to store nuclear wastes! But more. They would be mixed with that other bane of western civilisation - sewage sludge. This would make the desert green again. And any other toxics could be accommodated. After all, the radiation would keep the place secure against intruders. He mentioned cadmium as a suitable mix.

He wasn't straight. That much I felt, as well as a general nausea, as if an aura of negative energy emanated from his presence. I bristled at the mention of cadmium. What did he know? As if in telepathic response he volunteered he had connections with the nuclear industry and knew of an accident in which cadmium waste had been produced. It was a neutron absorber, wasn't it? I pretended ignorance, said boron I knew about. Robert had told him there was no way Greenpeace would support his 'solution' to the world's waste problems. Indeed, he could expect opposition on the high seas if he tried it. I told him PERG would not be interested in any assessment. I had travelled the Sahara. People lived there. People with little or no representation in governments. We did not believe in foisting our risks onto others, however few in number.

Bijou regretted our closed minds and we parted. Before parting, Marek turned and said, 'Be careful, Peter, these people could cause you a lot of trouble'.

Robert and I needed a long cold drink afterwards. 'He's a Mason, of course,' said Robert, 'and he could read our thoughts'. We both shivered and laughed. Robert then told me of his first encounter with that particular energy. After Durham he had worked for the Order of St John, on a respectable famine relief operation. The director of that operation had obviously become a mentor and father figure to Robert. On one occasion he had brought Robert into his office and the two had discussed telepathy and the reading of minds, which he then demonstrated. He had intuited Robert's latent ability. He called in a woman assistant and asked Robert to tell her something of what was going on in her mind. The woman was in a distressed state, and Robert immediately had access to intimate details of her life. He refused to participate, and left the job shortly thereafter. Robert added darkly, that was the first time he had met such evil. Bijou was the second.

We walked across Trafalgar Square and down to Westminster Bridge. It was a cold spring night as Robert related these parts of his past. He then talked of his growing relationship with Maida. He was madly in love! I could never take Robert and women seriously, although serious they certainly were. It was his constant romanticism. He was always in love. Each one was always the most beautiful woman in the world. I was not tempted to inquire of other qualities he appreciated. Even so, the prophetic vision was being fulfilled. He talked then of a strange experience at Maida's flat.

He had stayed over a few nights ago, after a long planning session for the chimney climbs. Maida had wanted a candle but had finished her supply. Dave, her 'estranged' husband might have one, and as he was away, she asked Robert to have a look in his room. She didn't like to go in there, it gave her the creeps.

'Peter, this is no ordinary drop-out. The room was meticulously neat. There were shelves of herbs and bottles. Many poisons. Hemlock. Nightshade. All neatly labelled. Ninja throwing stars on the walls. And a samurai sword. Peter, Maida says he made it himself. It was superb. And there were books on ritual magic and a large pentacle on the wall with the sword. The guy may be a freak but he is more together than he looks'.

I was stunned. I had not then told Robert of my vision. I did so. We now had our assassin. A kook, a ninja freak, some throwback from past lives, living only a block away from Sue.

'But surely', I reasoned, 'he's no warrior. No training. He's just a freak. He won't have the skills. He doesn't look like a marshal artist, doesn't walk like a fighter....'

'Ninja were masters of disguise', countered Robert. 'They had to look that way, to be above suspicion. You don't get permission to make your own sword unless you deserve the honour. To do otherwise would be sacrilege. He would know that.'

I remembered the last time I had been there, catching sight of the transformed pile of metal, now a gleaming bike, an antique Vincent. Robert added that when he shared his perceptions with Maida, she related how there'd been a rumour he'd offed someone with the Hemlock as an experiment.

I took a taxi back to Northchurch Road, relieved at the light in the window. Ian and Merrilyn were home. They also had some news. Speculation on Murrell's death had continued apace. The trail had led to a firm of private detectives in Essex, the boss of which was rumoured to indulge in black magic, and one of whose operatives had committed suicide a couple of weeks after Murrell's death. The word was that this firm had been 'contracted' by the security services and had done the leg-work of keeping all Sizewell objectors under surveillance. The killing might have been a cock-up, but there was also speculation of a ritual murder, the date and manner of death having Wiccan significance.

My rational mind finally gave in. Now must begin the most careful planning.

8

Divine Intervention

The following weeks were intensely stressful as I tried to organise my time, always with the thought, 'am I covered?', making sure I had no periods alone and sufficient for the 'frame-up' to work. Meetings were scheduled with officers of the Trades Union Congress concerned with the Holliday Committee, at the Department of the Environment concerning radwaste, and with the anti-PWR consortium of Local Authorities. I cancelled a trip to the USA to attend a conference on sub-seabed waste disposal, and one to the European Commission to investigate avenues of research on agriculture and wetlands.

My work was suffering. I had several acupuncture sessions with Gaby Hock to try to balance out my system. It was extremely hard to keep the vast amounts of references and data afloat in my near-memory sufficiently long enough to get a coherent piece of written work done.

I took a long weekend break in the hills of Wales, travelling up with Ron, who was also in need of recreation. Since the early days of the rebirthing groups in Oxford we had been using a small cottage in the rocky terrain above Harlech as a retreat and gathering place for spiritual renewal. Gatherings had been rather varied. At that time, the cottage belonged to the mother of a member of the group, Crispin Idiens, who was much taken with mind-expanding drugs, substances, plants and any kind of yogic endeavour that would take him 'out there'. If the gatherings had had a focussed leader, then there had been times of extra-ordinary magic. Not in areas of supra-normal experience, but in the simple contact with the elements of fire, earth, water and air. There was a purity in the hills behind Harlech, a timeless quality. Though no wilder or more natural than some other parts of Britain, there was an indescribable ancient emanation from the land. In hidden corners behind the high stone walled boundaries of the fields stood several large single standing stones and the circular remains of iron-age round-houses were scattered along old drover routes. The pale light of early spring, yellow lichens on grey rock, blackwater streams straight off the peaty uplands, these delights would feed me.

The cottage carries the name 'Hendre Dyfrgi', which means winter retreat of the otter. The homestead was several hundred years old, of a time when the plain of Morfa Harlech would have been maritime marshland and otters plentiful. Quite why otters would have retreated to the hill I do not know. There was little water and no obvious food.

Hendre abutted into the slope of the mountain and at one end the long low sitting room had a cave-like quality as one could see from a small window at the side the steep grassy bank dropping away several feet from the endwall. The walls were a metre thick and the deep windows channelled the light into the room. Often the whole mountain would be curtained in mist. There was an energy in the hill that was thick and dark, a base note in the symphony of energies in the surrounding outcrops, one of which was topped with an iron age hill fort. This energy resonated with the deep slow breath of rebirth. The soul would be drawn down into deep waters wherein lay darker elements of the psyche. This energy confronted, as if there was no escape, and often enough I had quickly left the house, feeling discomfort, and walked the windy ridge to the north above the steep woods.

Ron and I had gone out along that ridge on the evening of our arrival. The woods always drew us. I have found nothing to match their qualities of mystery. The oak and ash are old and the rocks so steep there is a likely continuity of woodland here, a long genetic lineage with the first oaks after the ice age. About a mile along the escarpment the pattern of pale greens of budding twigs is broken by splashes of white where giant geans, flowering wild cherry, rise and compete in height. I have not encountered such large cherry trees elsewhere. They are the favourite nesting site for a small number of herons, perhaps because the leaf comes early. We counted the nests. Each year there is one less. When we first came the Morfa was a chequerboard of pale browns, yellows, and greens, where gorse and sedge, willow and myrtle dominated the rough grazing and only a few of the fields had been reseeded to the monoculture of evergreen rye grass. Now the rough fields were few, the wet patches drained, the monotonal green in dominance and doubtless the frogs and toads and eels, food for hungry heron chicks, much reduced in numbers. Even here, on the very edge of marginal economic production, the relentless march of efficiency held a once poetic culture to ransom.

On the crest of the ridge, half-a-mile to the north of Hendre nestled a deserted cottage, 'Erw Wen', fair meadow, with the roof still sound. It stood above the steepest woods, with no access from the hills behind and only an overgrown bridle path wound to it from the road below. There was no electricity or water to the site. An old holly graced the curtilage to the front, its branches arching over to touch the roof. Ron and I had fallen in love with the place and made contact with Lord Harlech upon whose estate it fell. The estate was in financial difficulty and many properties were being put on the market - we had made an offer, having had the property valued and a loan arranged for that sum, but he had sold to some lawyer from the city at twice what we could raise. Now we approached the old house with sadness. In would come a road, electric wires, piped water.

Still, the owner would need a strong inner constitution. The door to one of the back rooms slammed shut as we left. There had been no wind. We did not know the history, but there was an angry female presence that was reluctant to leave.

Further along the ridge the energy of the land changed, becoming more open, drawing the spirit up and out toward the heavens. Here was an abandoned homestead, more dilapidated, a consolation prize, should we raise the money, but alas, not mortgageable. 'Llidiart Garw', the rough gate, smaller, single room with attic-space, timbers now rotten and a foot of cattle dung on the floor. Another year would see the roof gone. The cottage had little to enchant the spirit, but the land, although grazed short, held two small meadows that outlooked the Snowdon peaks across the Dwyryd estuary. In daytime, the grey clustered villages around Penrhyn hardly intruded upon the grey-green shaded hills and woods and with a little mist the vista would have been little different in the time of Glyndwr, or further back to Arthur and Merlin's mythic wanderings. This was a place to have a fire-pit, for ceremony, for yogic retreat. Such were our dreams.

At Hendre this time, however, there was no particular focus for the gathering and I found the company difficult. Crispin,, seemed to drift from one drug-induced experience to another without any sense of progress, of growth or change. There were several others from the Oxford group. We had spent two close years together, but somehow, I felt they had all got stuck, as if unable to break through to the next phase of growth. The closeness that we felt was real enough, but it did not seem to go anywhere. Yet were they not more at peace with themselves than I? Their relationships sound? Content with their roles in life, their work, their children? Maybe it was I that needed the growth, and they were fine, normal. Whatever, there was too much alcohol and dope for me to feel comfortable.

Cannabis, like tobacco, was, to my feeling, a sacred herb, an ally that could bring vision, and not to be constantly used as an intoxicant. There was something about such social use that seemed to subtract a very fine quality from the interplay of energies within a group. I preferred the hard edge to be softened by breathing together, when it seemed all senses sharpened but with the heart expanded to soften something much more fundamental than the soft-focus warmth of the drug-induced huddles. Ron was content to submerge into the haze and the arms of a longstanding girlfriend.

The moon was up and full and I left the cottage and drove south and across the toll at the Mawddach to the slopes of Cader Idris. I climbed briskly in a light bright enough for shadows, up the steep ridge to the summit which I

135

reached by about 2.00am. Mars and then Jupiter followed the moon across the arc of the ecliptic. Close to the summit I had checked my pace. I felt a challenge, a voice resonating inside, 'What are you doing here?' It was not a hostile presence, not friendly either. I proclaimed my right as of any man, and remained, finding a small cradle of rocks out of the wind. I watched the stars fade with the dawn and Venus rising, until the sun came up in a brilliant diamond of light in the clear pale sky. On the way down I saw my first wheatear of the spring, a male bird handsome in his grey and white and black and hint of apricot. A newly arrived willow warbler sang in the thickets by the car park, where I sat for a while, before moving off.

Undecided. Hendre did not appeal. I was too hungry to spend the day in the hills and the thought of scavenging among local Welsh village shops for half-decent bread and provisions was too much. I had enough of my gear for it not to matter whether I returned to the house. Ron could go back with Carol. I phoned, then headed in a fast drive to Oxford. It had already occurred to me that for the first time I was out and had been alone for several hours. I had not thought of Oxford, of crazed Ninja assassins, astral warriors, adepts and Masons, committees, meetings, models of oceanic complexities.....I drove at speed to keep my mind free, with my old white Volvo 144 having great trouble with the corners on the tight roads down to Welshpool and beyond into Shropshire.

Something steadily dwindles in the land from the western seaboard of Wales to the border country, until finally, on the stretch between Birmingham and Oxford, a flatness prevails that is more than the superficial terrain. It is a flatness of energy, like a flat musical note, a failure of resonance. Occasionally an old great oak will stand out, staghorned, beleaguered by acids and oxides in the air, last remnant of the time before roads and cars, before sprawling cities and myriad central heating systems belching their unseen sulphur. There would have been dark forest here, glades where the old trees fell, dappled light and green herbs for the deer, where wolves kept hidden 'til the night and a hunting moon. The land would have sung its harmonies.

When I first taught I knew that the more I awoke in my students a love for this harmony, the more sadness I would bring to the world. They would become like me, an old Indian longing for times long gone, of the forest, of beauty, of ancestor spirits. And around them would prosper the new age of golfers and surfers, skiers and paragliders, with their fast cars and......fuck it, always the same refrain, can't accommodate to it, if its not pylons here, its golf courses there, everywhere something to offend the critical eye. If I don't get out of this I'll die a bitter old man..... maybe not so old.

Oxford approached and I took the western ring to come down the Botley Road. Here the planners had brought the pylons to a halt two miles from the city, but not enough to save the grand vista. Another half mile of buried cable is all that it would have taken. Who cares?

Why head for Sue's? Some deeper intuition. Mind beginning to play out scenes of confrontation with a samurai-wielding nutcase, stepping to side, under the swing, turn and punch to the kidney, follow through as he falls, double punch to the neck. Stop. Clear the mind. Thought is creative. Get back into mantra, it must become second nature. Should I tell Sue? Or her best friend Shirley? If I ended up without an alibi I could call her, ask her to go round. What difference would it make, two scared women?

I have come direct to Sue's house. It looks quiet. Fast drive, not yet 9.00am. Kids must be up. Looks quiet. Milk not taken in. Go round the back. Door locked. No sign of anyone. Could she have gone away. I've been out-of-touch for a week. Maybe to parents. I knock. There's a shout from the road and the kids run up, followed by Sue.

'You're up early'.

'No bread, so we made a special trip to the French bakery. Croissants. Want to join us?'

There was a lightness of heart in her. Over breakfast she enthused about spring and crocuses in the Parks. The room was pungent with hyacinth. I began to thaw.

'Peter, I want you to know this', she said with a sudden serious note, 'I had a dream last night. I want you to know that we are totally protected. Jesus is looking after us. You don't have to worry about us.'

She had dreamt of witchcraft. What precisely, she did not elaborate. I told her the story, Ninja and all. She was unmoved, such was her trust in Him. Things with the church were going well. She had decided to be confirmed into the Catholic faith. We didn't talk further of it and all went for a good long walk in the Parks, feeding the ducks, a poignant occupation that always led my reflections to earlier happier years. Still, no lumps or tears, lots of running with Owen's ever steadier legs - that joggle no adult can emulate, both fluid and floppy with the sideways judder that rocks the head.

After lunch, later, back in my East Oxford room, after a moan to Roger about neighbouring kids having stolen my Campagnolo wheels from the shed and a bonzai from the rear garden, I settled to work. My sister phoned. A few days before I had asked her to see what she could find out from her Wiccan teachers about the Chapel of the White Lady.

Her voice was full with concern, 'What are you guys into? I asked Bel, and he said all hell broke loose in the room, chairs flying, crockery breaking.'

I said I couldn't explain over the phone, I just needed to know, it was a kind of a quest. I recalled 'Bel' had carved Ron a wonderful Green Man which he wore as a pendant and talisman. I hadn't met him. Sue's people kept to themselves.

I had also shared the whole set-up with Roger before leaving for Wales. He had talked with Bruno. Bruno had talked with the Gods. Firstly he had asked whether the threats Peter imagined were 'real'. He had expected a resounding 'no'. The Gods, by the way, always replied in a code of knocking sounds on the wooden artefacts of his altar, one for yes, two for no, three for maybe. He was surprised to get a 'maybe'. Second question had been, are the threats coming from the direction Peter suspects. A 'yes'. Third question, was Roger at risk? Answer, 'no'. This communion had swung Roger's scepticism.

'Lets go see Bruno,' I said. Roger declined, but thought it good that I go.

I found Bruno at home in his small house up the Kingston Road, just around the corner from Sue. A rather haunted and pale-looking American whom I presumed to be living there with Bruno made his apologies and disappeared to the kitchen and we talked. He enquired after Sue and the children with his usual concern. I quickly got to the point, telling him of Sue's belief in her protector and asked for his thoughts. He was dismissive of Sue's faith. Hadn't Christians always had such touching faith? Never did them any good. He was not for turning the other cheek, and began to outline a strategy of defence.

Firstly, I was quite right to suppose that they could track my every move. But that could be disguised. He would show me how to transfer my aura to someone else. I had to pick someone I did not like.

'Hang on a minute! What happens to that unfortunate? They could get hit. Killed. Could they not?'

'Of course. That's why it has to be someone you don't like'. He was matter-of-fact.

'Forget it Bruno. Whatever you do, don't try to help me! I'll find another way'.

Bruno made it clear he thought I was soft and bemoaned the whole world had grown soft and Christian's were much to blame.

I didn't stay in Oxford. Robert called. He was departing for the north that night. Maida was going too. They had their target. Indeed, that night and the next day, there would be eight targets in eight different countries.

'I'm coming too', I said, and relished another few hours of fast driving to dispel my thoughts.

We met in London and drove north that night in hired transit vans, Ron and Maida were climbing, with two others from German and Dutch Greenpeace teams.

We had a couple of hours rest around midnight in an anonymous bungalow on a housing estate somewhere in South Yorkshire. I'd smiled as we'd entered the cul-de-sac, 'Malwood Close', a little cosmic sign that we were in tune. The house was teaming with people, associates of Robert from his contacts with the working class equivalents of those middle-class New Age followers of Native American teachings. Robert had once invited me to a Pow Wow in Brixton, where they were all dressed up in buckskins and bonnets, and a formidable drumming supported hours of dancing. The 'indians' were now acting base camp and look-outs. I had to hand it to Robert, he enjoyed himself in situations where I would curl with embarrassment.

Behind the theatricals, Ron was a professional. Gear was checked, maps and drawings pored over. By the time dawn broke, I was watching the four ant-like forms nearing the top of the stack. The setting was perfect for the cameras. Steam from the factory below clouded around the climbers like smoke from an inferno. It was cold. Everywhere was concrete, tarmac, jaded brick walls and metal mesh fencing, industrial single-sloped roofs in all directions, and not a soul in sight. They made the top undetected. For a full hour we strained to see what the hold-up could be, tense, awaiting the unfurling of a banner. This was the tricky bit, to keep the banner from blowing too far out, from catching, curling, anything that would obscure the message. Then suddenly a giant 'S' unfurled, and written beneath, 'Pure Rivers, Clean Seas, Sweet Rain...Greenpeace'.

That night, eight such climbs would be successful across Europe from Czechoslovakia to Denmark and France, and Robert would have his pick of the four letters he needed to signal 'STOP' and a photomontage that would storm the front pages of the world's press. Each film would be flown to Paris that day. Our volunteer pilot was waiting with his own plane and the film was in the can and on its way before they'd begun their descent.

I envied my brothers their more glamorous tasks. Partly the thrill of action, partly the heroes' return. My typewriter, despite being Olivetti's top-of-the-range ET 221 with its stylish dark grey cooling fins, didn't quite match up. Somehow the rest of the week settled to the production of technical analyses. We had commissioned the government's own institution, the National Radiological Protection Board, to carry out computer runs based upon our own parameters of a major aerial release at Sizewell, and having just received the data, they had to be deciphered and worked up into a form laypeople could appreciate.

During these days, Merrilyn was my companion and confidante. At night, paranoid thoughts would return. The Ninja kook would become real again and my mind would start its steady trawling of the year's events and discoveries, Masonic law, astral projection, thought control, Reissland's death in the attic, Murrell's murder, the surveillance of the Sizewell objectors, Shastraji's prophecy, as if trying to glean some clue, some part of the puzzle I had not yet seen. I was not sleeping. I could not find the off-switch.

In the last week of April my sister phoned and told me the Chapel of the White Lady was at Eton. Of course.

I found Robert the next day and told him. 'I know', he answered smiling, 'I've just been talking with Dave the Ninja. He told me.'

Robert had taken the bull-by-the-horns and on return from Maida's had hitched a lift to London with Dave. They had talked of ninja lore. At one point Dave had smiled and looking at him directly had said, 'Do you know, they used to use women?'

There had been a little friction between Robert and I after Maida had apparently complained of feeling slightly pressed by my sexuality. I had dismissed it, firstly because Maida was not the sort to keep her feelings from me and I was sure of our friendship, and secondly, because I doubted Robert had heard what she had said without his own filters operating. I was still surprised that Maida had said anything.

Robert had asked Dave straight, 'Where's the Chapel of the White Lady', and the answer had come without so much as a blink or a pause or question in return.

That night, the last day in April, I had had enough. I felt no desperation. Just a sense of the ridiculous.

I called to Babaji, 'What the hell! If you want me to act, you send me some help. What do I know. I've no siddhis. I'm no astral warrior. What am I supposed to do at the Chapel of the White Lady? This is completely out of my depth. If you want me to go there, you send me some help.'

I had had no contact with the avatar since he left his body. His small band of followers in Britain had been far more disturbed than I by his 'death'. Several of them had been disciples of the disciples of Bennett, well-known disciple of Gurdieff, and were now lost with nobody to be the disciple of. Patsy Clasen, who I had met in India at the turn of the year, had written to her former Gurdieffian 'teacher', an American who styled himself 'Dadaji' and claimed either to be the ultimate avatar of this age, the 'dattatreya' or 'adiguru', or at least to have privileged contact, I was never sure which. Dadaji had netted two of my close Oxford friends, Anthony Cheke and his wife Ruth, who had decamped to Daglingworth, the guru's ashram near Cirencester. I had not felt in any way drawn, and had noted, on Anthony's visits, how his energy hardly reflected the presence of a great teacher.

Dadaji wrote to Patsy, evidently after she had conveyed to him Babaji's demise. Patsy circulated a copy. It had this to say to those of his former disciples who had strayed into Babaji's camp,

> Dear Patsy,
>
> If you are going to keep trying to communicate to me, then at least try and be intelligent about it rather than just showing off and making emotional gestures. You have an intellect, so you might as well use it to discriminate and see the whole picture of things.
>
> Your Guru, Herakhan Baba, has over the centuries achieved great heights of personal power, but had not matured enough in terms of spiritual integrity and honesty and humility. His pride made him think he could do no wrong, but wrong he was beginning to go.
>
> 1. Herakhan Baba is Gorakhnath. This is the truth. He has periodically challenged Lord Shree Dattatreya's spiritual authority and has been periodically defeated in this attempt. Lord Shree Dattatreya is Adiguru, not Babaji.

2. Trilokh Singh Muniraj (whom Babaji left as leader) is an advanced soul, but also suffers from ego and ignorance that causes him to make mistakes in his overall orientation. He is certainly NOT Dattatreya Swamiraj. Dattatreya is Adiguru, the Master of Masters, and has never been a devotee of Gorakhnath Herakhan Bhole Baba.

3. Babaji was given one chance at the end through communication from me through Julian Romanes (who is Swami Vivekananda reborn) to stop lying about Adiguru Datta and mend his ways. Evidently his spiritual downfall and disintegration had proceeded too far to stop this process from culminating in death.

4. The situation of Babaji's Personality Cult of Himself, his spiritual movement, is that the ignorant, ego-ridden followers of his will break-up into factions of varying interpretations of events (none of which will be the true interpretation as given in this letter to you) and there will be increasing meaningless clashes of pride and orgies of personal degeneration as their deceased Master will not be able to help them, for he is himself right now in a terrible cosmic battle in his Soul as to the real meaning and value of his being. Babaji is 'burned out' like an electric bulb that took too much current. He is presently under repair and will not be able to help anyone at all for a long time. A return in 1989 is a bit optimistic and by no means assured.

6. Rescue is offered to stranded, shipwrecked followers of Babaji in the form of myself giving them an opportunity, which most will refuse, to meditate on the true supremacy of Adiguru Datta Swamiraja in spiritual matters.

As long as the followers of Herakhan Baba deprive themselves of spiritual research into these things and blot out of their minds all understanding of the history and ongoing events of the Nath Sect in India, they will wallow in their emotional states and it is unlikely that any of them will amount to anything good for themselves or others. Babaji as Captain of his ship forgot Who's ship it was, Who the owner is. So now his ship is breaking up on the rocks.

That you want to sit there in the Captain's cabin thoughtlessly trying to suck me into emotional affirmation of Babaji only indicates your own lack of intelligent observation of what is happening at Herakhan and with Babaji's various mislead devotees. Only Lawrence Young (Laxman Singh) has shown any capacity to register the truth of what is happening.

Another thing you and the others at Herkahan should have an opportunity to know is that it was only by a Mercy of God that Babaji died, for if he had stayed in his body much longer, wielding cosmic powers in a vainglorious manner, it would have entirely destroyed his Soul and sent him back to very low forms of life to begin millions of years of personal evolution all over again.

Furthermore, out of great love and affection for him (he and I are related closely from past lives, like father and son), I have asked God to bring him into my home as my son so his Soul can be restored to proper truthfulness and holiness. This is very possible. So, if he were to come to Herakhan in 1989, it may be as an infant boy in my arms, having taken normal birth here with me. To further him in this, he would have Shree Anandamayi Ma, who is now my infant daughter, as his elder sister to help him in his character development. Anyone who can meditate on these matters with deep sensitivity will be more than blessed. As for the followers of Babaji who insult me and pretend they are important beings with important opinions, they will experience great emptiness and sorrow, for truly their master cannot help them.

Finally, be it known that Dattatreya Swamiraja has given me complete spiritual authority over the spiritual development in the Western countries and for the New Age ahead. I am Avatar. I am Kalki Panduranga. Anyone who finds a way to recognise this will make great progress. Anyone who denies it will have to be taken care of through more ind-irect (sic) experiences, such as the following of nearly disintegrated ancient siddhas like Gorakhnath Herakhan Bhole Baba.

Each Soul must ask Himself or Herself what is the real aim of spiritual aspiration? Is it to worship Power and Miracles and Powerful, Miracle-working beings? Or is it to become one with God? There is a difference you know.

Love,   (it was signed 'chief')

These strong words had shaken a few, but not drawn them back. For myself, I had always regularly entertained the possibility that Babaji was a 'fake'. India was full of wandering saddhus with no record of their birth, many of whom were genuine miracle workers, capable of reading minds, sitting in fires, healing the sick. Besides, I had not personally seen Babaji sit inside a blazing bonfire. He had not materialised out of a ball of light for me. I had seen some minor bending of the rules of physics. Then there were the inexplicable little teachings with colour-coded messengers, but hardly the stuff of cosmic commanders.

It mattered not to me whether Babaji 'was' Lord Shiva, or a reincarnated Gorakhnath, whoever he was. I had seen what I had seen, felt what I felt. That was my reality. He had taught me, helped me. I had been there with his simple ceremony of honouring the divine source. I had seen his simple life. Witnessed his humour, the depth of his eyes, a faraway poignant look of care and concern and knowledge of what was coming to the earth. There were no jewels, no riches, no cars and aeroplanes. He did not seek a great following, and I never heard or read of him making any reference to who he was. It was the devotees that called him Shiva or God or a manifestation of the Divine.

Sometime after the 'death', or as the devotees would have it, when He entered his 'mahasamadhi' or great bliss, a middle-aged slightly-built Italian woman had returned from the ashram to London. John Chaney (Narayana), whom I had been with at Herakhan, had known her and he called me soon after she arrived. Her normal domicile was in a nondescript but largish semi-detached in Twickenham. Babaji had given her the name Harigovindi. We visited. It had been a delightful experience. She was a quiet unassuming person. I had not seen her at Herakhan, but vaguely remembered there had always been a coated figure huddled by Baba's veranda at all hours.

She related how Babaji had told her she was to simply sit there outside his quarters. She was not to go to the temple, or to do any work. To sit there was her work. Shortly before he died, he had called her to tell her that she would later be given siddhis and much work to do. He had been ambiguous, but she knew now he had said, 'after I have gone'.

At one point, Babaji had emerged from his 'kutir', the small room on the veranda overlooking the river gorge. She was sat at the top of a flight of steps up from the veranda to the temple precinct. Babaji was leaning on his staff and moaning and groaning as he had for days, much to the consternation of many of the yogis concerned for his health.

'Oh, Harigovindi, help me, help me', he cried.

She yelled back, with finger pointing accusedly, 'If you are Lord Shiva, you don't need my help'.

Upon which there was laughter, and in the blink of an eye he was flying past her and grabbing an arm, yanking her up and to the top of the steps, where he turned, winked mischievously, leant heavily on his staff, and continued to moan as he walked, 'Oh, Harigovindi, help me, help me'.

John and I joined her bubbling laughter. Later I shared with them both the turmoil of the past few weeks. Harigovindi just said to remember Babaji's teachings, 'I am in your every breath'. He wants us to be strong. And to keep the mantra, Om Namaha Shivaya, as protection.

John later told me some of his own history. He was now a rather skilled mender of broken washing machines. A job that kept him free, in his own time, to follow his path. He was training as a masseur. He knew John Taylor personally. They had once shared a dojo. It turned out Narayana had also taken Karate to beyond a black belt and not so long ago had his own dojo. It was a useful confirmation of Taylor's authenticity.

I liked Narayana's simple devotion. Every morning he would rise early and perform a 'puja', a devotional song to Lord Shiva, sung to Baba's photograph, and an offering of lighted camphor. Babaji had given him a special healing mantra, which he would have to repeat continuously 750,000 times before it would take effect.

Narayana had married Christina who had been a participant of our two-year Oxford rebirthing groups, and the couple provided another safe haven for my troubled mind. They had a modern flat on Richmond Hill to which I repaired on several occasions. Christina introduced me to astrology by drawing up my birth chart. At first sceptical, I had begun to work with it by reading Liz Greene's 'Relating'. That book had opened up new landscapes of understanding and new questioning on the nature of reality, the personality and the soul's journey.

I am an Aquarian sun. No surprises. Intellectual. Involved in science. Difficult to get in touch with feelings. Cool and distant. Eccentric. Independent. Revolutionary tendencies. Christina had guessed that, and my moon sign, within seconds. Moon in Cancer. Deep feelings. Easily hurt. Home life important. Early influences of mother and home crucial to balanced development. The watery moon balanced the airy sun.

I began observing the polarities of the zodiacal mandala in my friends, lovers and associates, and more particularly, in myself. I had been lazy in this regard. Having devoted years of study to the classification of birds, mammals, plant life from plankton to pomegranates, I discovered the rich rewards of a systematic study of human qualities. It brought me a new compassion. People had their individual strengths and weaknesses. I had so often projected my own standards, naturally my strengths, and judged others that did not meet them. I began also to see myself more objectively.

If one were to engage in only one act of systematic self-knowledge, my recommendation would be to have an astrological chart drawn up, and to purchase Liz Greene's 'Relating'. I will select but one aspect of many,

> One may perform a very useful exercise by examining the position of Saturn on the birth horoscope, and then examining the charts of partners, relatives or associates to see whether any of their planets falls within about eight or ten degrees of one's own Saturn, in the same sign. Also significant are planets which are directly opposite one's own Saturn, one hundred and eighty degrees away. The angle of ninety degrees is likewise significant. These three aspects, or angular relationships - respectively called the conjunction, opposition and square in astrology - are the commonest of all the aspects of chart comparisons; and they inevitably occur in relationships which somehow force the individual whose Saturn is involved to examine himself and his own responses, so that he may discover something about the workings of his shadow. In any relationship involving these Saturnian aspects between charts, we can anticipate a good deal of shadow projection. The important thing is for the individual to recognise that he is the source of the problem, through his defensive or over-critical reactions, rather than to blame his partner for whatever discord develops. One must also learn to live out the meaning of the Saturn sign, even if it is awkward and embarrassing, rather than to run away from it and then resent it when it is expressed by others. Here at least the shadow can be recognised and given room to breathe, which is an excellent remedy for many of his less attractive qualities.

By the spring of 1984 I had worked a little with the symbolic map of my personality. Enough to see the projections of Sue upon me more clearly than mine upon her. Her Venus in Aquarius was opposite my Saturn in Leo. As a Capricornian sun with its roots in tradition and caution she found it difficult to live that part of her creative woman that needed the airy freedoms of Aquarius. That part, at least, was projected with resentment on to me as a restrictive authority-figure (my Saturn). For my part, Saturn in Leo left me with deep-seated self-doubt and a drive to compensate by superior competences. I had stayed with those skills, my scientific and analytic mind, of which I could be sure, whereas the Leo beckoned toward something altogether more centre-stage dramatic, creative and artistic. This accounted for my senses of resentment, though well hidden, and not directed personally, whenever others were unlocking such qualities.

In truth, in the scientific realms in which I worked, and had gained by now, some standing, I was an imposter. I am not a scientist. Apart from my brief survey of tree-hole communities when I successfully correlated insect larvae diversity with circumference and aspect of the hole to the sun, which, in any case, had been done many times before, I have never 'done' science. In my work I have relied certainly upon an understanding of scientific theory and a memory for facts and relationships, and upon an instinct for the hidden and not yet known, but fundamentally I have been a linguist and an actor. My scientific degrees were linguistic exercises in critical review. My performances on television, in public inquiries, on tribunals and commissions, those of an extremely well-briefed lawyer, the ultimate actor. Which is not to say there is no dedication to truth.

There are many who decry astrology as fancy, particularly in the scientific professions. Yet virtually all the early great scientists were also astrologers. Copernicus, Galileo, Kepler, even Newton. To critics, Newton replied, 'they have not studied it, I have'. Those who now decry it should take time to approach its art with an open mind and a month of study. When once admitted by sheer quality of self revelation, it then cannot fail to face the inquiring mind with the deepest of questions of the nature of reality and human evolution.

How is it that the personality, and I was later to learn, the path of the soul and the lessons of this lifetime, can be read in the pattern of stars along the earth's ecliptic? Or in the rising sign on its eastern horizon and on the western declination, and the sign at its mid-heaven and opposite, in the pattern of angles between the planets and their seats in the respective twelve divisions of the zodiac? A few minutes or few miles either way in space and time is enough to alter the delicate relationships.

For me, now, it is not that energies of planets or stars 'affect' us - for even the launching of a ship, no more than metal and wood, is the birth of an entity with a fate that will unfold. It is more that the planets themselves are part of a larger cosmic play in which we are all part. What is in us, this mind and its many thousand aspects, is also 'out there', linked by symbol, governed by inscrutable law. Events in the psyche coincide with events in the heavens because they are linked to the same reality, an unfolding of time and space and numerical relationship. Thus, Saturn as a planet shares with other elements of the Universe certain qualities, and all those elements dance to the same unfolding choreography in time and space: the metal lead, the crust of the earth, the structure of the state, traditions of culture, the limits of time, the Grim Reaper and karma, the limiting concepts of mind, the supporting skeleton, the testing of strengths and the Devil himself, all relate to the tenth division of the circle and the numeral 10, which the ancients called Capricornus, the mountain goat.

The relationship of the planets, the moon and the sun, to that tenth segment, is that of an unfolding cosmic play that is *their* evolution as much as ours. What is happening in the macrocosmos above, though far removed from our conscious perceptions (and I doubt it is the inanimate cosmos our limited concepts and perceptions assume it to be), is subject to the same laws that operate in the microcosmos of life on earth, and just as much in the cosmos of the human mind as in the interplay of physical bodies with physical things.

Our current priesthood of science would have us see ourselves as separate from the stars, see the galaxy that contains our zodiac as a Godless or Loveless self-assembly system, its rays and energies as simple waves or particles. For them there is no 'mind' out there. The mind, which they never explore on inward journey, is to be located in the brain, which is as daft to me as locating the orchestra that plays a symphony for radio in the little box of tricky soldering that receives it.

Astrology is on its own path of rediscovery. In ancient civilisations it was not built, as today, just upon meticulous observation of personality and correlation to celestial patterns, but upon an intimate knowledge of the mind's expanded state, of explorations into the unconscious, the dwelling place of archetype, and of astral journeys far out into universal matter. The interconnectedness of all was a direct and living experience and fostered by the experienced adept, not restricted and kept secret.

Which brings me to consider again our dear friends the Masons. Here we have secret teachings, acknowledgement of gods and demons, archetypes that have been revered since the first dawn in Sumer, then Egypt, Greece and Palestine. It would appear that behind the closed lodge doors there are adepts and initiations. And all of this within the serried ranks of the military-industrial-complex that fosters the scientific world view upon which that alliance depends for its technological 'progress', and yet which professes a philosophy that would have no magic in the Universe! The warrior and merchant classes may pay lip service to the mythic religion of the masses, and subvent the work of a spiritless science, but they themselves hold to and practice magic and arcane ritual. Major generals and bankers, chief constables and Prince Royals, all sit secretly with the Gelli's and other throwbacks from the times of the Templars and the Knights of St John. But to what purpose?

On May 6th I had a call at my phone in Oxford. It was Bhavani. She was at Heathrow Airport.

'Baba told me you need help'.

9

The Chapel of the White Lady

Bhavani was dressed in long flowing chiffon-like white robes and her shaven head was bound in a pale peach-coloured cloth. She was accompanied by a tall Dutchman called Jon, one of Babaji's yogis. She greeted me warmly. We spoke little by way of explanations. I felt no need to ask for details. She had been going to New York and obviously Babaji had diverted her here on route. I told her about the chapel quest and my fears about the Ninja. She wanted to travel to Oxford and go round to Sue's immediately. She said little more, other than I must remember she carries no money or possessions and that I need to look after her for a few days.

In Oxford she is received warmly, and a pot of herb tea prepared as we all sit in the small kitchen at Juxon Street. Sue appears self-conscious, but friendly. Bhavani radiates a deep peace that dispels any urge to make small talk. Before the tea is poured, she rises, takes Sue by the hand and beckons me to follow into the adjoining room. She sits us down, still holding our hands.

'You two have been together before. Susan you are still afraid of this man. It was in wartime. The Crimea. Peter, you were gravely disturbed, sent mad by it all, and quite violent, a danger to her and to the children. You had to be separated, you went to an Institution. The parting was deeply painful. It hurt you both very much, especially the pain of the children. Peter, the war destroyed you. That fate is keeping you apart now. You have to be very patient with each other'.

She reached into the single small bag she carried with her and drew out a red silk scarf with Krishna motif and looped it around Sue' neck.

I had a mental picture of looking through a fence and feelings of being caged and shut-off from love and from my children. Rage at the unseen hand that parted us. We were both in tears as Bhavani held us.

I left her at Sue's while I finished up what business I had in my workroom. She had asked to meet everyone. Ron and Robert would come up from London. I checked Maida was home, and that we could meet there. She was happy to cook some food.

The past life stuff about war and separation felt unreal. I had no feelings of memories of that period or that place. Yet the images Bhavani had evoked did have a resonance deep in my psyche. Did such patterns repeat through lifetimes? Were Sue and I still caught in psychic consequences laid down in some previous encounter? Curious how souls find each other in this crazy global theatre.

At Maida's, Ron, Robert, myself, the Dutch Yogi and the two women crammed in to her small room and ate supper on the floor. Very little was said. Bhavani then asked Maida to fetch Dave down, and he came in behind her, looking decidedly bemused. Bhavani rose and took out another scarf from her bag, this time purple and with Buddha motif. She stretched with her extended arms barely reaching to Dave's head and looped the scarf about his neck, and still holding on to each end, said,

'You have been outside for a long time. Now you are included. You can let go of the past'.

Dave's eyes welled with tears. Awkward, he turned and left without a word. Bhavani then matter-of-factly gathered up her things and indicated we must make haste to London. Robert stayed behind and arranged to meet us in the Greenpeace office the following day.

In London Bhavani over-nighted with me at Northchurch Road, and the Dutch Yogi decided to look up some friends. She handed me a mimeographed sheet with the heading 'Network of Light'.

> As it is Shiva Himself who ends the cycle of destruction (Kali Yuga), it is Shiva who brings in the next Golden Age, the one ending and the other beginning simultaneously.

> We are now in the midst of the greatest such upheaval - rebirth into the Age of Aquarius, of Universal Brotherhood and Universal Consciousness. Aquarius is the bearer, not of water (Baptism of water for the previous Age of Pisces), but of Amrit, divine nectar of light and love, Premjyoti. Amrit itself comes into the body (in the pituitary-pineal area) only following the awakening of the Kundalini energy and the constant surrender of the whole being to God, so that God can purge and purify the channels through which He (She) can then pour. It is Shiva alone who awakens His divine fiery, dangerous Shakti, Kundalini, and draws Her to Him from the base of the spine to the Sahasrar or the crown Chakra.

> Along the way is a great Revolution, a stirring up of the whole being in order to cast out the poisons so that the purified fluids

can transform into Amrit. This revolution is now happening on an individual, group and planetary level.

At this transitional time, there are many, many lightworkers, (on and off the planet) who have the natural ability to bring in light from above and pour it into this realm. They are often of the astrological sign Aquarius or have strong Uranus in their birth chart. They are also natural telepaths, like living lighthouses.

All of us, as we surrender to God and the higher channels, open, become more and more able to link with others and transmit Light (Jyoti), Love (Prem) and Power (Shakti) in the living network of light.

This netowrk has been alive and functioning on this planet since Egypt, but it wasn't till the late 1960's that this New Age was really initiated and this Old-and New Knowledge began to intensify and circulate both upon and above the whole planet.

In 1970, the Lord Himself, Shiva (to the American Indians, the Great Spirit - MahaDeva) entered a body to personally transform the physical realm. (How blessed are we who have seen His face, heard His voice, touched His feet).

He told us then to learn to hear Him in our hearts. There will come a time', he said, 'when that is the only way you can hear me'. That time is NOW.

On my way back to America on December 31st 1981, our Lord gave me a vision of a Great Circle with Native Americans and people from all over the world in it. He also sent the terms 'Empowerment' and 'network of Light'.

Since then, my chief role, both in America and here in India (yes, even in Haidakhan) has been to gather people together and to help activate or intensify the working of the network.

Much work has already been done all over the world in expanding and intensifying this subtle telepathic light-body on this planet. The 'Network of Light' is not an exclusive organisation, but a living communion of all groups and individuals who are tuned into the higher vibrations of love, light and unity, those who consciously serve as agents of God.

We are the living points of light that make up this network - our sacrifice, our love, our meditation, and our work, our openness to our Lord creates the 'space' for our Lord to pour through. Our bonding, our reaching out, our love for each other, create the channels for the light to flow. We must keep the channels between us clean and open.

There appeared a part missing, for the second sheet began in mid sentence, evidently about Babaji 'leaving us only after New year 1984, a key year in all world predictions. It went on,

> When He exploded out of His body, like a star going Nova he activated with that tremendous shakti the MahaTirtha of Haidakhan, the tirthas all over the world - from Vishvanath and Kedernath to Mt Shasta and Mt Sinai - all the dhunis and lingams, the spiritual centers and shrines of all in the world who seek peace and unity. The shrines we each have in our hearts were exploded in the same way, as numberless people have already shared with me. The shakti, the growth, the transformation are more, not less. In some way, our empowerment and our work have just begun.

> This September ('83) I took part with Luli (Shirley Brinks) in a 'Peace Mission', driving across America from New York to California, stopping many places and inviting many different groups to link consciousness with us in all-night peace meditation on the night of the full moon (which was right in the middle of the 3-day Peace Yagna at Campbell Hot Springs). We asked people to center on the havan. All the later reports included accurate and similar descriptions of that fire. We all experienced great power and love that night. I was then instructed to 'do it every full moon'.

> Before He left His body, Babaji had us meet together several times empowering our worldwide organisation, unifying us and increasing our awareness of each other, and preparing us to meditate for a link together all over the world. Since he left His body, and especially here at Haidakhan, I have experienced greater power and light, exploding especially (for me) from the dhuni He built with His own hands and empowered before His departure as 'Mahashakti Dhuni'.

> I experience a seed of light, love and power in the heart of the dhuni a subtle lingam above and including the dhuni, that acts as a center and amplifier, like a living crystal. I have seen it intensify even as I sat beside it, scarcely able to handle the brilliance. It connects with all the other points of light and it is a powerful focussing point for all of us who have been there.

The full instruction is that every full moon we all gather - either in our centers or with others, wherever we are - and we invite other groups to link consciousness with us. We focus on Babaji and the lingam of light above and including the dhuni. Then we focus on those here, those we have linked with in other Babaji centers, then other individuals and groups throughout the world and light beings on all levels, letting our visions be guided by our Lord from within. At some point, we see the planet bathed in a robe of light, love and shanti and be aware of all those over the planet who are linked together in this vision. This is to be done specifically every full moon and in addition, on all major holidays. Include in the vision whatever centers are most potent for the specific occasion (for instance Bethlehem at Christmas). On July 1-7th there will be a great Rainbow Gathering in America at Mt Shasta in California. On July 4th at noon (Calfornia time, Greenwich minus 7) we will join in silent prayer and meditation, just as I have described, sending light, peace, love, universal brotherhood. This will be followed by chanting, including Om Namaha Shivaya. There will be a flame (large dhuni) and a giant crystal to focus on (subtly, America is the Land of Rainbows and Crystals and Dancing Lights). Please join us - in the body if possible - otherwise in meditation.

I will see or feel you all in my prayers and remember you in our many circles at full moon.

And if our Lord permits, I'll see you in Haidakhan for Christmas 1984.

> Bhole Baba Ki Jai
> Jai Maha Maya Ki Jai
> Jai Maha Shakti Ki Jai
> Jai Vishva
>
> Bhavani

I had a reaction to the constant capitalisation of Him. Too much reminiscent of schooldays religiosity over Jesus. Babaji deified. I felt rather protective toward Bhavani as a 'light worker', and found it hard to take it all seriously. Flakey New Age crystal charging, while all about, the sea gets dumped on, forests slashed and burned and ecological Armageddon draws ever nearer. Who am I to judge? Maybe it is the only real work, this light of love. Whatever, I have simpler tasks that demand less than a pure heart.

The next morning we met Robert and Ron at the Greenpeace office in Graham Street. Bhavani had asked to meet everyone in the office. Her presence had a profound effect. I recall Pete Wilkinson, Reg Boorer and Toni Mariner, three of the directors and the three of us brothers all standing around her in Reg's design-room, a circle of men around this diminutive nun, when she began prodding Pete in the midrib saying 'such a lot to let go of, such a lot to let go of' and Pete's face beginning to crack as if he would weep and saved only by a joking remark from Reg. I know they were touched deeply but had no language with which to say so.

That night we met at John and Christina Chaney's flat. Bhavani, Jon, Ron and myself. We were to drive to Eton the next day. Robert would travel separately by train and meet us at noon.

I had no idea what to expect at Eton. None of us had been there before. We did not know whether the chapel would be easy to find, but I assumed it would be the chapel of Eton College, the public school. I asked John if he would check it out. I cannot remember now why I assumed, or knew, that John Chaney had 'the sight'. He sat down to meditate and I listened carefully.

'Yes. The Chapel. Near the Chapel is a courtyard. It has a pattern, like a chessboard or something, the pattern of a cross. I can see a clocktower. Ah, yes, the power point is not in the Chapel. I see a fountain. And columns.'

With that we each retired into our meditations for the night. I sat before my favourite photograph of Babaji, taken a short time after he arrived. He is young. Handsome. His eyes alight with fire. This is Lord Shiva! But what does he think of all this here, of Pan and Arthur and Albion. How far can I trust John Taylor. He himself has a hard time with Pan. Babaji, 'where are you in all this?'

Before my weary eyes, Babaji's beautiful countenance sprouted little horns and a distinctly mischievous look.

The next day dawned bright and blue and clear. A wonderful spring morning. John Chaney said jokingly, he would stay behind and 'guard our backs'. On the motorway west I could feel his presence behind me as I drove. Ron and Bhavani sat in the rear and the Dutch Yogi beside me. A short distance out my old Volvo was passed by a speeding white car. I felt it come up behind and watched it carefully as it sped away. It was an unusual mark, a Ford Xr4i with dual tail spoilers, white with gold trim.

We took the exit for Eton and approached the town across water meadows. The chapel was easily visible rising above the other buildings. As we were about to leave the last of the fields, there was a white car, the Ford, parked off the road, with the driver hidden behind a newspaper. I remarked to the others that the car had passed us earlier.

Eton College reminded me of Oxford colleges. It was centrally located, not separate from the town. Its period architecture glowed a warm buff yellow in the sun. The college was closed to visitors until 2.00 pm and so we wandered off to meet up with Robert and have a leisurely lunch. We ate in the open air at a pub by the river. The day was crisp for early May, with the first swifts circling overhead and buds not yet in full burst.

Everyone is feeling light. There is no plan and no talk of a plan.

As we amble back to the College, a file of Eton schoolboys, dressed in their black and white costumes passes us. Across the street, two boys in olive green military uniform, hands in pockets, shuffle gravel with their feet as they talk. Here will be schooled the bankers, the major generals, the aristocrats, ministers of government, mandarins of Whitehall. By the College entrance, where the Chapel is located, there is a graveyard littered with massive tombstones. A cluster of large cherry trees is profuse with blossom. With one accord we enter and take handfuls, which Bhavani collects in the folds of her robes. She is wearing brilliant white with a deep purple shawl.

The entrance to the Chapel is easy to find. To one side there is a large white statuette of Mary looking down at us. We go inside and the long aisle is full of light from the stained-glass windows on either side. Above the altar is a large arched window with the stained glass depicting the crucifixion. I notice the cross is rose red. As we move down the aisle, Bhavani's attention is caught by something off to our left. She moves between a row of pews to the wall, where there is a mural depicting a scene in which a maiden, presumably Mary, is kneeling before two bearded Patriarchs. One man holds what appears to be a scroll, which he is handing to her.

Bhavani shook her head. She knelt, muttering under her breath, and made some small ceremonial offering of petals at the base of the wall. The three of us brothers approached the altar and knelt down. I said a silent prayer to Mary, that we might be of service, that we might be instructed, and offered forgiveness to those who might have abused the power of this sacred place.

We left the chapel and began to wander aimlessly about the courtyard. The day was still. My mind had gone completely blank. There were patterns of dark and pale flagstones. There was a clocktower to one side with an archway leading off. I remembered nothing of John Chaney's vision. Robert disappeared through the archway and a moment later called out to us to come. The archway led to cloisters. In the centre was a grass lawn and in the centre of the lawn, a fountain. Robert had taken off his shoes and was walking on the close-mown green, despite the 'keep off the grass' notices. An old woman had appeared and fussed about him walking on the grass, then became agitated and asked him to leave. Ignored, she departed trough the archway.

Robert called excitedly, 'this is it. There are Masonic symbols carved on the stones'.

Each corner of the square of stonework around the fountain had been engraved with glyphs of some kind. The fountain had three tiers of round stone forming a tapering cone, and a gush of water arose from the top and fell over the sides to the tier below.

Bhavani approached the fountain, took off her sandals and placed them beside her as she sat down in lotus position, pulling the purple scarf off her bare head. A great 'aum' resonated from her belly and filled the air about us. We stood silent in the shadow of the cloister. Over to my right I noticed for the first time another figure in the shadows. He leaned forward with a camera and telephoto lens pointed at Bhavani.

Bhavani rose and began to strew her petals in the fountain. The first tier and the second, but the third she could hardly reach. She tried repeatedly. All of our attention was fixed. It was as if the earth itself stood still in waiting, and when she finally reached the third tier, and we released our breath, it was as if the land sighed its own release.

I approached the man with the camera. He spoke first, introducing himself as a freelance photographer with the National Geographic. He had an American accent, but there was something veiled in his countenance. Photographers of architecture do not normally use 35 mm single lens reflex cameras with telephoto lenses. I was sure he was the man in the Ford. He asked if this were some kind of ceremony.

I said, simply, 'This site is sacred to the White Lady. It has been abused and we have come to ask forgiveness for those who have misused it. We are Yogis sent by Babaji.'

His face gave no hint of surprise or bemusement. He asked for the name of the woman performing the ceremony and I had to spell it carefully for him. And he asked only where she was from, to which I replied, New York.

We left Eton. Bhavani came with me to Islington and I hugged her and held her close before she went to her bed. I had a strong urge to unwrap her shawls and draw her away from her nunnery. She felt the sudden charge of energy between us, and I wager I saw a flicker of longing. She had not been a nun all her life, indeed, she had grown-up children long flown from her nest. Next morning I took her and Jon to the airport.

As they left I suddenly felt a foreboding, and the one word, 'backlash' came to my mind.

10

Beaten

The day after Bhavani left, on May 11th, I received a call from Central TV. They urgently needed to collaborate on the issue of waste disposal sites on land for low -level radioactive waste. This issue had become intensely controversial, with the government having announced its preferred site for drilling and investigation in the brick-fields of Bedfordshire. The county had been galvanised into opposition and Central were filming the public debates and providing background to the issues of risk. I had already declined involvement in the debate, partly because of the work overload, and partly strategic. Having been appointed to the government's review of sea-dumping, as well as advising the Department of the Environment on its radioactive waste research programmes I did not want to spread myself thinly. Much as I was clear about what I wanted to see, if I was active on too many fronts the image of 'anti-nuclear-at-all-costs' could also be counter-productive.

Central were desperate in their pleading. There were no scientists with my level of technical knowledge who were willing to become involved. I agreed to help. The main plank of our argument was that if it was low-level wastes, it did not need burying. Already 99.9% of the radioactivity in nuclear wastes (designated medium and high level) was destined for long term above-ground storage where it could be monitored and controlled. Burial brought with it all manner of uncertainties: groundwater penetration and movement, bacterial activities, chemical changes, not all of which could be adequately modelled.

The real reason the industry wanted burial was that once the industry had gained planning consent for even one site of relatively innocuous material, their public relations campaigns could claim to have overcome the political and technical obstacles and 'solved' the problem of the disposal of all radioactive wastes.

I did an interview for Central, who sent a team down to my room in Oxford (there was later to be a major televised debate with Harwell scientists). I then had two days of meetings with Clif Curtis, an American lawyer and Greenpeace's international conventions expert. I would be working with him for the next six years in the battle to amend the dumping conventions such that we may never worry about a return to radioactive disposal in the oceans.

During these few days after the visit to the Chapel I had felt distinctly negative presences in my room. The few minutes before sleep came were the worst, when at one point I jolted to the sensation of hands about my neck. But, of course, there was no physical presence. I asked Gaby if I could sleep in the temple room at her house. Surely there I would be protected from outside influence.

The first night, again just on that border of sleep and wakefulness, my sense of peace and protection was rudely shattered by energies that rattled the window panes and flew about the room. My aura weakened and I felt forces penetrating, assailing my defences, powerful and mocking. I appealed to Babaji more in sorrow than anger. Could even he not protect me from this evil? Even here in this pure space? There was no answer. My ordeal lasted an hour. I was too tired to sit upright and my mantra of protection would fade as I dropped off, only to be assailed again by invisible presences. I despaired. Was this the dark night of the soul? The fate of all the saints, the trial and ordeal of faith? For some stupid reason I began to cry for them, for every saint that had ever struggled toward that divine love. Not that I felt one of their number, but in admiration. I laid my defences down, surrendered to the mantra, like carrion to the wind, but with my point of consciousness intact and inviolate.

I stayed with Gaby those few days. That first attack was not repeated. On May 14th I was on the night ferry to Ireland for a meeting with Irish politicians at the Silver Swan Hotel in Sligo. We were to discuss energy policy initiatives in the European parliament.

I had asked a friend from the Oxford rebirthing group, Anne Marie McBurney, with Catholic roots in both Belfast and Donegal, to come with me and we would drive on to spend a couple of days with the West Cork community. I was conscious that having set so much in motion with the gathering in March, it was important to follow through and offer them as much support as possible. Leonard Orr had always stressed the importance of long-term support in the rebirthing process. Besides, I needed the company and the break from the intensity of London and Oxford.

Anne Marie had felt closely guided by Babaji through her rebirthing journeys. She had had a long and difficult separation from her husband, who had also been with the group and whom I knew well. She was now living with my friend Martin (who had been with us on the first attempt at the Ben), one of the few who had made the journey to Herakhan and spent time with Babaji. Anne Marie had just returned from several months in the Swiss ashram dedicated to Babaji, and for the first time I saw an authority and presence in her that I instantly responded to. I asked her to co-lead with me a workshop in Cork.

There had been a mutual sexual attraction between us, but I had always maintained a reserve around the group in Oxford, where partners regularly moved round like musical chairs. I still could vividly recall Anne Marie's delightfully white and shapely back, like a large shell in a dark cave of a room in which we had just had a breathing session. In those early days, however much of a spiritual journey began with those first few sessions, there was for most of us, a sexual awakening that was both innocent and erotic. The breath would fill the heart with love and wonder. The relaxation of the body brought a sensual openness, and the rest was just a touch away. Perhaps that's how it should always have been. Yet there were other realities of the adult world that intruded with difficulty upon those moments, like fertility and contraception. By some grace, the Oxford group had avoided unwanted pregnancies, and had evolved toward a responsibility and commitment in partners. However, we maintained our safe distances and slept in separate rooms.

On the journey south from Sligo we over-nighted in a small bed-and-breakfast north of Limerick. The day was still, and we detoured to a round-tower we could see standing by an inlet of water in an otherwise featureless bay. We clambered around the ruin and boulders between its walls and the flat sea. Even the gulls were quiet. Anne Marie lay down at some distance, and I too, was compelled to lie on my back and close my eyes. I had no vision, but the most extra-ordinary sensation through my body to my genitals. A wave of dark sensuality caused me to stand up and look over to the supine female form by the tower.

Anne Marie rose too, and laughing, said, 'Peter, we'd better get out of here!'. She too had felt the pulse in that otherwise featureless land.

I had always supposed the round towers to have some rather mundane function. But they could have held but few people if meant as protective keeps during raids. Perhaps signal towers. And perhaps another mystery to do with that energy, now long lost.

A few miles further south I was remarking upon how familiar the land felt, although I had not seen it before, when my attention was drawn to a large monastic building flashing through the parkland trees to our left. The feelings of having been there before intensified, but there were no visions. Perhaps my long felt sentiment for Ireland had its origins in former lifetimes doing my monkish thing. Japan, Tibet, why not Ireland in the 13th century? It was no more than a vague intuition, and one not particularly welcome. I hated the western monastic tradition. They it was that cleared the remnant forests, exterminating wolf and bear. The only part of it I could admire was the earliest times of the bee-hive dwellings when monks were yogis. Skellig Michael and Gouggaine Barra and the times of Columba.

But from whence came the tears, when as a student I'd never miss the Irish night at the Greyhound in Oxford's old Gloucester Green, when always at the end some song' was sung in Italian to the bazuki and bodhran and the fists would rise praising Garibaldi and the triumph of the revolution?

We had twenty four gather for the workshop in Glengarrif, twice the number of the March gathering. Word had spread out to the 'blow-ins' of the hills and bays of West Cork. Few native Irish speakers answered the call. There were French, German, Dutch, American and English, with initially only Mary O'Donnel a native. Jeremy Wates was a very English refugee enjoying the simple life, having built a small wooden shelter in woods he had purchased. He and Mary were the backbone of the emerging Earthwatch, a new consciousness of ecological politics in Ireland's normally sleepy and traditional western counties.

Half-a-day on, an exhausted but intensely joyful character by the name of Desi arrived, having trekked in circles through the forest. He was an uneducated man from the furthest western promontory of Allihies, 'All-is-His', he said with a wide grin. He trained horses for a living.

What had I to teach this man, whose heart was full, whose being vibrated with the energy of life and the land? His breathing sessions released much grief from childhood and time in the army, and I marvelled at the power of spirit that so much trauma, so much cause for grievance, had not closed his heart.

The group were growing closer in the shared journeys. They had met in pairs while I had been away. There was such strength and independence that I felt no concern at passing to them such powerful tools. We practiced cold-water rebirths in the dark pools of the mountain stream, with Desi sitting naked for hours afterward on the rocks, fed by the inner fires the technique could generate.

Late that night, around the fire, and after Anne Marie had gone early to bed, Jeremy told me of an experience he had had on a mountain further to the west. It was called Hungry Hill. He had been told often not to walk there, that the energy was very dark, but had set out across the hill with a friend. At a point remote from the road, he had suddenly found his knees giving way as if under a great weight, and being drawn down to a drowsy sleep. His companion had hauled him up and virtually dragged him off the mountain. The legend was that in the time of the great famine many had died in the vicinity and it was the repository not only of grief but intense anger at the British. He related how in the famine, caused by a collapse of the potato harvest due to blight, the English landlords had still enough wheat to feed everyone, but, of course, nobody could afford to buy and so it was exported. I asked to be taken there the next morning early.

I was awakened at 4am with a cup of tea. A small party of seven had gathered. I cannot find a word for the feeling of togetherness I experienced that morning, of the rightness of my role, of the caring and respect shown toward me, as if I knew what I was doing. I had no thoughts of what to do. An invisible wire subtly tugged me in the direction of the hill.

We arrived along a lonely road to an occluded sunrise of mild western drizzle, the kind that soaks everything through. We left the cars and headed up into the mists on the flanks of the mountain. I knew we were not to go to the summit, but somewhere along the side facing the bay, of which we could see nothing. I small featureless cwm drew me on, and I began to gather small knots of dead grass and little scants of wood from the once burnt now whitened stems of heather that lay among the fescue. Pipits could be heard in the mists above, but all else was shrouded and soundless.

I bent down and formed my bundle, no more than a kindling that by rights should have been well sodden, but which caught from the match and burned magically unconsumed as if time were suspended. Mary's voice rose in Gaelic lament to sound the mists. An exquisite aire. At its close, another song, in English, poignant and clear, from Dee, red as any Celt, the gravely heartbreaking voice of a professional singer, a Song to Ireland, a ballad to the West and to Mystery. At its close, the magical fire still burned and we stood, arms linked and offered our silent prayers and I said, 'for forgiveness'.

On our return, another fire smouldered and flared. It was directed at me.

'How dare you come over here, acting like some fucking English Lord. What right have you in these lands?'

It was Anne Marie in full fury. Then tears. We held her as ages of grief consumed her small frame, of her youth in Belfast, of a hate never allowed to be vented, good Catholic as she was, of a love never able to speak its name, a world of traitors and histories, invasion and conquest and of those who would never surrender.

Jeremy became morose. What good was this? What meaning could a little fire add to such historic barbarity? What use our small forgiveness, our little ritual? He did not believe in magic. Only political action could be real.

162

I could only answer simply that we could not know more than we were guided to do. If we, in one small space and time could clear our minds of this one turmoil, go through to forgiveness and peace with each other, then could it not, like a ripple in a pond, go out as a wave upon the consciousness of this land? I believed so. We could never know for certain. Just one small act among many. Now let it go. There was much to be done.

Jeremy and I parted outside the offices of HOPE in the white buildings of Harbour View, Bantry. Such a small town, so far from the hubs of power. Staffed by workers of such intelligence and skill that in any walk of life they could rise to the heights of their profession, yet were here engaged upon a rebalancing, through the tending of gardens or a self-built home, time with children or the making of music. Here were the seeds of real community. People not closed, not certain of their creed, open to spirit, to the need to know oneself, to release old habits, old ways of seeing, old barriers to unity. Here I was welcomed for the first time for what I had to give personally, not for what I could do for them on some impersonal far away legal battlefield. Here there was a wisdom and maturity that did not seek new gurus, new forms of religion, but which could acknowledge the divine in all paths to knowledge, and more, hungered for it. I was at once, both their leader and their servant. I gave what I had been given, and I received in plenty of their own wisdom, their discoveries, and their humanity. We also had a lot of fun.

There was one strange episode that evolved then and played out through 1984 and 1985. Mary and I had been drawn to a large property for sale on the bay, called Ardnagashal. It did not lead anywhere, but in the year that was to come, after the events of the summer, I was to return several times, with Sue and the children on occasion, with Anne Marie and Martin, and to send many of my friends and fellow teachers. I feel it as a failure now, that there had been a key that could have been turned but one that I did not find. Babaji had answered clearly and simply, 'buy the place'. It was a large sum, £80,000, but not so large for a communal effort. I think the failure in me had its root in my having nothing of my own in the way of financial resource and the egoic inhibition at calling others together in a community that would so clearly benefit myself. And perhaps also, a need always to be free of responsibility, and a fear of getting bogged down in the daily running of things.

In those early intimations of communal needs was born a knowledge of what was lacking in my life. The Oxford rebirthing group had fledged its young on the world and they had dispersed. That caused me an unending sense of loss, a subtle and unexpressed grief at the absence of familiar friends, of people who knew me and with whom I was at rest. More, I needed the constant impulse of others toward self-knowledge to help drive my own. I needed challenge on my own hidden patterns. And I needed to dance and to make music and to see children laughing and happy on the knees of a circle of multiple 'uncles' and 'aunts' who would be in their lives, watching them grow, marvelling at their feats and follies. My friends in Ireland already had the beginnings.

As we were getting ready to take our farewell, Anne Marie came into the gathered circle with a lamp of camphor, and singing the mournful and haunting mother-aarati, hymn to the Universal Source, she moved around the circle wafting her free hand over the flame as if spreading the light out among the group. The ancient Sanskrit devotional song had been sung every morning to Babaji as manifestation of the Divine Feminine, and before his coming, for millennia in the eastern fastness of the Himalayas. The lovely chant now drifted out over the hills and burns of Glengarrif. My dreamsense of East and West meeting, of the inter-penetration of cultures was born in the purity of that moment. To these hills could come the medicine ways of Native Americans, the yogic secrets of the east, Buddhist knowledge, with the essence of each contributing to a new cauldron of rebirth. Anne Marie had sung the ritual without forethought or plan, where I would have held back with the caution of one wary of all religious ritual, however nourishing it might have been to myself, wary especially of seeming to evangelise any particular form. It was received as a great jewel, and I noted my unnecessary inhibition.

On return to England we drove to Oxford and I had a brief sojourn with the children and Sue. The stay in Ireland had dispelled some of the previous paranoia. The Chapel of the White Lady seemed like a distant dream. In London, ahead of me, were meetings with the TUC and the National Union of Seamen. The Central TV programme would be out at the end of the month. I would visit the NRPB to discuss statistics. There were meetings in early June with the DOE to discuss their new computer model of land-based disposal options. On June 16th I was to talk at a conference entitled AT in the 80's, on where Alternative Technology was going, and many old friends from the 70's energy campaigns would be there, people with whom I had long since lost touch.

Tukaram was also coming over for a series of workshops that I would almost certainly have to miss. Perhaps I would get to go to an evening. This did not seem a time for further delvings into the psyche. It was a time for political action. Yet one person was drawing me, a woman to whom Tukaram went for guidance, a professional psychic called Gail Ferguson. I had booked a session with her on the 7th June.

Into this apparent normality, intruded only the realities of my two dear brothers. Despite the successful Acid Rain campaigns Robert was still uncomfortable in the UK office and planned to move to Amsterdam and

164

renewed battle with Tioxide. Ron had settled behind his secret plans for the Ben, the timing of which I did not know. Merrilyn had begun to feel an estrangement, borne of my time away in Ireland, perhaps also my commitment to forms of personal growth that contrasted with her own steady and slow unearthings via counselling and analysis, already four years on, twice a week, 25 quid-a-time. However much I loved her tendernesses, I could not cope with emotional sensitivities. I had crossed the sexual boundary with too little awareness of her great vulnerability and of my own psyche, still locked in combat and unavailable for love.

I look back now in horror at my diaries of those years. The pace of life, meeting after meeting, air travel and hotels, the vast amount of intellectual work, and especially the weeks away when I would not see the children. I would not do that now, not for any cause, but then I could hold the fiction that it was for them, for all children, and I would even look to the real heroes of political work, the activists in South America, Africa and Malaysia, where to be involved was to place yourself under threat of death and certain imprisonment. England was tame by comparison and I was grateful not to have my own courage tested by such certainties.

As it was, the uncertainties of the situation in Oxford, the interplay of ordinary and paranormal realities, the thrashing work schedule, the terrible sense of loss around the children and my absence from the rhythm of their lives, quickly sapped the energies gathered from the trip to Ireland. Once back and alone with my thoughts, surrounded by piles of papers and reports and a programme of reading, note-taking, analysis and re-assessment that stretched for months ahead, the paranoia re-asserted itself. What had we set in motion with our ritual at the Chapel? How would they respond?

Late on the evening of my return to Oxford, at that moment between last wakefulness and sleep, the vision of the children and Sue cut to pieces and blood everywhere re-appeared. Fool that I was, I was alone. Roger was away. I had let my alibi slip. I got up. I could ring Sue's friend Shirley and ask her to go round. Sue had told her what was going on. Shirley was no stranger to psychic phenomena. Or there was Anna, upstairs in the top flat. She would take me in. We had had the occasional erotic encounter and the thought of her wispy long body enchanted. She was one of life's great treasures, a dedicated nurse, with a great love of old people, a woman of deep compassion meshed with commitment and skill - and of classic beauty, tall and slim with a perfect sallow complexion and delicate bone structure, yet so locked away and awkward physically. I had marvelled at such proportion and had I been more at peace with myself, more at one with my own sexuality, would have made more journeys to the top of the house and her delightful room resplendent in reds and golds and all manner of weaves and fabrics from the workings of her creative and recreational talents.

I dressed. It was not so late, perhaps 10pm. I hesitated in the hallway. The stairs beckoned. Would Anna be welcoming? Would she even be alone? I went out into the dusk and walked down past the east end of the athletics stadium and over waste ground toward the river. I was overtaken with visions of suicide, a mental impulse to throw myself into the dark water and surrender this life. I had fucked it all up. I had reached my limit of transformation. The work, what was it all worth? I had fallen into the trap of fighting enemies, of opposition, and thus forfeited my own creative powers. They would win. So what if we close off the ocean for dumping. The waste will go on accumulating. Millions of tonnes of the most powerful poisons known to man. Plutonium, Neptunium, PCBs, Dioxins. Every year, thousands of millions of tonnes of carbon dioxide pumped into the atmosphere, swamping the natural global fluxes and the capacity of the oceans and forests to absorb it, and sulphur, nitrogen, mercury and lead. Population set to double in the next thirty years. In Matthew's lifetime. No oil left by then. If we have no nuclear holocaust, then it will be a slow death by degradation. No rainforests by the turn of the millennium. The lungs of the planet cut away. The fight was always lost. So what if we stop nuclear weapons, nuclear dumping, fast reactors, plutonium production....without a massive change in consciousness the whole thing is finished.

Babaji had prophesied such a massive shift, a cleansing, but only after immense and instantaneous destruction. Ninety per cent of the world's population would be wiped out. Was this no more than a teaching device to keep us from projecting our work into the future? Tukaram had said, check out what you are doing now, if the world were ending in six months, would you still do it? That is how you must live. I certainly was not doing that. In Ireland, maybe. But right now, I would be with the children. And what use was I to them? Locked away, so little play left in me. So fucking serious, so little laughter for so many years. And now that I could feel the change, feel the softening, the opening, I was cut off from them. The same with Sue, she is never there to see the other side of me, only ever draws out the judge, the self-righteous, the critical disapproving father.

The water beckoned. In the willows a robin sang a few notes, kept awake by the artificial light from the city's glow. Suicide was a mental indulgence. The physical barrier was too high. I was glad not to have a gun, such a thin web between life and death hidden in suddenness, disguised by artificial form, unfamiliar mechanism. I had a picture of Sue's house flash before me, viewed from the dark garden behind, a sense of sleeping children within, and I began to run. Back up to Iffley Lane, back to the house in Bullingdon Road, best to phone first....no the house had been dark, Sue would be asleep, best to go round, to stand guard.

I drove across town and parked away from the house. What use was this? I am no martial artist. One year of Tae Kwan Do in Germany. I would be no match for even the most rudimentary of assassins, let alone the advanced. But I had to be there.

I entered the garden from a low wall at the rear by a graveyard that abuts the old but still active Lucy's foundry. There were no lights on in the house. Suppose Sue were with her lover! Well, that had happened before, when I had raged, even clocked him once, lightly on the nose. A superior judgemental wake-up kind of knock. He even thanked me for it much later. My history of violence. So easy to frame.

I called lightly and began throwing small stones at Sue's bedroom window. After several attempts, the window came up, without the light going on, and a weary voice said, 'you'd better come in'.

We sat in the kitchen while some tea brewed. Sue wrapped in her dressing gown saying, 'Peter, please stop worrying about us, we are quite safe, I know it. I want you to leave us alone for a while, until this blows over.'

'I have to stay. I have to. I had such a strong vision that he was coming, that he would come tonight, and I just could not stay away. I have to be here.'

'No. I don't want you here. I want you to leave us alone. It doesn't help. It will disturb the children. Talk if you want, but then I want you to go.'

I didn't have much to say. I sat silent with the tea. My mind blank, until I said, 'I'm not going, Sue.'

'Then I'll call the police.'

She was determined, I could see that. It was no idle threat. There was a quiet resignation in her. I thought it over. It was close to midnight, would they even come? There was no scene, no row. And how could she do that? Before, she had turned to lawyers with the threat of divorce and all that crap about 'unreasonable behaviour'. She was so fucking conservative, so bloody traditional. It was a betrayal, to call in the state. Then suddenly, an internal light flickered. The police! Perfect. Call them. Let them in on it. It was like discovering an hitherto unseen chess move. Check-mate!

'Okay, call them. That's fine by me.'

'I mean it, Peter, I don't want you to stay here'.

'That's okay. I won't stay here. I'll talk to them and then leave.'

She called Shirley and asked her to come round, then she called the police. Shirley arrived within five minutes and the police did not take much longer. It must have been around 11.30pm. The date I am not sure of, around the third week of May. There were two. A man and a woman, the man tall, distinguished and intelligent in appearance, between forty and fifty maybe, slightly tanned, not at all like your average copper on night shift. The woman young was exactly to type. I did not see numbers on the shoulders of his uniform. He asked me to be sensible and leave the house.

I assured them I would leave, but only after making a statement. He at first indicated an unwillingness to cooperate, but when I intoned that nothing would make me leave until I had done that, and it would take only a few minutes and I wanted him to record it, he relented.

I related slowly....'I believe my wife and children are under threat of death. I have reason to believe that someone will try to kill them and put the blame on to me. I want that to be recorded. In my work I have affected the interests of powerful people. There is a lot of money at stake. I work for Greenpeace and I have been working on issues of nuclear waste dumping. I am also doing work for the Sizewell Inquiry. These people have already killed one scientist who worked at Harwell and who had turned against them. He was called John Reissland.'

The woman took down the statement. He answered in a quiet, considerate voice, 'I can understand what you say. I know of your work. I have attended some of the meetings at which you have spoken.'

This surprised me. I assumed that he must be a member of Special Branch. That they must have been monitoring the house.

He asked, 'Can you tell me who these people are?'

I answered in one word, 'Freemasons'.

He showed no response, but the woman looked up from her notes and turned to look at him. Nothing was said. I got up, thanked them, and left. I went back to Bullingdon Road and slept soundly.

Next morning I awoke and felt well-pleased with my move. I worked through several papers, then phoned Sue. She said she'd be happy to see me for lunch.

168

Sue related events after I had left that night. The officer had asked them if they believed my story. They had said they did. He had then said, 'But of course, if he was going to do it, then he could say all this couldn't he, as if he were trying to create an alibi'.

I was stunned. How could a police officer say such things to two frightened women late at night! He must be involved.... the quick response to an otherwise unremarkable domestic scene.... the obvious seniority of the officer.

Sue re-affirmed her absolute faith in their safety. As we were sitting in her front room, Dave the Ninja walked past on the other side of the street, still wearing the purple scarf. He did not look over. He appeared entirely unaware of the world that spun about him not fifty feet away. I left and walked through town.

My mind refused to take in the latest twist in reality. The police, at street level, at least, had always had in my mind an aura of dependability and above, all, total straightness. A naiveté that a decade later seems inexcusable in someone politically active. This had been the uniformed police and seemed all the more at odds with my construction of reality. I imagined the scene that I had not been party to. How could anyone have said those things to Sue and Shirley?

It dawned upon me slowly that my brilliant move had been easily countered, and that with the collusion of the local police, the impending framing for murder would not be at all difficult. I could not contemplate the risk that an alibi would be enough, or that I would always be covered.

I could not bear going into my office. I had walked like an automaton and was now back in East Oxford. I headed for the river. There was only one way out. I could take my own life. Short-circuit the game. At least Sue and the children would be safe. I was beaten. As I stood by the river, not knowing if I had the courage, or whether, being a good swimmer, my body's automatic responses could be so over-ridden, I had the sudden thought that if 'they' were there watching me right now, then I could 'talk' to them.

The moment I opened my mind to that possibility, the input came thick and fast,

'You cannot win. If you commit suicide, we will still take out your family. You know we can adjust the evidence. It will look like you did it before taking your own life. You cannot win.'

'What do you want in all this?'

'We want you out of the political arena. You are way out of your depth. We can take you out at any time. You must simply resign. We don't care what you do in the Himalayas. We are not interested in your spiritual work. But the political realm is ours. We don't want you messing around in things you do not understand. Resign and we'll spare your family.'

There was no fight in me. No questions left. 'I resign. You win. I am outplayed.'

11

The Action

I cleared my desk of papers. Everywhere there were piles of documents and notes. Seven years' work. There was a sense of emptiness in the room. A spirit had left. A purpose and an identity. I refused to think of where I would go, what I would do. It was over, and a deep sense of acceptance arose in me. How could it be otherwise? I was simply out-classed. They had ultimate power in the political realm.

I called Pete Wilkinson and asked to meet that evening. Then Ron. Robert was away on Humberside. I arranged to meet Ron at Elaine and Alan's flat in Highbury. He sounded disturbed himself and said he had been about to ring and come and see me, it would be good to meet.

My meeting with Pete Wilkinson was brief. We were friends, and I did not have to go into details. He knew little of the psychic world. I told him that I had had threats to my family that I believed were real, and that I had no option but to resign from the Holliday Commission, and from all further nuclear work. We had earlier that month prepared a budget for the next year of attendances at the London Convention, where I would lead the Greenpeace team fighting for a ban on nuclear waste dumping. Pete was shocked, and did not try to dissuade me of my course.

I arrived early at Elaine's and told her of my decision. She had been my close companion and confidante for the past few months, having sat with me through innumerable committee meetings with the scientific establishment, the TUC and government, as well as the hours of driving from one place to another. She knew the stresses. At times, she had had to go to meetings in my stead, and make excuses about other work, when in fact, my system had simply not been up to the strain. She wanted me to meet with Alan. He would have another perspective on things. Much had been happening in the Greenpeace office, and she bade me not to take precipitate action until we had all met together.

Ron arrived later that evening. He looked pale and worn. He asked us to sit down and Elaine poured us some brandy.

'It's all off,' he said, flatly. 'The Ben. I've called it off. I had a meeting with John Taylor last night. They had a message from Pan. Someone would get hurt. And something about it being too invasive. Things had changed. We needed to do something more gentle. Something about a ceremony at a power point. St Marylebone, or somewhere. Say it with flowers. I've had it with this astral crap. Can't handle it anymore. I can't risk someone getting hurt. Pan, Arthur, Neptune, I don't want to know any more. I saw George and Pete this morning, and I've just got back from Waterloo. I met the Germans from the train and I had to tell them it was off and why and they just dumped their gear and walked off'.

The 'Germans' were the back-up team of climbers newly arrived for preparations for the Ben action. I still did not know the plan or the timing. Ron had told people only on a 'need-to-know' basis. He divulged to us then that he had bought a London bus as a cover for a route in from the street. No more dinghies across the river. Thousands had been spent. Everything was ready, but they had not fixed the date, which for extra-security, he would have decided at the last minute.

We talked over the possibility of doing an 'action' in the form of ceremony. Ron could see the point that Taylor was making. But he had received short-shrift from the Board. He had to tell them then of the astral surveillance and John Taylor's role. 'You should have seen their faces!'

Perhaps they thought he'd gone mad. They had scoffed at the idea of flowers and ceremony.

There was a glimmer of humour as we conjured up a picture of Bryn Jones, Reg Boorer, Toni Mariner and Pete Wilkinson confronted with the stories of Pan and astral warriors. This was the hard-drinking, junk-food, socialist wing of Greenpeace and it was clear to Ron that he should start looking at another profession.

George Pritchard, nuclear campaigns director, had already been told of the astral surveillance. He was less disdainful. He had once or twice in his life touched 'otherworld' realities and knew better than to dismiss them. He had insisted on a meeting with John Taylor, before the action is cancelled. Ron would take him to Delafield Road that night.

I decided to get back to Ian's house. I had contacted Merrilyn, but not yet told her anything of the developments. Robert would be back the next day, and we arranged to meet with Alan Thornton, who would also be returning that day. At that time Alan was somewhat estranged from the Greenpeace operation in the UK, although still one of two trustees. A schism had developed in basic philosophy and approach. Alan was Canadian, a lover of wilderness and mystery, vegetarian, and socially quite shy and unassuming. Yet, beneath that genuine sensitivity, lay also a steely determination and at times, quite ruthless purpose deployed on behalf of the planet he loved. He was in the midst of setting up what is now the highly successful Environmental Investigation Agency, the form of which we had many times discussed, and only the pressure of work had held me away from embracing more fully.

Alan would later be given the task of cutting away much of what was old and beyond its time in Greenpeace, and of fashioning a more professional organisation. Within a year, the old board of macho warriors, so unsuited to office life and with no managerial training, would be replaced and professional office managers, press officers and fundraisers brought in.

When I arrived at Northchurch Road the house was unlit. I was surprised therefore, when fumbling for the light switch, to see Merrilyn seated in the dark by the window, curtains still undrawn. Her face was wet with tears. I sat down, initially wary of closer contact, not sure how close she wanted me to be. Her hand reached out sideways toward me, though she stared steadily ahead.

She had decided to go back to Australia, 'Life feels so very empty here. Peter, I have lost my sense of direction. I have wanted so much to settle and to have children. I shall be too old. I wanted that so much with you, dear Peter. The world seems so dark.'

I told her I loved her dearly. But I knew we were not meant to be together in that way. I wanted no more children. It was enough of a task relating to the Matthew and Owen. I felt a deep intuition that for all her sensitivity to this land, she belonged in Australia. I would miss her. I wanted always to be close. I had no wisdom on the role of sex, whether lovers or not, I did not care, but I did not want to lose her friendship.

I cried with her. I knew one day she would find the happiness she sought and doubted because of the way relationships were, there would be a place for our friendship. I told her, much later that night, as we lay quietly together, that my work was over, and of Ron's decision. She related her time while I had been away, time with Joanna Macy, of 'despair and empowerment' workshops, and the 'council of all beings' and how much she wanted to work with Joanna. She talked of each person acting and embodying in song, poetry, music, dance and mask, the shadows of their being, dancing their despair and their empowerment and of crying for the earth and for humanity, and of allowing all beings to speak in the circle, each person identifying with a form of life and speaking for that being in the council. Macy was a Buddhist working with western psychology and process. Part of the dream unfolding, of a planetary wisdom crossing cultural boundaries, responding to crisis, drawing from all the ancient teachings.

I felt far removed from that kind of work. That was where real progress lay, in changing consciousness. My work was no more than plugging a finger in the Dyke. Joanna Macy worked at Findhorn, and I resolved to go one day. All I knew was of fairies and giant cabbages. As Merrilyn talked of the workshop and the people there, my own sense of isolation grew. Perhaps the future lay in forming such 'seed communities'. If they survived the 'great cleansing' that was to come, then they would germinate as a new consciousness. What use was it to try to head-off the holocaust, clean up this or that patch of ocean? Better to retreat, prepare for a future of widespread destruction, wait for the 'great humbling' and a new receptivity.

The next evening, Ron, Robert, Elaine and myself, met with Alan Thornton at the flat in Highbury. Elaine had related the background to Alan for the first time that day, but thought each of us should go over it again. I related the story of the vision, the Ninja, and my final capitulation. Ron drew a quick history of the astral surveillance of the Ben, and added that he had just returned from a meeting with John Taylor to which he had taken George. George had been convinced that the 'action' must be switched to something softer.

Alan paced around the room for most of this. He is tall and lean, with a haunted look at the best of times.

'It's such an obvious 'sting'', he began. 'You guys have been taken. It didn't take much. They get someone in the office. It's obvious where the main initiative is coming from. You three are crucial to the nuclear campaigns. They find out you're into this New Age stuff. Gurus. Red Indian Medicine Men. Buddhism. Karate. There's not much they don't know. Last week we pulled three more bugging devices out of the walls.

'Listen. They have a whole psychological warfare unit. Developed since the war. They started it in the fight against Hitler. Both sides were engaged. They'd dream up elaborate scams. These guys have got tremendous resources. Masters of illusion. Like a film production company. They can go anywhere, do anything. Nothing to stop them, no accountability. I've been having talks with people close to MI5. They were getting worried by Greenpeace's success. When the campaigns started to focus upon the military, the subs, the nuclear tests, plutonium production, they began to realise they couldn't afford to just sit back and watch. So at the end of '83 they set up a special unit to counteract Greenpeace. This has all the hallmarks of their operation.'

He added, rhetorically, 'What do you know about this guy John Taylor? He comes out of the blue. It's an obvious set-up. You guys are vulnerable, stressed out. He's playing a double game. It's a well-orchestrated sting and after only six months work they've taken you out'.

We were silent as Alan sat down. At each point he made, my mind had silently interjected, 'but you don't know *this*, you're not aware of *that*'. There was much to consider in what he had said, but I was not convinced. I stayed silent.

Ron was the first to speak. His demeanour had changed. He was suddenly charged-up, as if in response to an affront. 'Okay, okay, it's on! I've had it with all this astral stuff. I don't know what's real. I should have trusted myself. We didn't need their help. I need to trust my own intuition.'

He was happier. The glasses were brought out and we drank to the success of the Ben action. I remained non-committal. There was too much that didn't fit. I was in no mind to argue any points. Alan assumed the 'sting' had consisted of purely psychological tactics, the power of suggestion and staged appearances. He did not know enough of the detail to take on the reality of psychic techniques. In the euphoric atmosphere that now prevailed, I could not persuade my mind to start its catalogue of events, the many cross-correlations that ruled out such a simplistic explanation. I needed to go over the whole thing with the assumption not of psychological warfare, but of psychic warfare, and see where that left me. I needed to consider the possibility that within that context, John Taylor had been either an accomplice or an unwitting dupe, used by those far more adept than himself.

One factor I was instantly conscious of, was that Elaine did not want Alan to know of her own psychic experience, one of the few facts that would have been close enough to him to have swayed him toward another analysis. Still I elected not to say anything, I needed to think things through. It was perhaps not necessary to say more. What did it matter whether the security services used psychology or psychic means? It did appear to have been a well-orchestrated 'sting'.

The next day Merrilyn had a publisher's meeting in Oxford and we drove up together. I was still feeling dazed and at a loss. While she went to her meeting, I phoned Sue and said we'd pick the boys up and go out for the afternoon. I then went down to the river. I had talked over the whole history with Merrilyn on the way up. I was convinced now that if it were a 'sting' then it had been a cleverly constructed game played on psychic wavelengths. But the Ninja was real. The Chapel, none of which we had related to Alan was real. The police and what had been said. Bruno's confirmation. I remembered the 'maybe' reply to the question on the reality of the threats. Had that 'maybe' depended upon my response?

I sat down in the warm sun and closed my eyes. In all of this I had felt so far from my master and teacher. I had called out and heard only my own echoes. Was he no more than a puffed-up vainglorious interloper, as Dadaji would have it, now fighting for his own cosmic existence, and unable to help? Alone in my empty mind, I breathed the sweet spring air in deeply, becoming aware of every birdsong, squabbling ducks, distant laughter from punts on the river. The sun came from behind high clouds and warmed my face to a smile.

'Everything is me. No boundaries. I, and the world am one. There is only one humanity. All else is illusion...' These truths filtered in with the sun's rays, an invisible impregnation of spirit.

One humanity. Love thine enemy. What was I doing engaged in battle? But did not Jesus also kick over the tables of the moneylenders in the temple? The earth was my temple. Love....how to love enemies? Not to see them as separate. The truth hit me as if the sun itself had flashed upon a dark night.

'I and they are one'.

I went into deeper meditation, expanding my consciousness and opening my aura, lowering all psychic defences, all barriers and boundaries. I repeated the mantra, Om Namaha Shivaya, and then whispered loud, 'I and they are one'.

Now there was no 'they', only an 'us', one humanity. The sun had risen inside me like a new day. Such a simple realisation, yet the whole world had shifted on its axis.

Merrilyn and I had a pleasant lunch with Sue. The children met her for the first time, and we made the journey down to Hampshire to visit my parents. I felt free and light and cut out all further thoughts on the issue. Matthew and Owen were glad to see their grandparents, with whom they spent little time. I could tell my father and mother were intrigued at what they thought was the possibility of a new woman in my life, but I did not elaborate on the relationship. I realised Merrilyn was the only one of my women friends or lovers whom I had taken to meet them.

We returned to Oxford at sundown, dropped the children off and headed back to London. Merrilyn had loved the boys, but could feel they were wary of her. I realised how much difficulty they would have, and any woman would have, if I did enter into another committed relationship. They so wanted Sue and I to get back together.

On leaving the house in Oxford I could sense that the psychic air had cleared. There was no threat. It was as if the Masonic mind had quietly evaporated.

It was Saturday, June 2nd. I had a meeting planned on Sunday with Robert in the Greenpeace office. The diary for the next week showed a meeting on Thursday at the Department of the Environment to discuss their computer model of nuclear waste dispersion known as SYVAC, and on Friday, the Holliday Committee would meet at Congress House. I realised then that I would be attending. I was back. I also had a meeting on Thursday over lunchtime with the psychic counsellor, Gail Ferguson.

On meeting with Robert, I learned for the first time of what had happened when Ron had taken George to see John Taylor. He had made nothing of it at the meeting with Alan. It was a tidal mark in my relationship with Ron, as if our spirits began ebbing away, pulled by the invisible moon of his mistrust, or perhaps it was a simple need within him to be his own person, free of other's thoughts and agendas.

On meeting with the two, John Taylor had asked Ron if he would be willing to go 'out' and meet with the masters themselves. They would tell him clearly what was meant. Ron agreed. Only years afterwards did he relate to me in detail what he had experienced, such had been the cut-off on this issue following the meeting with Alan.

Initially Ron experienced no sense of travelling. He had been guided out of his immediate reality, and very suddenly found himself underground with a sense that it was below a sacred site such as Stonehenge. A frightening green-eyed monstrously semi-human form had greeted him, to which John had exclaimed, 'Don't worry, that's Pan'. He had then been taken to another presence, in a large hall. A presence so awesomely powerful that Ron could do no more than kneel and lower his head. Nothing was said. Then he was out on cliffs overlooking the sea. He was joined by someone he did not know. An elderly man who explained to him that Parliament was also a sacred site, sacred to many people, especially old people in Britain. To storm that site, to invade it with masculine bravado would do nothing to help the cause, indeed, it would be counterproductive, it would alienate a lot of people. Better to do something more gentle. He would be shown where. A power point above which flowers should be laid.

John Taylor had interjected, 'That is the poet John Betjeman, he spoke to us before'.

George's ears had pricked up. He issued a challenge, 'If that's John Betjeman, then ask him whether he liked what I had sent him'.

The reply came clearly, yes, 'you know how much I like wild flowers'.

That had convinced George, who had been a friend of Betjeman. He had sent a posy of wild flowers to the funeral. John Betjeman had died only some months previously.

I shared with Robert my sense that to go ahead with the action was wrong. Robert replied that each of us must find our own wisdom in all of this. I told him of my conviction that the episode with the Masons was over and that I would get back to my work. He was pleased. He seemed distant, however, and a little forlorn. He had his own troubles within Greenpeace and would be leaving for a new post in Amsterdam. I would miss him.

I re-entered my world of scientific review and consultative meetings. The DOE was genuinely seeking my input. David Lewis and Frank Feates had made great strides to open up the workings of the government departments concerned. They listened to criticisms of the fragmentation of the research and monitoring efforts, of the evaluatory systems for the so-called 'Best Practicable Environmental Option', a framework for comparing waste disposal strategies, and new research was by then being commissioned to give the Department its own body of knowledge from which to compare solicitations by industry.

At the TUC meeting, I found my other committee members respectful of my efforts and a slow acceptance by them of the sociological perspective of environmental impact. They were, to a man, 'hard' scientists, meaning 'experimental' reductionists with good grounding through biology or geology in the solid science of physics and chemistry. They had had little contact with what they called the 'soft' science of sociology. At first they had thought sociological impact ought not to be part of their remit at all, as it was not 'scientific' and they should restrict themselves to scientific methods. Such was my task of education! They had virtually no knowledge of the large body of analysis that had become a 'sociology of science' and which had long ago buried the myth of a value-free methodology in any branch of the sciences.

In my efforts to argue my point I had painted a simple picture, 'Suppose I take several tonnes of household rubbish and decide the best practicable option is to dump it in Salisbury Cathedral. I explain to the parishioners that it has been totally sterilised and will harm no one and that this way it won't take up productive farm or building land. To many simple Spanish fishermen, the ocean is their Cathedral'. I made headway. Social impacts were given equal standing to physical impacts.

I was concerned about the marine science, however. My colleagues and I had by now built up a large dossier of criticisms relating to ocean modelling. The three professors had done no such homework, nor could they be expected to. They had full time offices to run in the Universities, besides sitting on innumerable other committees. When I had asked about their own secretarial and research support, from students for example, they had joked heartily. It was worrying. There was no sure way of evaluating complex scientific models unless one worked into the original material upon which it was based. I sensed problems ahead.

On Thursday, June 7th, I had my first meeting with Gail Ferguson. It was in a small room in a suite of solicitors' offices in the unsalubrious Craven Street that runs to one side of the Charing Cross Hotel, and between what was then a massive re-construction site for new offices and hotels. I still have the tape of our meeting and the noise of traffic outside.

Gail was a great and wonderful contrast to the grey suits of Whitehall and discussions of SYVAC. She was, I guessed, in her forties, dressed as only American women seem able, where even something simple, like tweed skirt and pullover, a return to her Scottish roots, doesn't actually work. Perhaps they think the same of British women. I have never been able to pinpoint the failure. It is a bit like knowing someone to be a spy because however well-briefed, some slight inflection of the accent is missing. And I could not decide if I fancied her. She was attractive, but cool and matronly. I was still prey to brief fantasy.

We talked. I was keen to get her reaction to the astral wars. She was a renowned psychic, famed for working with the Los Angeles police department, for locating lost properties and peoples. But she did seem very straight.

She confirmed my analysis of the use of psychic techniques by the military. Affirmed that the Russians were far more advanced than anyone else. But quietly requested that we turn to more personal matters, and that I close my eyes, relax and she would ask some questions, and she herself would then open her intuition and see what could be seen.

She quickly tuned in to the difficulties with Sue, and said how patient I would have to be to win back her confidence. She laughed at her internal picture of my colleagues in the research group and accurately described their difficulties with my intuitive modes of action. I had not thought of myself in that way, but it was true enough. I 'knew' when something had mileage in it, and recalled Roger dismissing a distraught farmer who had called us from Scotland because his cows were dying and he suspected a nearby incinerator. Roger had seen some press clippings in which the Scottish agricultural department had dismissed the farmer's concerns and

179

suggested it was poor husbandry. I knew it was not. I could tell from the man's voice that he was a good farmer. I could not persuade Roger that we should follow it up. Years later that farmer had made his case, with the help of Canadian scientists and the discovery of dioxin fall-out on his land, and the incinerator was forced to shut-down. Although in fairness to Roger, only after a long-running legal case fighting for compensation, which ended only a few months ago this year, the High Court ruling there was no evidence it was chemical contamination that killed the cattle, and he lost the personal case.

Gail turned again to Sue and Owen, saying that whatever Sue avoided in me, she would have to deal with in him. I did not immediately see it, feeling only that Scorpionic edge where Sue's rising sign met his Sun.

The next week-end saw me in Oxford. I received a call from Robert on Sunday night to meet on Westminster Bridge as early as I could the next morning. I took the children down and we arrived at 6.00 am. The world's press and TV were already on the bridge, cameras trained on the Ben. Ron and Renato, a Swiss climbing partner, had scaled the Ben at 4.00 am, taking only 17 minutes to reach the clockface. A large Dutchman had been found chained to the roof of the service lift. Pete Wilkinson had driven the bus, out of the top of which had come a ladder, and as the bus had stopped at the regulation halt by the clocktower, the climbers had gone for it. Robert had watched amazed. The ladder from the top of the bus to the clocktower, with its scurrying figures, seemed invisible to the few policemen about.

We shouted up from the street and Ron waved back, to the chidrens' great excitement. The pictures flashed around the world. Thatcher was raised from her bed. Round Two, a knock-out.

Ron had been set for a week's embarrassment of the regime. The banner read, 'Time to Stop Nuclear Testing' and the media teams had been given packages to hand out on Britain's weapon test programme in Nevada. Reagan was due to arrive for consultations with Thatcher in two days time. However, later in the morning the pair had witnessed a van which they took to be a Greenpeace van, do a 'U' turn on the bridge and knock over and injure a cyclist. Ron had been concerned, recalling the astral prophecy.

A police siege-negotiating team had arrived and attempted to talk them out of remaining aloft. They focussed in on the 'accident', appealing to the climbers, now they had made their point, not to further endanger safety on the bridge. Ron could see below, in the grounds of the Parliament, an SAS team with balaclava disguises, ready for action.

He told me, only during the writing of this book, for he was convinced he had told me before, of an incident at the foot of the Ben, at about 8.00 am that morning. There had gathered a group of well-dressed men and women. They formed two concentric circles, linked hands in silent meditation and then looking up, began to move, one line clockwise, the other counter-clockwise. It lasted a few minutes and when they had finished, they waved happily and went on their way. I asked him how he felt.

'Not good at all. Something very negative. And what was odd was the timing. They must have got themselves together very quickly, so many people, probably from all over town, because it was still early, they couldn't have had more than two hours to co-ordinate it'.

He then related how he and Renato had been afflicted by an intense cold, despite it being June, and how Renato, whom he had always known as a hardened mountaineer, began to complain he was freezing and sounded distinctly feeble. Disturbed and feeling quite dazed, Ron decided to descend later that evening. Pete Wilkinson was disappointed. Of the accident, they could get no information, and in fact, although reported in some of the papers as severe, there was no casualty to be traced in the hospitals that day.

Looking back on the event now, perhaps the tricksters were still active that day, and the accident had been a ruse. Perhaps it was just another coincidence. I marvel at Ron's presence of mind through those tortuous months and the focus required. But on reflection, I still ask, how much of that was our own needs for action in the face of the monstrous political forces at work in 1984? How much was our own catharsis? It would take almost another decade before a nuclear test ban was forced upon a reluctant Britain by the more progressive regimes in Russia and the USA.

We three brothers met later that week. Ron told us of the final week before the action, how Pete Wilkinson, in a fit of frustration at the twists and turns of the tale, and the pressure of secrecy and paranoia, had said, 'okay, if its back on, then we tell everyone in the office, no more secrecy, everyone is in on it, they can all come on the bus'. Ron had been devastated. He thought for certain it would all be blown away, that they'd simply be stopped on the road. Yet not a single obstacle manifested.

12

Completion

The rest of the summer of 1984 was a refractory period of quiet on the psychic front, although much of the political work reached its culmination. PERG had presented three large bodies of evidence to the Sizewell Inquiry, and Gordon Thompson came over from the USA to act on behalf of the Town and Country Planning Association; the Holliday Committee work continued with visits to Harwell, where the waste drums had formerly been packed and to the MAFF marine laboratories at Lowestoft where the computer models of ocean dispersal were developed; the Black Inquiry took its final submissions; and I developed Greenpeace's scientific inputs to the Inter-Governmental Panel on radio-active waste dumping for the UN's London Convention meeting in the autumn.

Robert moved to Amsterdam and co-ordinated various actions in the campaigns against acid rain and Tioxide. Ron led a number of climbing assaults upon European cathedrals and chimney stacks, highlighting the damage acid rain caused to Europe's architectural heritage. The acid rain campaigns, in conjunction with initiatives from many other environmental organisations, and, of course, the Scandinavian governments, led to commitments within the EEC to reduce sulphur dioxide emissions by 30%. The Tioxide campaign was successful, with the banning of all sea-dumping in the German Bight of acidic wastes from the paint industry. In the final stages, Robert had co-ordinated actions against Kronos-Titan, the main company concerned, and I once more reflected upon how our opponents tended to appropriate the names of the Gods for their own projects and operations.

In the summer and early autumn there were no indications of otherworldly developments. I was able to finalise the political work without interferences of any kind. However, the summer was not without difficult work in other realms. Sue and I took the children to France for three weeks, staying for some time with our guide and teacher Tukaram, and attempting some more consistent work on our relationship. I went to Ireland and led three three-day rebirthing workshops on the west coast, taking Matthew and Owen, who was then well over two-years old but not yet weaned.

Though mercifully devoid of the darker elements, it was not an easy time. I felt greatly in need of further guidance, yet meditations brought nothing but an empty silence. One curious episode underlined the strange relationship that was now to evolve between myself and my divine preceptor, Babaji. Elaine Lawrence had accompanied me to a session of the Sizewell Inquiry at the Maltings in Suffolk. She had preferred to stay outside in the car during the meeting, to finish some paperwork, and then go for a walk. What then transpired she was not to tell me for several days, as she wrestled with its surrealistic quality. She had been outside the car, briefly, for a smoke, and heard what she at first took to be the car radio. On re-entering the car, from the dash upon which I had stuck a small photograph of Babaji, came the clear message, 'tell Peter I can't talk to him right now, tell him not to worry, everything will be alright'.

Which to some extent, it was. Sue and I took time together and my time in Ireland nourished a more giving part of me and helped counterbalance the mental and political world of work to which I had been so wedded. In those few months, there evolved a certain spiritual synthesis. I know now, in retrospect, that was why Babaji could not talk to me. I had to find my own way through the moraines of past teachings. The Lord of the Dance may set up the theatre of challenge and illumination, but at the end of the day, he must leave us alone to make of it what we will.

I look back now with embarrassment on my notes of rebirthing trainings I attended in the process of my own eclectic seeking. Leonard's work had spawned many imitators, some of whom I knew as friends. Some leaned toward the rather rigidly mental approach to enlightenment where the 'basic truth' of the Universe is that 'thought is creative', and others, rather fewer, such as my dear Tukaram, worked the other polarity of intuition, where the divine play unfolds and the seeker surrenders like a dancer to the rhythm. In the former, spiritual work focuses upon a 'cleansing' of the emotional body in a dual process of working with the breath and the mind's programming. States of deep relaxation and energising of the body-mind trigger a sequential process which will highlight crucial life-decisions, especially the points where key negative thoughts have crystallised and energy flow has become blocked. The mind's computer must not only be wiped clean, but re-programmed with positive thought.

In my own youth I had developed a constant disparagement of my body. It was 'too' thin, awkward, not manly enough, not substantial, and most especially my hands too long, effeminate, my face too lean, gaunt, and skeletal. I had recalled each point in the crystallisation of body-awareness, mostly around my schooldays with my lifelong friend Christopher, who constantly remarked on these qualities, as if he, the superb athlete and model of physical attractiveness for women, had to make sure that I, with my undoubted mental prowess, should not have the slightest of gifts from his own realm of competence. In consequence, my body had grown tight, I could not dance, had no rhythm, constantly doubted my attractiveness to women, could not relax into the deeper joys of sex, and realised at the age of thirty five, that I had been virtually all my life 'anaesthetically orgasmic'.

Thus, a great part of my 'spiritual' work focussed on healing the relationship of my mind with my body. In that, the breathing programme worked wonders. Sensitivity to touch increased, and in the surrendered space of a rebirth, with the connected breath circulating ever greater charges of pranic energy through my system, my whole body became orgasmic.

It is easy for me now to forget just how much I did have to work on freeing myself physically, and easy to dismiss the quaint and simplistic western mantras that Leonard's acolytes had invented. I recall that on the first of the long retreats, in the spring of 1980 at Barton Farm, Bradford on Avon, Leonard's second workshop, how the joys of innocent body awareness overtook my tightness. There was a refrain that stuck for weeks, as a popular tune might....'all the cells of my body are daily bathed in the perfection of my divine being' and I recall singing it in a shower when the curtain parted and two laughing voluptuous women joined me in the song and the shower. And in Leonard's circle later, full seventy people, and a plethora of full-breasted Californian beauties, feeling afflicted, whatever the holy Sanskrit mantra, by the constant hunger of the eyes for their curves and hint of nipples. There was a sharing in the circle, each person honestly divulging their immediate feelings and thoughts, so many fears, expectations, spiritual questings, and when it came to me, the inescapable admission of my affliction.

Leonard simply asked, 'so who will give Peter the breast?'

A forest of hands shot up. Across the room was one of the Californian beauties, perfectly shaped, long flowing hair and I chose her. There was a silent pause of expectation.

'What, now?'

Leonard nodded and I crossed the quiet circle as she whipped off her top. I cradled in her lap, looking up for-all-the-world like a babe at her breasts and taking the nipple. As I suckled curled on her lap, a wave of red heat rose from my chest to my mouth, dissolving age-old cravings and traumas of denial. The room stayed quiet and I know that for many it was deeply moving. From that moment the hunger and affliction ceased.

In this process an innocence dawns that, in the right company, can make sexual contact blissful and free of the guilts and doubts and oughts of adulthood. Such intimacy posed potential problems for the rebirther. The surrendered state was a vulnerable state that could arise in even the first encounter. It was, in a sense, artificial, and left the rebirther in a position of some responsibility. Practioners quickly evolved professional codes of conduct. When we began in England in 1980, we were all pioneers. There were no professionals. It was not a therapy, but a healing journey together, a community of spiritual brothers and sisters. However, many were to make it their life's work, and a 'rebirth society' and 'certification' processes were set up.

Such a course was not for me. However, I agreed with the general supposition that the rebirther stood in a position of responsibility and power, by virtue of leadership, greater experience, and perhaps also, the magnetic aura that the strengthened energy field can bring.

Thus, where 'clients' were involved, such as people who might come to me for individual sessions, and those who were part of the groups which I was leading, I was careful not to cross the delicate boundary between intimacy and shared sexuality. Where that boundary lies is not always an easy matter to discern. Strangers might, in general, keep their clothes on and invite no more than a supine hug at the end of the session. Although I recall one woman I did not know, who had entered what Leonard dubbed a 'spontaneous' rebirth during one of his rare discussion circles in Oxford, and whom I took to another room, at his request, to complete the cycle, who was then so overcome by the sensual energies in her body, that in a great act of trusting friendship, and still fully clothed, I might add, wrapped her legs about my midriff and culminated in a spectacular groaning orgasm. I felt distinctly honoured!

On other occasions, relationships with some women I knew rather better, developed into naked huddles and exchanges of energy. At other times I'd laugh at the New Age euphemism 'let's exchange some energy', but in truth, that is what it was about. I was more inclined than some to keep my penis away from its natural inclinations. I was helped in that endeavour by a physical relationship with a bisexual woman friend, an experience of liberation from the expectations of where things should go, for I had no reliable antennae for the symbolic meanings the act of penetration might have for the women I encountered. This was another area of growth through which I would make but gradual progress.

In the innocent interplay of physical bodies I learned to laugh and relax, to feel and focus upon the immediate, to surrender to energy currents that could flow between man and woman, to savour and marvel at their subtlety and the blissful spaces that would on occasion expand beyond the personal, beyond time and dimension, leaving a deep sense of awe and mystery and togetherness. However, in my unintegrated state, I was denied this in my more committed relationships, with Sue or with Merrilyn, where many and varied fears still held sway. There were other women with whom I had deep friendships and with whom the physical interplay, whether as lovers, or intimate occasional sleeping partners, enabled a gradual evolution of feeling to take place, but it would be well into 1986 before I began to feel an integration of freedom and responsibility in my sexual affairs.

I was close to two other women at this time, Tine Andersen and Manami Suzuki. We were to become close friends as well as occasional lovers, and there was a curious absence of feelings of attachment, possessiveness, or jealousies related to any other relationship they might have. This in itself was a liberating experience and caused me to reflect upon the source of those negative energies that arise within more committed relationship and which had wrought such devastation in my relationship with Sue.

I would constantly dwell on my own inadequacies in this regard. I wanted a monogamous relationship, and for all the fears that it still brought up, I was still holding out for this with Susan. My friend and colleague Jackson Davis was a welcome counter-balance to the New Age shoulds and oughts with which I harangued myself. Although only six years older than I, it was sufficient to mark a generational shift, and he was determinedly old-fashioned on these issues. We would talk for hours between sessions of the London Convention and its interminable working-groups and drafting committees, not about the intricacies of this or that scientific or legal analysis, but of our histories with women. He had a simple and avowedly male philosophy: fear was natural, it had a function, and where women were concerned, it was genetic, a preserving of the hard-won territory of making sure it was your own genes that got inherited, considering who was doing the providing. Thus, for Jackson, the whole area of territoriality, with its emotions of nausea, dislike, fears, jealousies and angers, was perfectly normal and acceptably human.

I needed not to judge my unevolved state, but I could not settle for a life built upon emotionally charged territorial boundaries. It was the root of the fear that needed addressing, and that lay in my own fears of incompetence, of comparison, of being found wanting and of being superceded.

In the early years of rebirthing I had had a vision of myself at the age of three, looking down a staircase in a darkened house. At the foot of the stairs my mother was breast -feeding my baby brother. A tangible energy flowed between them, an energy that I had not savoured. I myself had not been breast-fed, as mother had given up shortly after birth. On investigation, elements of our family history had revealed themselves. Robert had been seriously ill a few months after his birth with 'pink disease'. The cause was not then known. The illness was triggered by the presence of mercury in a proprietary talcum powder and only affected those sensitive to the metal. It was usually fatal and the only treatment was

24 hours-a-day nursing. The eyes were very sensitive to light and the skin developed a pink rash. Mum brought Robert through it.

I refelt that time. My usurping younger brother had unlocked a level of physicality and feeling that I had not. It had two consequences. One was a deeply rooted expectation of being replaced by a male who had something that I had not, and the other was a vicious jealousy that brooded through our childhood when I locked Robert out of my adventures, and then surfaced in fits of violent rage directed at him in our adolescence. The jealousy focussed on a soft and vulnerable helpless act that Robert obviously became equally afflicted by in his need to secure that attention, and was fuelled by my own stance of un-needing, as if decided then and there at the top of the stairs, that I must not need, that his very life depended upon me not needing. In my stoic isolation grew seeds of immense resentment.

Had not Sue simply played that all out again? The karmic power of expectation and repressed creative thought had brought her Stephen into my life. He had a boyish lostness, a femininity of music, a frailness of frame that had wroughtt such rages of derision in the first years of their relationship. Now she was with him, and I trapped again into un-needing. It was my story. Why had I blamed her? I had raged so much about betrayal. So much mother-stuff to work itself out.

It was to this that the work with Tukaram addressed itself. And with Sue, the patterns related not to her sexuality, with which, however unevolved, she was remarkably at peace, but to issues of freedom, authority, boundaries, acknowledgement and of being 'seen' for who she was. In her suspicious state, she could find no trust of me, no let down, and to approach her was like approaching a fortress above the walls of which the maiden would appear and enquire, 'what is it you want?'. Her suspicion that I, and perhaps all men, wanted 'sex' as if it were a thing to be dispensed, never quite left her. Had I the patience urged upon me by Gail, and by Shastraji, I might have won through, but that was my great failing.

There were other areas of 'spiritual' endeavour that related to the accumulation of negative thought patterns. One prime one being that of money and possessions. I had neither. There was definitely more to it than the aspirations of saintly simplicity that resulted from my African expeditions. Firstly, I needed to have a greater command of resources in order to work: I needed a large, safe, reliable car, smart clothes, and a computer to replace my now obsolete typewriter. Secondly, my family circumstances required considerable amounts of finance in addition to my own needs, where by now small bedsits were proving cramped and unproductive.

The first wave of rebirthing teachers held what seem now rather obviously naive American views on wealth: it was our natural state of being, there was more than enough for everyone, and not to have it therefore demonstrated an un-evolved state dominated by unconscious negative thought patterns that prevented one's natural birthright coming to you. The first task was to unearth the negative thought patterns. This we did through the familiar techniques of recalling points in the programming, the passing on in particular of parental thoughts, habits, fears and instructions. One's overall sense of self-worth played a key role. Also, there was a constellation of thoughts waiting to be unearthed around what the psyche would expect to happen if you did suddenly have wealth, which surprisingly for most people, held an expectation of animosity, jealousy, and loss of friendship. Money, in English culture at least, held a great deal of negative expectation and large quantities were therefore best avoided.

My mother was desperately cautious, accounting for every penny, never spending anything on herself. My father, the breadwinner, would periodically sink the ship, usually over a highly disadvantageous car deal, never saved, and spent what he had with no thought for tomorrow. As far as he was concerned, all years since 1945 were 'borrowed' time and he was thankful for each one. He had been given nothing, and he saw no benefit for his children in piling up any kind of inheritance. My own cautious and meticulous accounts, and adult life devoid of possessions, savings, investments, pensions and insurances, began to look less like a rational response to international justice and the crisis of the Third World, and more a reaction to my childhood, especially the teenage years when mother would confide in me the detailed accounts of her struggle.

The way through, it was deemed, was via positive 'affirmations'. Once the psyche had been shaken and stirred by the dynamic breathing, the computer could be reprogrammed. I have notes of the weeks I spent in this endeavour.

'I am now ready to receive a brand new Volvo 145 GLT estate, onyx green with pale brown leather seats, sunburst alloy wheels, right now, today'.

The affirmation was a twofold device meant to stir-up counter-thoughts, as well as a radiosignal to the cosmos that, thought being creative, it could not possibly ignore. One workshop leader encouraged with 'be realistic, expect miracles' and another, one of the rebirthers who I had met at Herakhan, John Paul Collard, felt to be a little more realistic and give the universe sufficient time to respond. My Volvo changed to a low-mileage second hand deal, and a time by which delivery should be affected, namely 31 May 1984.

The Volvo was about 2 months late. It was a 1975 model, GLE (perhaps a better option, injection but not high compression), without the alloy wheels, but green with leather seats and a sliding sunroof, high-specification model with relatively low mileage and full service history, that I bought for £1500 off a titled banker who had been its sole owner. I was pleased enough, that being the most expensive motor I had owned, and it was every bit as good as a new car, except, of course, it wasn't. I realised then that I could not cope with the reactions of my friends, most of whom scratched a living with their plethora of new age crafts on the periphery of organised economic society, or of my compatriots in Greenpeace and other environmental and socially aware organisations. So much for self-esteem!

On the finance front, a transformation was under way. My gross income had moved to above £30,000 per annum and brought with it the pains of tax and VAT accounting. However, I was using a good proportion of this to employ others and commission work. There was still something in me that felt distinctly uncomfortable with a high income. Of my personal monies, I began to pay my enterprising friends for massage, homeopathy and acupuncture, and the craft-inclined, I commissioned to make things, - shirts, pots, little items of furniture, and I developed a philosophy of appreciation of high quality, natural fibres and woods, and artistic design, and a belief that if everyone would further their development by so allocating their disposable income, the world would rapidly become a better place.

Slowly, I developed a better relationship with money. It could be a positive and creative force for good. I had a growing expectation that as people came to see my natural wisdom and creativity, they would donate large amounts for my direction.

Not wishing to draw the reader too far into the future, I can say that whatever unconscious blocks that then remained, and I have even now not entirely seen their faces, and much as my attitude to money transformed to the point that I very quickly lost all sense of dread and cautious counting, large amounts did not come my way! But, by the close of the period to which I wish to extend this analysis, which is to the summer of 1985, I had become much more relaxed, some did say well-dressed, with a guiltless liking for a good car, a good computer and a finely cut suit, and with modicum of savings and stock market shares to my name. I thought then, this was spiritual progress, but I will not now interpose any wisdoms I may have learned since!

I will say, that in the encounters with Gail Ferguson over these two years, the first raps upon knuckles did occur. As a professional and highly adept psychic, she obviously had considerable opportunity either for self-serving interferences or mischief. In her soul, however, she was a Taoist, leaving in her actions as little footprint as possible upon the sand. She chided me for the occasion, which I will shortly relate, when racing for a plane at Cork airport, tired and with sick children, I had coupled mantra with the creative image of the plane waiting delayed on the tarmac, and we had arrived five minutes after due departure, to be waved speedily through without even so much as a ticket check, with our plane and a full load of passengers delayed by some technical hitch.

For Gail, I had no right to assume that my needs, however pressing, were above those of a planeload of people, even to delay them for five minutes. There was no telling what one's own actions could set in motion. The psychic powers of the mind could be used for healing and good, but were better disciplined to impinge as little as possible upon the physical world, or the lives of others. I began to re-assess the obsessions of some of my fellow rebirthers with affirmation and creative visualisation, and the goal-oriented spirituality it encouraged. It was very American and very materialistic. Harmless enough if the visions are related to a 'willingness to receive' - of cars, or sexual partners, jobs or positive bank balances, but there begins a slippery slope of re-organising the universe of other people according to one's own fancies.

For the most part, looking over my lists of desires and wants, they were harmless enough. The key element in manifestation was to actually get away from the 'desire' or the 'want', and replace it with 'I have'. Tukaram would say, 'In the wanting is not having'. Thus, 'I always have exactly the right amount of funds in my project development account', is, naturally, always going to be true. It is in the same vein as 'I am always in the right place at the right time successfully engaged upon the right activity' and simpler, 'I always have what I need'. These are good antidotes for totally powerless wishful thinking. I note that I went further and affirmed, 'my new age institutes are now extremely successful and a major economic and moral force' and that 'I have personal resources in value in excess of £3 million, on or before May 31st 1994'. John Paul liked to give deadlines. Perhaps I just didn't repeat that one enough. In fact, I never could get into the 'writing affirmations' that others would spend hours doing, in an effort, usually successful, to re-programme their mental computers.

I have no doubt that all this works, provided there is sufficient discipline in the application. One has to root out all counteracting deep thought structures, and that is by no means an easy task. Further, within many affirmations made by simple mental, oral or written means, there lies, at the inception of the act, the unacknowledged thought that one lacks something, and unless carefully done, the lines become powerless exercises in the face of a deeper emotional sense of lack, with its uncovered thoughts of unworthiness and negative expectation.

The techniques further fall down in failing to get to grips with symbolic thought made of images and archetypes that may have no syntax and logic to unpack them. This, I feel, was Leonard's blind spot. Here Tukaram was more in tune. He would work more with images and action, using theatre, dance and music to great effect. With Tukaram we would build pictures of mother and father, for example, constellations of qualities, negative and positive, and then of ourselves, and note the transferences and inter-relationships. Finally, we would create from our own list of negatives, an image, a monster of a shadowself, which we would then interact with. Tukaram called this game 'the monster hunt'. Once named, the symbolic creature, if creature it was, would be studied for its methods, of how it maintained itself in the psyche, how it was 'fed' and kept alive, for it always had a function or 'pay-off' for the psyche; and then, of what behaviours definitely would not feed it. The monster, at first befriended with compassion, would be starved out of the psyche by doing exactly the things it hated and by removing those habits which fed and nurtured it.

My monsters were several, for they varied with time and the unfoldment of the rebirthing process. I recall the Black Panther, a creature of the jungle that would slink its way along the boundaries of the world of men, proud, isolated, yet somehow always yearning for the warmth of community. I starved it by opening to community, to groups, and when leading, which could be yet another of its isolationist tricks, dropping social barriers and boundaries of physical contact.

In the first Irish workshop in which I introduced the hunt, my friends quickly discovered that their negative shadowselves had great similarities to their political hate figures of Thatcher 'the milk snatcher', or 'rooster' Reagan and we all had a good laugh at the social realities created by negative thoughts. If we were going to change our political leaders, we would all have to go back to the projectionist inside and stop fiddling with the screen!

Susan and I spent a productive three weeks at Tukaram's place in France working on our shadows, our respective patterns of expectation and our distance from each other. Tukaram lived in a small chateau called Justiniac on the edge of Cathar country in the South West near Saverdun. I could not contemplate exploring that country further and opted out of a trip to Montsegur, having strong feelings to keep whatever memories it would unlock for some later time.

South West France nourished us with its hot sun and rich country life of hoopoe and hen harrier, the meadows still whole and full of flowers and insects, larks and buntings. There were fifty or so people staying with Tukaram. The food was excellent and for three weeks we ate no dairy products yet feasted upon all manner of wonderful rich salads and oriental dishes. No pressures of households to run or children to feed. Everyone worked a few hours and all tasks were completed with a minimum of effort. There was much joy and laughter, as well as the tears of revelation and letting go of the past.

Susan, sadly, maintained her distance. I could not find a way through. Tukaram said to me, simply, 'she is a young soul', as if that would explain why she seemed unable to see the necessity of breaking through to each other. And to me, sitting one afternoon quietly under trees on the lawn, he turned, and said, 'you've never really been real, have you?' It went like an arrow to my heart, and my breath came in heaves and sobs, as if releasing years of the grief of separation, of acting, of a constant self-consciousness, never coming from my centre with any kind of spontaneity.

I returned from France to meetings with the DOE and Holliday Committee work, and then on August 4th departed for Ireland with my two boys. I had left the ferry booking too late and so we flew club class to Cork city. The next day saw us on the heights above Gougaine Barra lake. About twenty people had made the pilgrimage to this sacred site of the earliest Christians and we made a celebratory fire for Lammas.

The West Cork group had organised three workshops of three days each over the sixteen day period, and many people came to all three, such was the commitment to growth and self-knowledge. I had planned the final workshop before departure. I wanted only participants who were already familiar with the breathing techniques and therefore having released the heaviest of blocks to the flow of energy. We would have a 'fire ceremony' on the final day of the 18th August, and the workshop would take place on the farthest western point, at Allihies.

I recall that a wiry wizard of a local man, who had taken part in one of the earliest workshops, but since kept his distance, was reported to me as remarking, 'what does he think he's doing, f'kin fire ceremonies! And we suffering three months of drought.' The west of Ireland had had no rain for three months. In many places the wells were dry and springs had stopped flowing for the first time in living memory. I thought no more of it, for the fire ceremony, the peace 'Yagna', as re-inaugurated by Babaji, was something I had long ago decided we would do.

The work was intense. I had always maintained a policy of allowing children to be present at the workshops. That way, most couples could attend. We now had regular attendances of over thirty adults, and there could often be ten to fifteen children, ranging from babes in arms to early teens. It meant that much of the quieter more focussed work could only be done late at night when the children had been bedded down. Work in the day required a strong focus and a surrender to the noise and 'disturbance'. This had its advantages, as we could work on individual resistances to the presence of children, and also on the quality of relationship between mothers and their infants.

With regard to the mothers, if they had come without their small children, then they felt liberated and discovered their old sensuous dancing selves, which was fine and necessary. However, when with their children, the reality of their immediate life was apparent, and for some this meant an imprisonment, with little support, where the children had robbed them of their youthful sexual self, and where smouldering resentments were covered over by oughts and shoulds of what were legitimate feelings. In these circumstances, for a woman to surrender in rebirth with her children present, to go 'off-duty' and then to feel their gentle presence as they tuned in to her peace, was a truly wonderful experience. There was a great deal of stress in the lives of many couples, and also a great deal of love and commitment. I was ill-equipped to offer much wisdom, but I could feel the power of the breathing and yoga and the growing togetherness of the community.

Having Matthew and Owen with me brought me some precious moments with them, and Matthew, now seven, got to see an aspect of my work he would otherwise not have seen. Owen found it difficult, and he would not settle at night. At one point, he cried and woke me from much needed sleep and in the first moment of wakefulness I shouted at him angrily, and then as I saw the little man freeze and his body shake, I was overtaken with recrimination and held his untrusting body close and sobbed. The massive pain of separation and broken family raged again through my body, but was taken by the tears to leave an exhausted peace.

The final workshop at Allihies took place in a field by the 'dancing stones', overlooking a clear blue Atlantic. On the Friday before our 'fire' was due, I was moved to do something we had not done before. I arranged the group, about twenty, in a circle in the field, lying on their backs, feet to the centre, and I retired to a rock a few paces distant and played a few notes on my flute. The air and ocean were totally still. I drew the group into the connected breathing rhythm and guided them out of their bodies into an imaginary journey, first out over the ocean, looking down on the western tip of Europe, then higher until the blue planet could be seen in all its beauty, to be praised, to be loved and cherished as home, and then back over fields and settlements, towns and cities, and always through the eyes of love.

Half-way through the breath cycle I moved to join the circle and slowly lifted them up, still breathing, to sitting position, eyes open, hands linked, and then standing for a moment, when I broke the line and led down to the shore of the ocean, a place of giant boulders and rock pools, calm as glass, the fierce sun above and behind the line. I entered and waded waist deep to the centre of the pool and beckoned each one to follow in turn, whereupon I lay them on their backs in the cool water, dipping the crown and forehead under, until all the chakras were immersed, a hand held behind the neck, as they gently breathed the cycle, and floated them to the boulder shore, where each one would beach and crawl out like a seal and sit and watch as the others filed down for their baptism. At one moment, with the sun glinting on the water, the sky white with its light, and the shadowy figures silhouetted, I was transported in time, could feel Palestine all around me, and the great joy of this ancient work. There was a peace surrounding me. My beached rebirthees sat motionless, watching with love. The dove of great peace had descended upon us, a flame, a countenance, a blessing.

Thereafter, there seemed little more to do, except to sing and to dance and to eat heartily, for many of us had fasted the three days. In the evening we trekked out to a great rocky stack reached by a perilous looking swing bridge of a walkway. Far out in the Atlantic we could hear thunder, and within the hour before dusk, great boiling clouds rolled in. That night came torrential rain, and all the next day, with thunder and lightning all around. There was to be no fire! Instead we closed the circle in the village hall with more song and dancing, and ran wild along the shore as great rollers thrashed in with the wind.

It was to rain for three days and three nights. My children were well in need of being home. Owen had diarrhoea and felt very sorry for himself. On the trip out to the airport in the morning, my driver was unfamiliar with the narrow local roads and the high stone walls and hedges made navigation difficult. We lost nearly an hour in coming full circuit back into Allihies, and so began our rush for the plane and my determined mantra.

It was during these three workshops that a new seeing began. My friends in Ireland brought me many gifts, but the most valuable was that of allowing me to open a side of myself I had hitherto no experience of. For four years I had attended dozens of workshops and 'trainings' in my own process, from the smallest and most intimate of gatherings at Hendre, to the largest congregations of the EST of Werner Erhard and the LRT of Sondra Ray. I had experienced the mentally structured masculine processes devised by Leonard Orr, and his more ascetic programmes of fasting and working with the four elements of fire, water, earth and air, as followed by Babaji's devotees at Herakhan, and I had been shown the power of non-structured, intuitive work, by Tukaram. In all of that time I had rebirthed many people and been close to the process of hundreds more. A side of me had begun to emerge that was more feminine, nurturing of others, an intimacy of giving and being willing to receive. In

Ireland, I was given the opportunity to flower, to open to a cosmos where each moment's action would come of itself, without plan, without reason, and afterwards, without any necessity of analysis. On one level, I 'did not know what I was doing'. In that space, I saw great magic and great healing. I also could see that it was not I that did anything to heal or precipitate the magic. All that was required was to say, 'come, come together, let's open to the magic of this life, to the breath and to love'.

Ireland's great gift was the revelation of the divine feminine in the subtle energies of its land, the rocks and bright ocean of its western shore, the dark peatwater pools of its burns, the broad sky interplay of the elements. The gift of my friends was that of their trust in me to lead them momentarily, to show them what I had been shown, and to open to myself, to trust that part of me to surrender and follow an instinct of action. The healing power of the breath had its own wisdom, its own agenda of revelation. It needed no organised programme, no structured curriculum. We did not systematically regress into childhoods, or past-lives, we did not sit down and say, 'today, we'll deal with parental repressions or the birth trauma', although occasionally as a group we'd have fun drawing out the constellations of negative thoughts in that west-coast new-age culture with respect to money, or work, or sex. Each person would have revealed to them what their own psyche brought to the surface in its own time. Each group session would develop its own flavour, through synchronicities that would cause us to marvel continually at the magic of time and space that had netted us.

I learned that intuitive knowledge was a function not of wisdom or maturity, but of position. It came of a willingness to step into the centre of the circle and to stay focussed, open to the attention of each member of the group, and open to one's own deeper channels. The knowledge was there, accessible without effort, a clear channel of visual, or feeling, or auditory information that could at all times be trusted and given. Anyone who was willing to take that space and to trust could have access to knowledge.

In the years that we were to work together, I devised simple exercises to transfer this power in the group. I was aware from the beginning that this isolated community were embarking on difficult work and conscious of my absences as leader and guide, I needed to create as much self reliance as I knew how. The techniques were simple enough, and such a journey of self-knowledge required no more than two people in committed relationship. But in practice, experience counted greatly, as did the support of a larger group. Whenever larger numbers gathered, then subtle power dynamics inevitably surfaced. Few new age teachers dealt with it, or were aware of it. Men in a group are like wolves in a pack. Subliminal signals quickly establish who is top wolf, the eyes follow the energy, whether it be tone of voice, strength of posture, or subtler forms of commanding presence. Natural leaders always establish a 'seat', a position in relation to the circle, or occupy one that is predetermined by their organisers. I would allow these dynamics to establish themselves around me, and then consciously play with them, stepping out of the 'hot seat' and into the circle and inviting others to take the seat. I would have to deliberately stay quiet or avert my eyes so that other eyes were forced not to seek mine but to focus upon the other person. I set up dyads where everyone developed an intuitive skill, looking at the other person's eyes, listening to internal voices, or feelings or visions and telling what they 'see'.

In these ways we explored the 'divine' presence. We taught ourselves to listen, to see, to hold vision. We realised ourselves as part of a larger play, one human mind, one story unfolding, and in this work I came to make peace between the two warring factions of my own psyche. On the one hand the scientific, with its analytical approach to ecology, man's predicament, and the bleakness of our future, and on the other, the poetic, that which dwells in love, trusts its instinct, revels in sensual delights, and communes with the spirit of nature, where every animal and plant can be a teacher.

My work in Ireland was to continue throughout 1985 (it was to last seven years during which we worked intensely, and the group was to invite a variety of teachers to complement our rebirthing and yogic practices). Early in 1985 I asked my friend Suma, who had been in Herakhan during my time there in 1984, and with whom I had been close friends since our meeting at Gilthallion, to come and co-lead a residential workshop at Clonakilty, where the group had hired a large former convent. Suma had transformed her own life, emerging with the drumming and chanting group 'Prana', as a leader of rebirthing and voice-liberation workshops, and teacher of the North American Indian medicine wheel. It was good for me to share leadership with a woman so strongly immersed in the intuitive world. I enjoyed her ways. She, on the other hand, found the still-active analytical and generalising tendencies within me a bit of a trial. But then, I was to find that often enough, for women who went so deeply into the feminine could react with hostility to these masculine tendencies until such time as they could meet that more fully within themselves.

We were to move slowly through the realms of personal psychology into the spiritual marriage of East and West. I brought the yogic practices and insights into the workings of the mind, Suma the ritual magic of the medicine woman. Within the Irish group there were already some with advanced knowledge and practice: Charlie Stevens was a yoga teacher in Ballydehob, Toni Cohu a practicing Buddhist and Desi had been initiated with Guru Maharaji. Mary O'Donnel had an intimacy with the Celtic heritage and lore. Phil Kearney brought a knowledge of the western analytic traditions of humanistic psychology. Richard Hardwicke was to return to University (at Cork) and write his masters thesis in psychology on the rebirthing process!

I cannot say that anything very distinctive as practical spirituality emerged! More, that seeing the truths of such separate cultural relationships to the divine, and in the freedoms of our own growing trust in the immediacy of the universe, we were growing free of form and closer to that element of divinity which is formless, and which in everyday expression becomes rather ordinary.

Perhaps this growing freedom in myself accounted for a more peaceful co-existence with Sue. However, the autumn of 1984 brought us the trials of a young child with asthma. Owen had suffered from a severe cold, and on a day when I was visiting, he suddenly went into the dreadful spasms of breathing characteristic of a severe attack, but of which we had had no experience. I held him close as if he were rebirthing, and he came through that first attack despite the lack of medication. Sue had called the doctor, who arrived just as Owen was relaxing and beginning to sleep in my arms. The doctor took one look and without consultation called the ambulance. Owen's heart was still racing and he was exhausted. Sue went with him to the hospital.

I felt powerless and angry. Owen went through the additional trauma of the rush to hospital, of an X-ray and anti-biotics in case of bacterial infection, and an overnight stay. When I entered the John Radcliffe Infirmary the next day, I shuddered at the brutally heartless new building, monument to efficiency without feeling. Walking in to the hospital I had similar feelings to those I have around nuclear power stations and large industrial plant, it is an alienation, an unbelief that so deep a transgression is so unconsciously accepted as good and progressive. I determined that Owen's asthma would be treated with everything that alternative medicine could offer. Robert's son Aaron had suffered this debility and had been on drugs continuously for several years, Kim Narayan having no trust in alternatives.

We registered Owen for a course of homeopathic treatment, and took him weekly to the main osteopathic hospital in London. The homeopathy treated his overall constitution and the hospital worked on releasing the muscle spasms and holding in the chest and back. In this way, we were to keep Owen drug free for several years, with only the occasional resort to ventilatory muscle relaxants.

I am convinced that a contributory factor in Owen's illness was the emotional shock of Sue and I parting, or at least, the unpeaceful way in which we separated. Asthma may have several contributory causes, part genetic, part emotional, part environmental, and like many other elements of damage to our health and environment, not readily amenable to scientific analysis. My own feeling is that the suppression of grief or anger is the initial weakener of the bronchial system, and that genetic susceptibility in the form of allergic response, may determine the oncome. Allergens from the environment then play their role. We discovered from the results of a University blood survey in Oxford that both Owen and I had blood that was reactive to grass pollen, fungal spores and dust mite faeces, whereas Matthew was reactive only to tree pollen. Within the next year, I too had developed a mild asthma, enough to make exercise and sleep difficult at times, and for the essential ventilator at the bedside.

This aside, the weeks through to November were relatively uneventful and filled with finalising the Holliday Report and making preparations for the London Dumping Convention in 1985. Sizewell was now over, although the controversy over surveillance still simmered. At the Inquiry we had delivered our reports and they had elicited virtually no cross examination, signalling that our analyses were essentially correct. We had effectively debunked the nuclear industry's claims that the uranium fuel cycle was less damaging to human health than coal, oil or solar power, without trying to hide the impacts of coal and oil on climate and soils with their unquantifiable repercussions. We had presented in graphic terms the consequences of massive land contamination following a meltdown and loss-of-containment. And we had described the horrific risks that emergency personnel would face when so unprepared for such a scenario. Our work was to prove prophetic. In April of 1986 the world would learn through Chernobyl just what such an accident entailed, but at that time, such catastrophes were regarded as 'not credible' scenarios and not worth planning for.

In the final judgement of Frank Layfield, QC, the Inspector at that Inquiry, these risks were acceptable. But then, his job was not to gainsay government policy, which had already decided they were, as it had decided that the whole edifice of regulation, control and standards were adequate, and that nuclear power was an integral part of a balanced energy policy. All Layfield could do, within the terms of reference of the Inquiry, was to decide whether Sizewell was likely to meet these standards, which most of us would have agreed that it was. I had known this before, of course, having learned the lesson from Justice Parker at the Windscale Inquiry. Public Inquiries were window-dressing, they were not participation in government policy. At the very least they might prove an intellectual testing ground for such policy, and in one case, that of the absurd state of UK's emergency planning for nuclear accidents, this proved the case, with the debate having some later effect on procedures. At the end of the day, complacency on safety continued to rule, and ultimately only economics would cause the dinosaur to topple over. I vowed never to get involved in another Public Inquiry, and gave the subsequent Hinckley Point one a miss.

Things were more productive in the Holliday Committee. The PERG review had been finished and submitted. In the course of events, MAFF had passed to the Committee a first draft of its environmental impact assessment, dubbed 'Review of the Continued Suitability of the NE Atlantic Site'. Remember, no one had then done a proper environmental impact assessment according to international guidelines, that is, where the potential damage to the environment is quantified. The MAFF review had contained no 'collective dose' assessments, and on my behest, the draft was sent back and they were requested to produce the calculations, itself a relatively easy affair once the individual doses had been calculated. With the latter, it is immediately apparent that individual doses to various fish eating populations around the world would be a very tiny fraction of the so-called safe 'dose limits'. With the former, however, figures could be produced on how many deaths could be expected worldwide when these tiny risks were integrated over the number of people exposed to them. This number ran to several tens of thousands.

In addition, we had built up a detailed critique of the modelling exercise itself, having unearthed recent research on hitherto unexpected processes at the deep ocean and continental shelf break, and Elaine and I had collated what little research had been done on the relatively neglected issue of social and political impacts.

In the finalising of the reports, Fred Holliday faced the predictable dilemma of how to respond to the inputs on marine science that neither he nor other members of the panel were in a position either to refute or to agree with. Initially, they agreed to five paragraphs summarising our criticisms, each dealing with a major area of uncertainty in the model. When the final meeting with the TUC came round at Congress House in November, Fred showed me the copy minutes before the meeting, apologising for what was now a single sentence on general uncertainties in science, and urging me to go with it on the grounds that all my other points on the social impacts had been taken on board and were sufficient to sustain the final conclusion that sea dumping should cease until a full impact assessment could be compared with the alternatives. It would be enough to sink the dumpers.

I was angry, but decisions had to be made in minutes. Fred urged me not to resign or to write a minority report, that this would weaken the overall case. I recall him adding that he was no believer in resignation as a tool - and that years later, when as Sir Fred and appointed to chair the government's Joint Committee on Nature Conservation, he realised how powerless the committee would be, he did just that. Much to my later regret, I relented. Our months of work thus disappeared from view, although not entirely lost as they later formed the backbone of the case at the London Convention in 1985.

I made a further error when Bob Clarke, who hardly agreed with my views, offered me space in the Marine Pollution Bulletin, a key professional journal which he edited, an offer I failed to take up due to the intense pressures of time and emotion that were to follow later that November.

The Holliday Report precipitated the government's Best Practicable Environmental Option review in 1985. I was initially involved. Indeed, the whole Holliday Committee was asked to reconstitute in order to further the work. I decided not to, and the idea sank. I was already convinced that the BPEO methodology was flawed. It would seek to quantify the impacts of each option, doses to workers in Britain being weighted less than doses to children in foreign countries and future generations. But the weightings would, of course, be of an arbitrary magnitude! As expected, the BPEO found that sea-dumping compared favourably with some options (except deep disposal in mines), but if the weighting factors had been 100x rather than 10x, the result would have been different. These factors had little or no basis is science. The DOE team quite simply decided what results it wanted and chose the numerical factors that would deliver the policy it already had. Late in 1985 I resigned from the Research Advisory Group, and the event was reported at length in the newspapers. It was evident to me that the earlier openness shown by Waldegrave, Feates and Lewis had been superseded, and to stay on would have meant collusion.

Having laid the foundation of the scientific critique of the ocean dumping programmes by the spring of 1985, it was essential to prepare the political paths for its effective use. I spent three weeks in California writing up the critique with the help of Jackson Davis at the University in Santa Cruz where we was a professor of biology. My colleagues in Greenpeace and Jackson in the USA worked ceaselessly. Remi and Hans cajoled the Spanish speaking world, the Africans and the Nordics, whilst Jackson toured the Pacific. In six months I travelled three times to Madrid and once to Vigo and Santiago de Compostella, to Washington, Bremen in Germany, and for two weeks in the northern towns and prefectures of Japan.

In the London Convention meeting of the autumn of that year, the scientific critique of the oceanic modelling, and in particular, the estimate of worldwide 'detriment' in the form of 10,000 cancers, was sufficient ammunition for the majority of states to justify a vote against a lifting of the moratorium and to demand further analysis. We had effectively won, because we knew the high cost of storage and keeping the option open would lead the dumpers to develop alternatives. I published the critique as a PERG report, but it should have gone to the Marine Pollution Bulletin, even then. It would take another seven years to finalise the legal battles to outlaw all radioactive and industrial waste dumping at sea, but essentially the war was won in 1985. I hope to write about these scientific issues in more detail another time.

There was one amusing anecdote accessible to the layperson. Early in 1985 MAFF delivered their final draft of the assessment (for the Nuclear Energy Agency) in time for the Scientific Group of the LDC. There was a major discrepancy with the draft to which I had access in the Holliday Commission at the end of 1984. In that first draft the maximum dose from the dumped material occurred only 90 years after dumping ceased, and was located in the fisheries of the southern Arctic Ocean around Norway and Iceland. I presume this was out of consideration of the 'conveyor belt' phenomenon. In December 1984 the Nordic Environment Ministers had made a formal complaint to Britain about the radioactive contamination from Windscale's discharges persisting and measurable off their coasts and in their fish. In the space of only three months, MAFF had revised the scientific model of ocean circulation, such that the maximum dose now occurred after 200 years, and not in the northern oceans at all, where the contamination now failed to surface, but carried all the way round to upwell in the Antarctic seas! I was able to present these two drafts to the Convention. Needless to say, few people at the LDC meeting, especially few Nordic people, were convinced by such rapid scientific progress.

The victory at the LDC would have far-reaching consequences for the scientists engaged upon ocean modelling, more particularly those specialising in radioecology. One of the leading experts, a Prof. Goldberg in the USA, complained of the drying up of funds for research and PhD studentships, and hence recruitment to the profession. I termed the syndrome 'Goldberg's Lament', applicable to any area of science dependent upon dilute and disperse practices of toxic waste disposal, where scientists come to have a vested interest in the continuation of bad practice. Inevitably, as with the sudden progress in oceanography made by the MAFF team at Lowestoft (with its new £5 million laboratory for radioecology), scientists are going to be compromised in their dealings with uncertain data and interpretations.

After the vote at the LDC I found myself sharing a lift in the IMO building with Dr. Jan Pentreath, one of the leading MAFF radioecologists. He hissed an angry farewell, muttering that their jobs were now on the line. As it happens, he need not have worried for himself, for much as Lowestoft got downsized, he was later promoted to chief scientist with the newly created National Rivers Authority, an organisation no doubt appreciative of his sterling work on assimilative capacities and acceptable levels of dose.

One final comment on the scientific issues of this time relates to the outcome of the Black Inquiry. This medical committee could only concur with the statistical findings. They then, contrary to the most basic prescription of science, held that there was no convincing evidence that radioactivity was to blame for the excesses. This judgement depended entirely upon the submission from the radiobiological professions that their models were adequate assessments of the risks. Black made little of our submissions on the scale of uncertainties in those models, except to call for more research. Again, political necessity overcame scientific integrity.

It is not that there is convincing evidence one way or another, it is that science, of its nature, cannot provide that evidence, and could say little more than that the null hypothesis, i.e. 'there is no link' is neither proven nor disproven. Scientists dealing with pollution seem to have a preference for the null-hypothesis, and this itself is a political act, if an unconscious one, for it may require considerable resources to develop the statistical power necessary to deny the null hypothesis. In the absence of that effort (expensive long term monitoring and frequent sampling), the null hypothesis stands.

In the case of the Windscale discharges and the excess leukaemias, the jury is still out 10 years later, but very little new research has been done and Black's conclusions still stand, based as they were upon NRPB's modelling exercises. A full-scale conference in the autumn of 1986, to which I gave a paper, and which was published as a major book by Wiley, still did not move this formidable edifice of belief. It is an issue to which I hope to return in more detail in other writing.

13

Poison of the World

On November 24th 1984 I attended the wedding of two of my friends in the chanting group 'Prana', Andrea and Tony, at Much Wenlock in Shropshire. Suma was there, and she introduced me to Gillie Starlight. I learned later that the old witch was up to her matchmaking, and much later the full extent of the weaves and webs that I was now about to naively stumble into. Gillie was a raven-haired Celt, short, strong and stocky, but nevertheless alluringly feminine. She had a fifty mile return journey after the ceilidh and no means of transport. I took her home.

Her place was an exceedingly small and remote stone cottage on Forestry Commission land at Hirnant behind Pen-y-Bont Fawr in the Berwyn Hills. Goleudy Sych, the Lighthouse. She lived with her two small children and innumerable cats and chickens. The house was damp and claustrophobic, every last inch occupied with the paraphernalia of a lifetime. Crystals, old Grateful Dead album covers, Rastafarian memorabilia, pyramids, Robert Anton Wilson books, jars of herbs and dried mushrooms, age-old twigs and flowers dried-dead in their vases, suitcases and open racks of colourful clothes, an open fire with stacks of logs, layers of ancient carpets and animal skins, candles everywhere and hardly a place to sit. It was in every respect a witch's den.

Gillie had known Leonard Orr, and although our paths had not crossed before, she had been to many rebirthing workshops. She also had photographs of Babaji on the wall and had organised a small altar in a cave of a room where the house met the slope of the hill.

We had a strong and immediate rapport and we slept together that night. She was of the moon, she knew her body, she could not conceive unless she wanted to. I was not unwilling, rather a lack of will in the matter. My sexual energy had seemed dormant, unfree, and I felt I had little to offer. But of what little I had, I did unconsciously give.

I kept asking Babaji, 'why have you brought me here? Is this where I am meant to be next?' Gillie had two small children in obvious need of a father.' I like these children. They need fathering. I'm welcome here and there's work to do. Are you showing me that this is where I am meant to be?'.

And there was much I could learn from Gillie about the ways of women. She was unlike any woman I had known. There was a wild almost frenzied look that alternated with a twinkling soft and seductive invite into realms of which I had no experience. She knew my thoughts before they were spoken, and those that politeness censored. She was of a watery place below this world and I bound to the interface, unable to dive deep for lack of air.

Would this be my journey? It was a frightening prospect. The house was isolated and tiny. There would be no space for my work. Was it then time to drop all of that, to make the journey inwards, to stay and chop wood and walk the hills?

I returned to Oxford after a couple of days at Goleudy. I was debating with other scientists at the Department of Engineering Science later that week. Remi had set up a meeting in Madrid for the following week. I also had an appointment to rebirth a friend who had been helping with some organisational work on the World Information Service on Energy, which I had helped to set up. And for myself I had an appointment with someone I had rebirthed three years previously, and who was now a practising homeopath.

Although I had known my friend and her husband, for some time, she had only just begun to approach me for help in her life. She had been casting around on the fringes of alternatives and politics, and during her first talk with me alone, she had said, 'I can make you feel things, I can make men cry if I want to, make them reveal things', and I had felt a sudden wave of energy wash over me. She emanated a magnetic wave of such power that had I let it, it would have drawn out of me all of my remnant sadness. I told her she seemed to have a need to impress and demonstrate her power, and that such a great gift ought to be directed, that she needed to cleanse her psyche of such petty needs of personal power so that her gifts could be put to good use.

We set up a series of rebirthing sessions. In her first, she had reconnected with a childhood experience she had efficiently suppressed. At the age of about ten in her native Portugal she had been visited in her room at night by two 'angels', one of whom she took to be Jesus. 'Jesus' had told her she was to be a healer. She was most annoyed and told him to get lost, she wanted to be a tennis star. On hearing of the vision, her parents, devout Catholics, were disturbed, Jesus being a rather unwelcome visitor if one wanted a quiet life in a Catholic country community, and the matter was not mentioned again.

She had several powerful sessions in which she dealt with deep patterns relating to sexuality, power, authority and men. A short while thereafter, she began training as an acupuncturist, qualified three years later as one of his best students, and was to go on to become one of the faculty teachers.

Of those I saw through the rebirthing process, a good proportion changed direction in their lives and went on to take up a healing profession - several homeopaths, acupuncturists, counsellors, analysts, masseurs, an apothecary. And many who already had such skills, came to add the work of the breath and elemental yoga to their healing skills. Simon was a case in point. He had only one session. Before that he had been a social drifter, on dope and reggae, turning his hand to bits and pieces of joinery, and generally at a dead end in his life. In just one session he contacted something inside that revolutionised his life. He took up a study course in Human Ecology at Oxford Polytechnic and enrolled to train as a homeopath, travelling out to see the master Vitoulkes himself, located on some rustic Greek island. As a homeopath he was now newly qualified and practising and I had asked him for help with my various surfacing ailments, in particular, an outbreak of coldsores and slight asthma.

Simon had made his allegiance to that school of homeopathy that believes in using the more powerful of the potencies at their disposal. For someone trained in scientific method and schooled in the traditional medical notions of the workings of the body, homeopathy cannot be understood, and hence is usually dismissed without investigation. Its fundamental precept is that 'like will cure like'. Remedies are made from substances that affect the human body in such a way that the symptoms they generate are similar to the symptoms of the disease one wishes to treat. Often the remedies are derived from highly poisonous sources. A case in point is the valued remedy Belladonna, from the plant *Atropa belladonna*, or deadly nightshade. Poisoning from this plant is accompanied by symptoms of fever. The practice is based not upon theory, however, but on systematic trial and observation, and it works. On that score, there should be no problem for modern science. Indeed, one would think true science would get excited at the prospect of discerning more of nature's secrets.

The problem arises in the preparation of the remedy. The substance in question is diluted by a process of separating 1/10th of the solution and diluting to the original volume and repeating this many times, the favourite dilutions being six repetitions (low potency), 30, 200 (medium) and even 1 million (high potency). This process is accompanied by shaking or 'succussion'. This inverse relationship of potency to dilution runs counter to any current scientific theory of cause and effect, and indeed, after a certain number of dilutions, the original substance can no longer be regarded as 'existing' in physical form in the solution.

Here, the so-called 'scientists' draw their line and state, 'this cannot be true' and seek recourse to other explanations, chief of which being that of the 'placebo' effect compounded by subjective unverified perceptions of the success rate. Of course, these are not scientists of the first order, but reactionaries afraid of new knowledge. A true scientist will accept the possibility of going beyond the bounds of present understanding, and that all progress in science depends upon a willingness to do this.

Beyond these bounds is dangerous territory. Pioneers always make mistakes, some may look decidedly silly when everything new has unfolded. There are vested interests which will snipe away at anything that threatens their hold, whether on prestige, power or markets. In the case of homeopathy, all three are threatened. Modern medicine has great prestige and for the individual this is acquired slowly and at great expense, medics sit in positions of power (witness the recourse to Sir Douglas Black over Windscale), and, of course, modern pharmaceuticals make a hugely profitable enterprise.

Thus, the true scientific response to homeopathy would be to put funds into trials which will substantiate or refute the claims, and most importantly, with an awareness of the limitations of the scientific methods available for assessing results. Scientific method is actually extremely limited where many variables operate, and homeopathic treatment, which does not prescribe the same remedy for the 'same' illness, but differentiates according to many variables in each case, presents problems for standardised controls. These variables may be related to personality, family history, or other influences that arise from treating the underlying potential causes of the symptoms rather than just seeking to alleviate them.

Furthermore, the healing process may be a long one, with initial results involving a 'worsening' where repressed symptoms arise, and eventual healing may involve such unquantifiable and subjective elements as mood change and overall sense of well being and happiness.

Such scientific trials as have been performed in recent years, and I have not had time to pursue my interest in reviewing them, have demonstrated homeopathy's success in treating such intractable conditions as asthma, which modern medical drugs aim to simply alleviate or suppress.

In my case, I had watched the success of homeopathy with my children. I could compare Owen's strength in relation to asthma with that of his cousin Aaron. In India in 1984 I had not taken anti-malaria pills, preferring instead a homeopathic preparation. None of these decisions had been easy or made with confidence.

I now approached Simon with much the same uncertainties. He was intent upon treating my most basic 'constitutional' weakness, but he did not let on how he perceived that, or what the remedy would be.

The consultation had been at midday on Saturday December 1st. I had been to see Blade Runner, yet again, that evening. I was then alone on my futon at Bullingdon Road and it was approaching midnight. There was a fracas out on the street. My normal nature would have been to peer out of the window. If it had been louts, I would then have called the police. I could hear obscenities being shouted into the letterbox of the house next door, which was occupied by a bevy of student nurses. The obscenities grew more objectionable. Something in me flipped. I jumped up, dragged on my jeans, a sweatshirt and trainers and stormed outside. On the steps of the neighbouring house I confronted two drunken yobs banging on the door and continuing to give vent to the darkest misogynist filth.

I challenged them aggressively with 'what the fuck to do think you are doing' and they went for me, fists and boots flying. There was a moment in their combined charge when I could have kicked to the groin and disabled one. I hesitated. As the other came at me I moved to one side and my knife-hand shot to his throat but stopped a fraction short. I was unable to strike such disabling and dangerous blows and from then on I was parrying for all my life was worth as they went completely berserk. I moved backwards out into the street, but as they piled in I was caught in the eye and nearly went down. I doubled up and weaved to alleviate the blows that rained down. At any moment I would be floored and the boots would go in. Suddenly neighbours appeared and in the pulling and pushing I dodged away, into the house, and telephoned the hospital for an ambulance. I spent the night there. My cornea had been torn by an assailant's ring, and it hurt greatly.

I was kitted-out with a black eye-patch, which made for a rather bizarre entrance when I met secretly with various diplomats and scientists later that week in Madrid.

Before leaving on that trip, I had a premonition of trouble. Madrid was a centre of ancient Masonic influence. How could I be sure that whole episode was over? Fortunately, I stopped off at Christina and Narayana's in London and over-nighted before getting the plane. Christina took me in hand. She went through the pattern of the year, remarking in her low-key, matter of fact way, that I seemed to be inviting conflict into my life again and that wasn't it time I saw the world as a more peaceful place. She pointed to the still strong remnant in my psyche of a need to prove myself, to take a stand, to test my manhood. I took the message to heart and meditated on clearing my mind of expectations of trouble from dark quarters.

Madrid was productive and trouble-free. Back in London I spent the morning with Narayana and I accompanied him across town on my way to Paddington. He had a call to make and invited me in as it might take some time. I found myself in a shared house, one room of which was a communal lounge. Before I entered that room I could sense what I would see. On a low central table was an enormous quartz crystal that stood at least 20 inches high and 8 inches wide. I had never seen the like of it. On the wall was a photograph of the great pyramid at Cheops, with what appeared to be a star in the darkening sky at its apex. Since the meeting with Gillie I had been sensitised to the Sirius mystery and the pyramids. She had told me of Robert Anton Wilson's stories of Masonic plots and links to Egyptian magic. Stephen Knight's book had revealed modern Masonic rites connected to the Egyptian mysteries. A few days before going to Spain I had met Hans on the Greenpeace vessel 'Sirius' in the London docks, much to the delight of Gillie when I made a call from the ship's telephone. The boat's name was a synchronicity - Greenpeace Holland, who had bought the ship had not renamed her, as had happened with the Rainbow Warrior.

It appeared that many questers, particularly users of LSD, had encounters with 'Horus' the falcon-headed God, before being led deeper into the Egyptian mysteries, or to their untimely death. Gillie had warned several times with her witchy cackle that such realms were not for the uninitiated. Now I was intrigued. Was this another quest that was beckoning? If so, how would I need to prepare? Would Gillie be my guide?

I asked Babaji for guidance. More, I made a strong plea, not so much out of any sense of desperation, but because I was beginning to feel a distinct fragmentation and lack of direction, a renewed uncertainty over my work and what I was meant to do. Gillie had been a strong challenge on many levels. There was an invitation to a relationship which if followed would mean a totally different lifestyle, a separation from my two boys, giving up all work toward reconciliation with Sue, perhaps even the giving up of science altogether. Babaji had been decidedly unavailable for several months, but this time he came through strong and clear.

'I will send you a messenger....black and white.' That was all I got.

On return to Oxford, I related to Simon my little encounter in the street. He apologised. He should, perhaps, have warned me. The remedy had been a 1M, high potency, Lycopodium or 'Wolf's Foot'. This innocuous primitive moss-like plant was used to treat 'cowardice'. Perhaps it was with this new found bravura that I decided to spend the New Year with Gillie. She phoned my office the moment I walked through the door, saying simply, 'you're back then!'. She would be having a small gathering of the kind of people I would normally steer well clear of, travellers, hill-dwellers, rock musicians, replete with their dope, their dogs, their mushrooms, their incessant reggae.

At this time, in the lead up to Christmas, I saw the film 'Amadeus'. The reviews informed it had been based on a play by Peter Schaffer, where the Masonic source of Mozart's psychic trials and eventual death was made much more explicit. The film triggered much in my psyche. Paul Schofield's characterisation of Salieri brilliantly displayed the tight Saturnine restrictions of tradition, power and authority, that I associated with Masonic structures of the mind, and how this strangled true genius, true inspiration and the workings of the divine. Mozart was more than open to these divine energies. He was an innocent fool, at times a slobbering idiot, out-of-order, emotionally uncontained, a ready receptacle to the dark feminine of disorder, and from this cup flowed divine music, written as if by unseen hands, melodies that flooded in from a distant universe and wrote themselves upon his willing soul. He gave to that source his total loyalty, his life and painful disciplines, and to humanity the fruit.

In Salieri's hate I saw the Masonic mind laid bare. It hates that which it has suppressed deep within itself. In its order it hates disorder. In its tight control, it hates the loose and the free. In its male isolation, it hates the female. That which it has exiled, it fears and therefore seeks to control. In the quest for control, it seeks magic and in the quest for magic it surrenders its soul. Its God then becomes a fabrication, a projection of its own mind, Jabulon, Jahweh-Baal-Osiris, the energy of the 'Great Architect'. It has exiled the dark feminine to the realm of underworld, of demon and devil. Women then become honoured only as mother to the son, or as the dutiful daughter. The maiden and the crone demand death of the ego, death to the ordered Cosmos, and therefore become enemy.

Here then was the mind of Gelli and his bankers, generals, secret service chiefs and politicians. Here was the 'magic' of Admiral Rega, 'El Brujo', the torturer of rebellious youth. And of George Bush, Vice President of the USA, friend of Gelli and the mafiosa Michel Sindona. Here was every group of men in positions of power and authority. Here was the coming war on the 'drug culture', the source of prejudice on gays, on hippies and travellers, and broader, the long opposition to womens' rights and feminine values. It has its expression in the workplace, in key symbolic areas such as the modern suppression of midwifery, and the resistance to education on the spiritual joys of sex and the significance of orgasm. In modern science it was played out fully in the repression and persecution of Charles Reich. This was a three thousand year old history, with its culmination in the Inquisition and the wiping out of nine million women like Gillie

Starlight, and the countless tribal peoples perceived as less than relevant to the unfolding New World Order.

It has its own modern mythic expression in the Star Wars movies. Of which, it was rumoured, Babaji had had some influence within the genius talents of Industrial Light and Magic. Daarth Vader represents the Empire of men removed from love and bound in hierarchy and power, the archetypal Mason. Luke Skywalker, the spirit of rebellion, the champion of the Princess of Light, the White Lady herself, must first centre and know himself to carry the fight, and above all, fight not with anger, but with love. In the end, it is not the power of winning and conquest which is sought, but the power to redeem the other that only love can deliver. And, of course, Vader is Luke's own lost father.

The task before us is therefore no less than the redemption of our lost fathers, a rebirth of consciousness such that the power of love can reach the interstices of the state, now as remote as any 'death star'. I still have not the wisdom on methods. I feel uneasy about the American myth of the armed rebellion and successful heroic combat. But even cinematic genius is constrained by market realities.

But where in this is Jesus? Another Skywalker before the Sanhedrin, but dying to himself, on the cross of material reality, by the sign of the Fish at the Cusp of the Ages. A Piscean martyrdom, of selfless love and a surrender to spirit. But now we are to enter another two thousand year cycle. So many questions for this New Age of Aquarius. Can love also wield a sharp sword? Or is to fight still to fall under the illusion of separation.

I spent a quiet Christmas with the children and Sue in Oxford, with visits to grandparents, and then headed up to Wales before New Year. It was the second New Year that I had spent away from familiar faces. There was a light snow, and I felt a slight dread of becoming snowed-in and having to spend more time than I had free. Gillie's friends seemed unreachable. Although I did not smoke myself, I could readily handle people being stoned out of their minds, but there was beer as well, and the combination had a fierce edge. Gillie was alternately seductive and distant and would disappear for several hours leaving me unsure whether she was out on the hill alone or engaged in some private liaison.

Late on the eve of New Year, we were all gathered about the fire, with most of her guests in a quiet snooze. She reached over an offering. It was Acid. The tab was black and white chequered. I took it, lifting it to the centre of my forehead, and whispered an 'Om Namaha Shivaya', gratefully accepting the messenger.

Gillie said, 'I think you had better have some red as well', and opened her hand to reveal another tab, a red heart.

I declined, 'No, pure Kali is the order'.

She proffered a wrinkled old mushroom, to which an involuntary nod caused me to accept. I lay back and tried to feel more at home. In that space of anticipation, I felt decidedly out of my elements, in a foreign culture and very alone. A decrepit all-in-one stereo system began to crank out a pitifully weak rock song. A short while later, still un-relaxed and my faculties entirely normal, an internal voice commanded, 'go to the temple'.

The prospect of the temple was decidedly uninviting. I had been in there earlier in the day and it was ice-cold. The fire had not been lit, and I did not feel confidant of finding candles. I reflected on my relationship with Acid. Dave had been heavily into it during some of the rebirthing years, and, of course, way before that. It was always around and he had often bade me try it. I had shied away without particular reason, just wary of letting go again into realms where my conscious mind had no way of directing its course. Except on one occasion. There had been a party and of the thirty or so people, most were from the rebirthing group and it seemed all were on Acid when I arrived. The house was full of figures seated on floors and stairs, crossed-legged, eyes-closed or vacantly open. I calmly accepted a tab.

Nothing much happened for a while. Then some faint calling, not a sound as such, but a siren heard on that inner plane - somewhere near, was love. Not around me, that was for sure. People were still sitting upright and eyes closed. I moved to the stairs, squeezed past the bodies and was drawn to a closed bedroom door, where I hesitated. There were sounds of warm laughter inside. My normal inhibitions rose. Group sex! Could I do that? No way.

But then I needed that warmth. Love was behind that door. I opened the door gently and walked in. Dave greeted me. His lady, January Jane lay on the bed. There were two or three others. I was relieved everyone was fully clothed. Nothing was said. Dave seemed to have been expecting me. He led me into the room, gently turning me round to face January on the bed. I stretched my arms and legs, suddenly feeling energies moving up my spine. I became instantly aware of every muscle and tendon, every point of contact with skeletal bone, and each state of tension at every joint. I could feel a contorted twist in my spine, where my hips compensated for one leg being slightly shorter than the other from a teenage accident. I was being shown just how difficult it was for energy to move through my tensioned system, how much energy it took just to keep balance, and which in normal consciousness I was so habituated to, that I could no longer feel.

Dave led me to the edge of the bed, all the while giggling and laughing. It was as if they had all been waiting and they knew what was now about to happen. Relieved again that my clothes stayed put. Should I have taken them off? I couldn't do that. Anyway they were all still dressed. Mind still fucking around with this! Dave guided me to lie on top of January who embraced me with a great smile.

Energy began to surge up my spine and fill my chest. It came in waves, like an orgasm building but which would not dissipate. I gasped and panted with the waves, longing for it to burst and ecstatic at its constant rising and continued building. The breath took over and I went into a rapid rebirthing cycle. January held me and Dave came close to my head. I was travelling the birth canal, all in glorious technicolor. In a moment I was out and huge hands held my rubber-floppy neck. I was entranced.

Then it was as if the film got fast-forwarded. I was beneath ground. In a coffin. My body was dead. Silent. Yet my consciousness, the merest pinprick of awareness was still there as witness, as if daring itself to stay until the very end.

There was a movement and sound by the door and I remember coming right out of the trance and urging quiet and total stillness in the room so that I could go back and witness that final point. I hung on as the flesh dried, as the bones became brittle, and was there at the very last when in a puff they crumbled to powder!

That had been it. A totally wonderful experience. Afterwards I had taken a walk and marvelled at the acuity of my visual senses, the depth and clarity in the landscape of trees and meadows by the river.

'Go to the temple, now!' Recollections disturbed as the voice repeated urgently.

I recognised Babaji's pressing intervention and quietly made my way through the cluttered kitchen and the little door to the temple room. I crawled into the cold dark interior and assumed meditation posture before the altar. I sensed a presence in the room. Suddenly I was surrounded by light and noise. It was as if the walls had become screens in a surround-cinema and on all sides a massive epic history of mankind unfolded. Only this was the history of the beast. Before me unfolded every act of inhumanity in all its gore and detail. Swords flashed, heads rolled and guts spilled. There was rape and slaughter in which I was at one moment victim, the next aggressor. The room swam with blood and reverberated with screams and wails and the thunder of battle. My spine weakened like jelly and I fought to stay conscious and upright as I was assailed by images of corruption and depravity for what seemed interminable hours.

The pain in my spine kept me conscious and determined to stay witness. This was all true, all me, there could be no separation. Then there appeared through the holocaust a vision of Babaji. He was on the altar before me. His hands reached to his chest and tore it wide open, and in a moment, a mere blink of the eye, everything was sucked in like a giant river disappearing into a swallow-hole in the ground. The room became instantly still, dark and silent.

I sat for a while and then unsteadily rose to my feet and felt my way out in the darkness through the kitchen to the sitting room. Gillie and the others were nowhere to be seen. The two children were asleep by the open fire and candles were alight all around. One of the childrens' feet was only inches from a candle. I took it and lit my way back into the kitchen. My inner voice urging me back to the temple and scolding my lack of trust and my judgements. I had looked around, the place was a tinderbox. Yet, had not Gillie lived here quite safely for years? My ordered mind. Could I not accept that the spirit protected her? I remained in the temple for some time.

The altar was dusty. The flowers long dead. The aarati lamp and little bowl for water did not sparkle with the care of daily polishing. My judgements again? Or was there something trying to filter through about the reality of Gillie's fragmented path. She entered at that moment and laid a small pile of wood by the fire, saying nothing. I did not feel to light a fire. I found my way back to the centre of love and acceptance in my heart and once more left the temple. Dawn was breaking. Again, Gillie was nowhere about and I left the house and moved quickly through the wind-sculpted larches and up the hill behind. Just as I was above the cottage and garden, I looked back. All around was normal vision, but spiralling up from Goleudy was a single thread of red light that disappeared into the heavens. I climbed further, heading for the summit of the mountain.

I moved quickly and easily, despite the unfamiliar and boggy ground. To the north, behind me, the sky was still dark, but before me the first greys were colouring the south-east. As I reached the summit I was exposed to a sharp wind in my face, which caused me to turn and hold my back to the wind. There before me the dark northern sky was a mass of rainbows.

14

Synthesis

Gillie rang me two weeks later. She believed she was pregnant. I was staying with Merrilyn in Northchurch Road, and the news had as much of an impact upon her as upon me. I could get no intuition. Logic told me it was unlikely. I did not want to put out any thoughts on the aether, other than to surrender to what would be.

She gave birth to this new soul in September 1985, naming him Elijah Seren Gwynn, after the star Sirius. Our relationship thereafter is another story for another time. Susan had a strange response. She had had little contact with Stephen for the past six months, but on hearing my news, she reconnected for just long enough, initially, to become pregnant and give birth to a baby girl whom she called Anna. And our relationship after that is another story for another time!

Of Gillie, I will say only one thing of relevance to this story. One day, early in the year, she rang with her voice of thunder and portent, and urged, 'Peter, keep out of this Sirius stuff, leave it alone, back away now before it is too late. They may not harm you, that is not their way. They will get the people you love. Leave it alone.'

I had been reading and slowly piecing together myths and connections, as if in preparation for another journey. After the call, I sat down, and simply asked, and was simply told, 'This is not your quest'. And I needed no second telling.

As little of these mysteries as I knew then, I know now. With the years has come no new knowledge relevant to that time, but some synthesis. Leonard had taught me a basic truth, that thought is creative. I am convinced that with appropriate discipline, the human mind can create material reality from apparent nothing. I have seen and heard enough to accept that a yogic master can overcome many of the physical realities we in our normal consciousness take for immutable laws. All matter, at a level of understanding now accessible to modern physics, is energy, merely a level of vibration. What was once thought atomic, that is, the smallest discrete units and building blocks of existence, is now known to be a constellation of sub-atomic 'particles', and even these, depending upon what instrument is used to measure them, can be seen either as discrete entities, or waves, as of light and other forms of radiation. Perhaps the day will come soon when physicists sheepishly admit their measurements were all illusions of light, created by the instruments they devised!

Matter is therefore simply energy vibrating in patterns of low frequency and is therefore, as the ancient yogis taught, an 'illusion' of light, or 'maya'. The dance of matter and all form is therefore a play, a light show. Herein lies the law of karma, of cause and effect. All that has gone before has created consequence and consequence plays itself out. Newton was not wrong. The 'mechanists' and 'reductionists' have not been wrong. Physical reality is a strong reality. Once something of weight has been set in particular motion it cannot be stopped without that force being transferred. To every reaction an opposite reaction. And so, with human life, actions mirror that reality. A deed of hate or anger is a reaction, a creative thought that seeks to alter the 'other'. And so are we netted by our past. And in the world of thought there is no time or boundary of place. That which has gone before is with us now. Thought is not restricted to the transmitter or receiver. Each of us broadcasts and each receives, whether we are conscious or not.

I have not the wisdom to know where God is in all this. The Sages talk of the Mind of God, and so perhaps we are being dreamed but slowly into our future. Babaji showed me the unutterable obscenities of our existence, the poison of the human mind, the totality of our dark history, and then, as Lord Shiva, he drank the poison of this world. His heart opened in one instant to embrace in love everything of what we are, from the basest to the highest. Some of his 'devotees' believe that 'He' came as an avatar to this world and that by his 'death' he took away enough of our karma to avert the great catastrophe that was about to engulf us. I, too, could easily believe this. I saw his human body wracked with pain. I saw, too, that he could choose to stay in a state beyond that pain. I have not the sight of the mystics. Others would see great beings come to the fire ceremonies. Perhaps Babaji was another astral warrior, fighting great cosmic battles on our behalf. Perhaps, as 'Dadaji' would have it, he was still not free of an egoic human past, and that he too succumbed to 'illusions'.

I do not think so. For me, Babaji was a teacher not a God or demi-God. I could not worship 'him'. I was no 'devotee' of Lord Shiva. I do not believe he asked that of me. And I do not judge those who do so worship his form. The path of devotion, bakti yoga, so little comprehended by the western mind, is a path to open the heart and to find humility. I have seen such beauty in those so devoted. In some I have also seen great hypocrisy and narrowness of mind, but then, who is to know where anyone lies on the great path, and what transformations may occur around the next corner?

If there is such an entity as Lord Shiva, Lord of the Dance, Lord of Destruction, then Babaji could act the part. He is reported to have said, in 1979, 'Now I will let the destruction begin'. He told us to prepare for the 'kranti', a time of massive destruction when the face of the earth would be changed and the great majority of mankind would be annihilated. Thereafter would dawn a 'golden age'. Those who would be left would have their consciousness cleansed by this cataclysmic event. When I took this at face value and asked for further knowledge, Shastraji rebuked me but gave me no wiser insight. Babaji was reported to have said that he would come back in five years time and that within that time the 'kranti' would occur. Some reported that he was to be found still in a physical body, by those who really needed to find him, in a remote temple in Nepal. Leonard made many expeditions. Some say he wrote to Shastraji many months after his 'death' complaining of the lack of conscious awareness in the ashram, and how he simply got fed up and had to leave in the way he did.

These things do not concern me. As my teacher for that time, he left me with what knowledge and wisdom I have, such as it is. My understanding is this: that 'Shiva' is an energy form, an aspect of the divine interplay of creative powers that we may call 'destruction'. Without destruction there can be no evolution. In the Vedic cosmos, the divine has three primal energies, Brahma-Creator, Vishnu-Preserver, Shiva-Destroyer. Behind this reality lies the great void, the blackness of the unformed, the divine feminine that is The Great Mother of All. The Hindu language and culture has ways of symbolising and relating to these energies, and these ways take a certain form that we may call religion, a way of relating to perceived forms of divine energy. These forms are particular to that culture. For myself, therefore, I had little interest in the forms. I was familiar with them, perhaps from former lives spent in Himalayan monasteries, and so I could approach them without fear. Even Kali represented for me an 'energy' in the form of 'the dweller on the threshold', the demonic female aspect of the destructive power that must be encountered on the spiritual quest. Kali slays the mind. Or at least, that aspect of the mind that is male, that seeks to discriminate between 'this or that', the aspect that maintains the separate ego. In myth, even Lord Shiva must surrender to Kali.

Having embraced these perceptions of reality, I was left with a deeper insight into our own culture. The western mind has attempted a coup. Many see it as the usurping of the masculine over the feminine. Ours is a culture where the male mind has run rampant: logic, academic analysis, reductionist method, manipulation, construction, engineering, control, hierarchy, God as spirit Father, the Great Architect, the Great Plan, and Armageddon if it doesn't work out. To gain such ascendancy, feminine wisdom was disparaged, and more, women who held to that wisdom were systematically eradicated.

I think it is more basic than this. The coup is not just the masculine over the feminine. I do not believe that men have ever had such power that they can have so easily and completely destroyed the wisdom that is the province of that powerful element of humanity that is natural woman. Women have to have colluded. They have lent their power to the process. They have willingly become men. It can be seen all around, in every school, in every University, in every business, they compete, anxious as any man to prove themselves, often even more so.

No, the coup has been against Shiva. The western mind has sought to amputate the Destroyer from our consciousness, to live for ever as the divine Child of the Creator.

Thus have the myths been rewritten. God exists now as the Father in his own right. There is no primordial source, no 'great mother of all' to which even He must surrender into nothingness. Spirit Father then begets a Son. The Son alone is capable of holding the divine power. To elevate the daughter would run the risk of elevating the natural female wisdom. A woman could not be relied upon in a coup of this magnitude!

Except as Mother to the Son. And not even natural Mother. Instead, Mary untouched by carnal unions, never other than girl and mother. Divine only as nurturing 'Preserver' of the Son. And the Son himself becomes the Christ, under the sacrificial sign of the Fish, another aspect of the 'Preserver' Vishnu. This is the energy of the heart, of selfless love, the love that sustains, that is everlasting, that guarantees the immortality of the soul.

But 'soul', has become thereby debased. True soul cannot resonate without the dark feminine as its base note. This false soul has become synonymous with 'personality' and a world religion teaches that God the Creator has reserved a room in some colossal mansion wherein this bundle of clothes will have its permanent show, a catwalk in the sky!

Jesus, you screwed up! Great Yogi you should have seen what they would do with your death. They claim you took their sins away. That you are God. That in you alone lies salvation. That no other aspect of God has validity. They claim you never made love. That she who stayed with you through it all was nothing more than a reformed prostitute, grateful for her salvation at your divine feet. In your Father's name they massacred their own womanhood. They took the land from the Red Man and enslaved the Black. They hacked down the forests and desecrated the wild places. For you and your blessed mother.

Babaji has been embraced by the same needy western mind, as some cosmic gladiator to be revered, yet another saviour. I cannot know what battles 'he' may have fought on our behalf, whether 'his' interventions steered us from a greater catastrophe than what we now face. But I do not think it is likely.

What merit is there for us if 'god-beings' fight our battles? For me, he was 'guru' as teacher. His life was a life of example. He lived in simplicity. His life was dedicated as one long song to the Divine, Jaga d'Ambe, formless Mother of the Universe. His life was love expressed. Not a pale love of sentiment, but the vibrant love of conscious union, an embrace of the dance of life and death, birth and destruction, form and the formless. Because he lived that love, he was one with the divine source, which *is* that love. In everything that I saw of him and heard of him, this love was manifest.

And I also hold to my reservation, as with Jesus, that there are things that I cannot see and thus cannot know, and for which my intuition is not necessarily a reliable guide. And so, there is also the possibility that parts of him were not at one with that source, just as there remains also for me a possibility that Jesus had things to work out. And I must live with these uncertainties.

I say that with a sadness as if demanding of sympathy. Nay! I *must* live with these uncertainties. That is my truth and I must embrace that truth as my life positive. Do I need to know whether this or that human form outside of myself was perfect or near-to-perfect? If I follow any teaching other than because I know it to be true from a knowing that is in my gut, firm as a rock, then where am I? I do not need Jesus or Babaji to be God before I can look at their lives, their teachings, and gain inspiration. I do not need a creed of any kind to know that love exists in the Universe, because I have felt it. And if there are those who would still say that love and light are mere illusions of the conscious state, just so many neurones firing off in the primate brain, and that matters also not, for is that not true of everything, that all form and concept is maya, that even love is an illusion?

Jai Maha Maya Ki! Glory to the Great Illusion!

If I have seen that love exists, I have also seen when it does not. That there are times when I feel it and times when I do not. Only spirit encourages me to choose the one as more real than the other, and Spirit has no name, no form, and comes of its own grace.

I will not stray from such insights as I had those ten years ago. I chose Babaji and not Dadaji. Jesus and not Mohammed. Buddha and not Jabulon. The latter, in any case, is by personal invitation only. When Babaji said, 'now, I begin the destruction', Pluto moved inside the orbit of Neptune, and by 1982 it was on the cusp of the eighth house, Scorpio, the sign over which it rules. Fourteen years from cusp to cusp. In the ancient picture of the world that is astrology, with its roots in Sumer and Chaldean wisdom, and developed now to a fine art by modern practitioners, there is a western wisdom of 'Shiva' expressed in the mandala of twelve houses, where the eighth house rules birth, death and rebirth.

The planet Pluto is named after the God of the Greek myth (Romanised from Hades, Lord of the Underworld). Here was a true lord of death and rebirth. As the older Greek and Sumerian matriarchal forms gave way to the patriarchy, the underworld, a symbol for the collective unconscious was given a masculine ruler. Formerly, this realm had its Queen. But of that I will write in another time. The Graeco-Roman teaching myth relates how Ceres (Romanised from Demeter) is out on the side of Mount Olympus, walking in the summer meadows of fruitfulness with her beloved daughter Persephone. Summer is warm, bees gather honey, flowers awake to the sun. Food is plentiful. If only......the natural human desire for it always to be like this. The desire to be with the 'preserver', Lord Vishnu, Jesus, the Buddha of Compassion, Mother Mary, forever who we are now, the good, the sun-light warm rays of the heart. Ceres is the Goddess of Fruitfulness. She rules the summer plenty. Not for her the deaths and decays of autumn, the rotten and flyblown, or the cleansing colds of winter, dark and purifying nights ruled by inconstant moons. She would keep her daughter to herself.

Dear Lord Pluto. For all his dwelling in the dark, among the undead thoughts of generations, archetypes of mind, demons formed from the condemned and exiled, he was lonely. And did not justice demand acknowledgement? Is not Pluto also part of the great plan? And so, in aggrievement he rode his chariot out and across the sky, until his lusty eye settled upon Persephone. My preferred version is that he then and there abducted her to his world. Others prefer to see him as seducer, but I will come to that. Persephone, then, against her will is held in the underworld. It is at this point Pluto tries his seduction. Some prefer rape, but I think persuasion. He needed time. Meanwhile, above ground, Ceres weeps for the Daughter of Fruitfulness, and searches high and low, neglecting her task of maintaining the world. Fertility declines all around. The harvest is poor. The ground turns barren as Ceres distresses herself. After three months, Zeus intervenes. He remonstrates with Pluto, tells him he's failed in his attempted seduction, his plan of marriage, that Persephone will not have him and he must let her go. Pluto tries one more tactic, offering the famished lady some pomegranate. She accepts this apparent move of kindness, unwittingly binding herself to him. She appeals to Zeus, who upholds the trickster's pact, and judges - she must stay for three months in every year with the Lord of the Underworld.

And so it was that humanity came to accept that summer could not be forever. That Pluto's realm would have its place in the order of things. The wise knew that in the embrace of death lay rebirth, in the process of death, a cleansing and a strengthening that would lead to regeneration. And for the unwise, those wistfully attached to the preservation of life, the matter would have to be forced upon them. In Masonic teaching, the myth of Pluto's seduction is used as a warning to the acolyte to spurn the advances of darkness and evil.

In 1930 modern astrology could begin to map the aspect of Pluto in individual and historical consciousness. The outermost planet was discovered and named by astronomers, completing the series, Uranus (discovered 1781) and Neptune (discovered 1845). Where Uranian energy can be seen to govern the breakthrough inspirations of consciousness beyond the confines of Saturnian structure and tradition, and where Neptune rules the submersion of individual consciousness with the All, Pluto stands as the apparent final barrier between human consciousness and the great void. In its highest expression it is the birth of divine consciousness, the realisation of unity beyond duality, but of cosmic proportion. Pluto represents that element of the divine play, Lord Shiva, that will intervene to precipitate this realisation. It is an energy of violent awakening that will burst through whatever layers and structures have been built up to protect individual and group consciousness from ultimate reality.

Some astrologers hold that we have become conscious of the planet at the time when our consciousness is evolved enough to handle the energies. I prefer a doctrine of co-incidence. As we evolve, our consciousness expands and telescopes are merely extensions of that. These energies have long been met and understood by adepts. Now, masses of people know of the planet's existence, and an ever larger number are embracing the higher teachings of astrology. Of course, for those who are not, the planet is just another ball of atoms, a curiosity of the solar system, with no meaning at all.

In the web of things, where everything interconnects, where the dance is choreographed not just for us, but the stars also, for we are not separate from them, then just as Pluto must move inside the orbit of Neptune, so must human life manifest a new step to the dance, a human form to dance Shiva's dance, and to teach the ultimate reality. This was Babaji's light-show, courtesy of the divine theatre company.

> 'Be happy! Be courageous! Live in Truth, Simplicity and Love. Be ready to die, to jump into the fire, dive into the waves. Do not be attached to this body, it is but a vehicle. I come only to serve. Serve humanity. We are all one.'

In the Hindu pantheon it is Shiva who drinks the poison of the world, such is the depth of his love and compassion. Babaji showed me in the vision that this was what I must aspire to. Not to believe that he has done some great deed of karmic cleansing on our behalf, but that each of us must work to that point of consciousness where we can include the dark as well as the light. It is said, in the heart of Shiva, lies Krishna. Was this not also the Christ-consciousness, to love the enemy?

At the end of 1984 these were but vague realisations. Perhaps we are God's dream unfolding and one day, that day of at-one-ment, we shall be co-creators potent in our own dreaming. But of the more mundane and immediate relation of human thought to human reality, I had become aware, that to engage in a contest with an enemy based on the supposition that the enemy was so powerful it had to be beaten, was to subtly give away all of one's creative spiritual power before the contest began. It was to perpetuate 'karma', action and reaction.

When first I engaged with the nuclear monstrosity at Windscale, it was in reaction to its power. This was the deadly possible future that had to be fought. It threatened everything. Through plutonium and the weapons programme it could annihilate human existence in an atomic war. Through accidental explosion or leaks it could contaminate vast tracts of land and render life a misery for millions. Through dumping it would despoil the oceans and their life forms for generations to come. Socially, the technology required a high level of central control by elite technocrats. Its complexity and danger rendered it beyond ordinary democratic control; it demanded secrecy, surveillance and social order, and the means to those ends.

In that combat, we had won a number of rounds, but were losing the contest. Life itself was over-shadowed. The social psychologist, P.D. Pahner, on contract to the International Atomic Energy Authority, had written, 'nuclear power may represent a symbolic threat of death....which has the power to undermine the very creativity of youth.' His report was buried by the industry that commissioned it. But how unscientific a statement! How can such a risk be measured, quantified, justified?

In my case, it was already true.

My whole psyche was consumed in reaction to the enemy. The opposition dictated my moves. Indeed, almost everything the environmental movement engaged with was reactionary and driven by fear. Fear of death and annihilation; fear of 'resource scarcity', lack and deprivation; fear of losing genetic integrity, of contamination, ill-health and especially cancer.

The gladiators of the movement would not themselves display these fears, indeed, I doubt that on a 'feeling' level they were real at all for the select group of warriors, whether scientific, legal or marine commando. As men, we were locked into a battle that demanded either the action competences of the cool professional, which my brother Ron displayed to perfection, or the ingenuity of the campaigns manager, forever on the telephone co-ordinating, planning, eye on the front-page and the column-inches, to which Robert had brought his own flare and genius, or my own combat arena of words. and concepts, cutting analysis and indictment and the claiming of the moral high grounds of international equity and environmental responsibility. In my world, especially, emotional realities were disguised and the choice of weapons that of the enemy.

Tactically it appeared sound enough, the power structures gave credence to nothing else. But strategically I had my doubts as to its wisdom. Already by 1984 I had begun to perceive the effects of this sell-out on my own psyche.

I had by then begun a steady transition in my motivation. I was no longer consumed by anger and riddled by fear. I had grown wise enough not to be 'attached' to the outcome of particular skirmishes. Where others would head for the bar in consolation, I felt free and simply began planning for the next campaign. In victory I seldom stayed to celebrate, or even to witness the execution. What mattered was the quality of combat, the degree of love and compassion that could be maintained in the face of many a pull toward judgement, condemnation and hate.

And of course, there were professional standards to maintain. I, and all of my colleagues in PERG, believed in the highest standards of scientific truth, even though we were well aware that it would always be relative. We fought for 'our' truth, and did our best to make sure that truth accorded with the best of theory and the fullest analysis of 'fact'. Of science itself, we believed its only safeguard as a way of knowledge lay in its openness, its plurality, and the freedom to dissent and be included as dissenters. Perhaps we were, and still are, naive, and that science, of its very nature, can never manifest those safeguards sufficiently, rather like a leaky set of nuclear safeguards - there is an illusion of the possibility of a perfected system, and that illusion is itself a great social danger.

Where I *was* sure, was that I was still basically a 'reactionary' and I had no creative power in my own right. This mattered little in the years to 1984. Others were more able than I, and would inherit the future. Alternative thinkers abounded: soft and intermediate technology, solar energy paths, regional self-reliance, organic farming, holistic medicine, education for peace, gender awareness, birth without violence, homeopathic medicine, traditional Chinese acupuncture, shiatsu, restoration ecology of wetlands and forests, trade-as-aid.....these were the birthing grounds of a future in which I would be content to pass my days as a worn-out warrior, an Horatio who stayed on the bridge, gaining time for the children to grow.

Such was the romance. And to my own children, if in the end the light failed, and science fiction futures unrolled their concrete mausoleums, lands devoid of wild forest, the rhino and elephant mere mythic tales, then I could pull out the photographs and say, I was there, I tried, many of us tried. There would be honour in defeat.

That latter romance died. I remember going with Tine Andersen to a 'protest' at Upper Heyford airbase where the US had located its forward deployed F-111 bombers. The protestors had turned out in good numbers for all the approach roads were packed with cars, all neatly parked on the verges. There were scuffles at the gate. Photo opportunities. Off camera, by the high fences to the west of the base, there had been a small cluster of caravans and tents permanently occupied in vigil. For that I had respect. Meanwhile, the mass protestors had their thrill and went home, taking their motors with them.

I recalled the Malville blockades and occupations and Babaji's words, 'I am for fighting. In the peace movement, blood has turned to water'.

If all of those cars had been left in the road, hundreds upon hundred and set alight, that would have been courageous. And as for my own courage, I would have little daydreams of driving a bulldozer through the fence and on through the parked F-111s until they were piled in a mangled heap. But I was no such warrior. Too scared of prison, of missing my children.

I came to believe that whosoever creates from his own power, and the other opposes, the opposer has already given away his power. We must create what we want and let them oppose it, or get locked into permanently opposing them and thereby losing ourselves, however many little battles we may appear to win.

For several years I had been invited to speak to the combined sixth form at Abingdon School, a boys' public school of the old tradition. The first lecture had been instigated to provide a democratic balance to lectures on nuclear energy and its future, then part of a road-show organised by nearby Harwell. I talked straightly of risks and benefits and alternative energy paths. Slowly this lecture metamorphosed to include the global threats to the planetary ecosystem that were then becoming apparent. And in my last lecture there at the close of this period it came to an analysis of where we had gone wrong.

I was speaking to about two hundred boys, and two or three masters sitting in. Several of the boys and one of the masters were in military uniform. I drew a circle on the blackboard.

'This is our Earth. Please tell me its gender.'

The boys looked nonplussed. I looked at them for a long time, then remarked,

'Where are the girls?'

Some shifted. Some giggled.

'It is as if you are afraid of them. That they might in some way hold you back from your learning'.

I told them, 'You all know that this Earth is female. It is Mother Earth. Suppose for a minute that she is your real mother. You know, so-called primitive peoples regard her as a real mother. Suppose she is a sentient being.'

'Then transfer to your real mother the way you are with this Earth. You take her completely for granted. You never send her flowers. No birthday cards. No thanks for the meals she prepares. No acknowledgement of her beauty. She is just there. It is your right. Everything she has is a 'resource' for your utilisation, your growth, your career. More than that, you no longer ask for what you need, you take it as of right. There is no question of thanks or gratitude.

'How is your mother now?

'Is she sickening just a little. Does she look sad, neglected, worn out? Does she go on without murmur because it is her duty. How long will she live without your love?

'Of course, if you have a real mother, she will not let you grow up like this. Not only because of her needs for love, but because of her love for you. You would be a monster child unless she broke through your unconsciousness.

'Some say, "Reclaim the Earth", "the Earth is your Mother", "you must take care of her, she is fragile". But I see differently. I see rocks that are hundreds of millions of years old, that once were great volcanoes, an Earth once laced by fire, sulphurous heavens, rain of cinders. I see mighty oceans that drowned whole continents, asteroids that wiped a whole dynasty of creatures from the face of the land and quakes that raised mountains and rifted great canyons. Ice that formed a hundred feet above where we stand right now, only 10,000 years ago, a mere blink of your mother's eye.

'Take care! This is no pale mother. No self-effacing Mary to indulge every boy-child among you. To the sensitive medicine peoples of North America, to Himalayan yogis and Mayan magicians, and to those in this land still gifted with feeling and prophecy, your Mother is growing restless. She sends you many warnings. This year violent storms and unseasonal frosts. Last year one whole mountain exploded to fire and dust. In her most violent rages and fevers she could vent a thousand volcanoes simultaneously, or sink this land by one hundred metres in an instant.

'But of course, I cannot prove to you that your Mother's actions are anything but random!'

I went on to describe the laying waste of this garden, of the tropical forests and the oceans, of nature 'conquered', agriculture overblown, everything laid out neat and square in the quest for order and comfort, safety, warmth, freedom from decay, from bugs and pests, and cancer. And how this was a flight from the dark feminine, from surrender of the male mind to disorder, and from women themselves, economically dominated, educated as men, the teachings of higher sex and orgasm avoided, for there lies other realms, and of the war on drugs and gays and 'travellers'. And finally, of the hidden worshippers of Masonic order, of their God Jabulon, of Calvi and the P2 lodge and the penetration of all of the upper echelons of western society with secret and magical devotion to the Great Architect, the archetypal Father.

'In the beginning, there was a sky father God whom the Greeks called Oeranus. He was married to the Earth Mother, Gaia. They were the children of Kaos, the formless Great Mother of All. Oeranus and Gaia also begat children, the earthly Titans. Oeranus, a being of the aethereal sky, did not like what he saw and withdrew. The eldest of the Titans, Kronos, was resentful of this distant father and decided on retribution. Some say he was abetted by Gaia. He caught his father asleep, and castrated him with a sickle. He threw the bleeding genitals into the ocean. The blood drops formed into Furies, demonic beings of retribution. However, from the genitals arose Venus-Aphrodite, floating upon a shell.

'Kronos is Saturn, Lord of Karma, the Grim Reaper. What is sown must be reaped. The initial rejection of the children by Oeranus begins the process of Karma. Venus is the love of the redeemer. Only love can redeem. In the modern myth of Star Wars, where Daarth Vader is this distant Father, Luke Skywalker is urged by Obiwan Kenobe to fight not with anger, but with love.

'We live in a world out-of-balance. Gaia is no longer respected as equal. She no longer sits beside the Sky Father as Earth Mother, honoured by all. She has been relegated of late to an 'hypothesis' on the part of some scientists now dimly aware of the repercussions of our depredations on her 'ecosystem'. Instead, it is Oeranus who is honoured, and not just in the old age of 'Our Father Which Art in Heaven', (Uranium is the Greek word for Heaven), but also in the metal Uranium, promise of a New World Order, the advance of science, the gift of atomic physics, everlasting energy source, the ultimate weapon for control of the earth and of the enemies of freedom.

'Yet, here lies a curious thing. Inside the nuclear reactor, so meticulously honoured by our men in white coats, the Uranium fissions first to Neptunium and then to Plutonium. These are known as 'daughters'. Only some of the Plutonium isotopes can be used for weapons or making fast reactor fuel, the rest is waste, along with many shorter-lived fission products, which poison the nuclear reaction. If you bury this waste, Plutonium binds to soil and most rocks, and thus remains in the Underworld, but Neptunium is not so bound, being extremely soluble, and moves with the waters, whether in ocean sediments or earthy groundwaters. If you model the distant doses of these poisons to future generations then Neptunium, which is more toxic than Plutonium, dominates the dose.'

I talked then of the astrological symbolism of Pluto and Neptune. And of the mocking of the Gods, so prevalent among scientists and military technicians. Of Hades the name of the French missiles with neutron-bomb warheads of the purest plutonium, of Poseidan and Polaris submarines, of Harwell's Pluto and Dido reactors, of the Trinity Tests and the Baby Jesus atomic bomb. And of the Revelation of St John, when in the end times, 'the heavens will be split assunder'.

'We face a world driven by men who seek total control of nature, of wild nature, and of human nature. Men afraid of disorder. They would rather annihilate this world, than confront their fear. That which they deny and repress into their unconscious, becomes grist for Pluto's mill. He rides again with his chariot now for all to see, on the tip of their weapons that would guarantee their freedom to control, yet he speaks not of order but disorder and chaos, of the uncontrollable, of the terrorist who gains access, of the panic on the button, of the computer fault that starts the count-down to destruction.

'And there lies Pluto's gift to us. Without this ultimate threat to our lives, would we now be waking so profoundly to the realities of oneness. Pluto, the Great Awakener, issues the challenge, 'wake up or die'!'

I have had no further invitations to speak at Abingdon School! Although I do recall, how before the lecture, the headmaster had warned me that it might not be possible to interest more than a few of the more dedicated boys in the tea and discussion that was organised for after school, but how the study was crammed, and the boys desperate for books to read, and how, somewhat wrong-footed, I could offer little more than Richard Bach's 'Illusions'.

At this time, too, I revisited Theikenmeer. It was winter and grey, and I had escaped from a conference on the North Sea and the Precautionary Principle in Science held by Non-Governmental Organisations at Bremen University. My friend from the battles of 1975, the Lutheran pastor Friedhelm Brockmann, accompanied me. The youngsters of my youth group had, after I left, formed a new nature-protection group for the region, engaged the support of local and national government, and with the help of the very people and machines that had drained and devastated so much of the surrounding landscape, they had dredged the lake out to its former size, and written a book about its regeneration, 'Das Zweite Lebens des Theikenmeeres' - the 'rebirth' of Theikenmeer. The new lake was now surrounded by reeds and emerging willow. There had been a rebirth both in the land and in the consciousness of those few young people, now at University and as engaged as ever on the 'environmental' mission.

I looked with sad pleasure at that misty landscape, so many fine memories of glorious afternoon light on the moor and the sedge. Of a time before that dark confrontation of soul, of time before thirty, of naive love and simple marriage before painful awakenings. I know now that Saturn-Kronos, Lord of Karma, then transited the place it held at my birth, in Leo and the Fifth House, completing a cycle of 14 years since its opposition in Aquarius when I was fourteen. Had I the guidance, I could have spent those fourteen years in conscious work with my karmic inheritance of doubt and fear, the need to control, the need to fight that which threatened, and the time of its return would have been a time of integration and strength to go beyond. But, for my generation, and for a while yet, there was no initiation into love, only war. Pluto also transited my Neptune in Libra, which is square to my Moon. Christina had said of this, a tendency to idealise women, to be deluded in relationship to the feminine. Pluto had a lot to shake up. And when, in 1982, he entered my seventh House, right on cue, Susan severed our sexual relationship and moved out. A death, an ending, and a new beginning.

Sometime in March of 1985 I found a message on my answer-phone at Bullingdon Road.

It rang out, 'Sirius Calling...., Sirius Calling. Peter, the answer to all your questions. Meet me on the first Saturday in April, at 7 o'clock in the morning, on Parliament Hill, underneath the big tree. Be there.'

The voice was familiar and yet I could not place it. It sounded as if the person knew me well. There was some affection in the tone. I went to Parliament Hill. Robert had been in England, having spent much time in Canada on Tioxide campaigns, and I had asked him to accompany me, but to stay in the car and come up later to the hill if I were not back. There was nobody about. There was not one obvious big tree, so I walked around and I waited an hour. Robert then joined me and we both walked around the trees but nobody made themselves known to us.

As we walked down Parliament Hill, which is a short cul-de-sac with semi-detached not-too-grand but comfortable houses, I noticed that the top house had a plaque.

'Here lived George Orwell'.

It sprang strongly into my consciousness. Was that the answer to all my questions?

I have not to this day been able to find out from whom the call came. The voice had a slight almost Irish accent, but none of my Irish friends admitted to any kind of prank. Besides, everyone knew how busy I was. I could think of very few people with whom I had discussed the Sirius mystery. I had learned of Orwell, that he had been engaged with Allied Intelligence during the war in a unit for psychological warfare. He would therefore have had ample opportunity to observe its people and its methods. From this he wrote '1984'.

Could it have been that Big Brother was a symbol for the Masonic order and its agenda of control? And more, did he decide that psychic warfare would be beyond the credibility of so many that he chose the allegory of electronic surveillance? Big Brother did not need two-way television screens in the astral world that had been revealed to me.

In July of 1985 the Rainbow Warrior was blown up by French Secret Service commandos while in the harbour at Auckland, New Zealand. My friend Hans Guyt had just left the boat with Fernando Pereira, the Portuguese cameraman, his very close companion, when there was a muffled explosion and the boat listed over and Fernando rushed on board and below decks to retrieve his precious camera and film. There was another explosion and the boat sank rapidly. The rest of the story is well-known. Two of the French team were caught and initially charged with murder. The French government put enormous pressure on New Zealand's government and the charge was commuted to manslaughter, to which the plea of guilty avoided an embarrassing trial. The two agents were repatriated to French territory and spent one year on a pacific island before being moved to France and eventual promotion. As far as I am aware, this action was not condemned by any other state, certainly not by the British.

The commando team blew a hole the size of a car in the side of the vessel, directly adjacent to the largest compartment under the water line, the engine room. If you want to sink a boat quickly, that is how it is done. We will probably never know whether they knew most of the crew were ashore so late at night. If you want to simply disable a boat, as the charge of manslaughter would require as motive, then any seaman can tell you, a small charge on the prop shaft of such an old vessel would do the trick. It would be virtually impossible to replace.

The murder of Fernando had a strong impact upon Hans and upon Greenpeace worldwide. He became bitter, angry and more determined and engaged with renewed vigour against the pipeline at Windscale, for which he spent three months in jail. The campaign against Mururoa was stepped up. Hans was not alone in his shock and anger. However, the French action, on one level, made Greenpeace stronger. In the period after 1985, membership worldwide grew enormously. The sinking of the 'Warrior' marked a watershed and the old Greenpeace was no longer recognisable.

Greenpeace became more of an 'organisation'. The next boat to be purchased was an hugely expensive ocean-going tug capable of operating in the Antarctic, and in the debate as to its naming, 'The Greenpeace' won out. There was also a debate to refloat the 'Warrior' and have it as a museum, but the 'romantics' lost that and she was laid to rest in deeper water as a wreck.

The French action was authorised by the Defence Minister, Hernu, known to be a member of France's most senior Masonic Lodge. The Grandmaster of the Lodge being George Mitterand, the President's brother. The head of the secret service, Admiral Lacoste, was also a member. At the time of Gelli's escape from the Italian magistrates, the French Secret Service were reported as aiding his getaway. I could not help but acknowledge the adeptness of this strike to the heart of Greenpeace. The 'Warrior' was disabled, and although the poster of the new campaigns sang loudly, 'You cannot sink a Rainbow', you can sink a heart. In those early days there was a spirit on the boats that began to fade. Ron noticed it in the subsequent North Sea campaign against the incinerator ships, in which he came close to losing his life. There were divisions and arguments and at levels that would often compromise the safety of his teams. Battles were fought with too much anger and not enough love, with moral self-righteousness, and above all, more and more with the weapons of the 'enemy', with science, cold reason and argument.

At this time I sought out David MacTaggart, who, after galvanising much of the massive change in management that followed the sinking of the warrior and the growth of 'the organisation', had begun his retirement from the role of 'godfather'. I questioned him late one night at his house in Lewes, where the International Office was then located, as to the spirit within Greenpeace. He got up, left the room for a moment, and returned with a small pouch. The pouch contained pebbles of different colours. One was black. One was white. And one was red. They had been given to him to safeguard. In advance of the desecration of Indian lands, they had been unearthed from the burial grounds of the Indian tribe whose elders had initially approached him in the boatyard at the outset of his own Pacific quest from the western shores of Canada. These stones had been with him since the birth of the organisation. He did not elaborate but bade me not to worry about what was at the heart of Greenpeace.

Robert and I also decided, around this time, to revisit Delafield Road, where John Taylor had been based. We had had no contact. However, Robert had some independent confirmation of the astral episode with Charmayne. Whilst one of the Greenpeace boats had been in Hamburg, Dave Greenway, one of the Zodiac operatives and a former Royal Marine Commando, had got talking with a seamen who turned out to have been on the crew of the boat that had been dumping and on which Charmayne had appeared as an apparition - he confirmed the story of the 'ghost', the return to port and the hands signing off.

We did not announce our visit. The house was exactly as it had been, and John Taylor welcomed us as if the whole episode had been not a year but only a week ago. He was still resentful of what he saw as lack of support, and expressed how surprised he had been that we had gone ahead with the Ben action in the light of the messages from 'the other side'. In his own life, little had changed. People still went out, but he did not indicate upon what task they were employed. When Robert told his story of Dave Greenway's meeting, John turned to Charmayne and said,

'Now do you believe it was real?'

Apparently, Charmayne had not then been convinced the episode was anything more substantial than a day-dream.

As I write now, I have talked with some of the leaders of Greenpeace today. Chris Rose, in the UK office, has taken a cold hard look at the past few years and seen that the organisation had lost direction and become too narrowly focussed upon results in the media rather than results on the ground. A rebuilding is under way, whereby results will be measured by actual change delivered on the ground. This will mean change at the heart of where the organisation has aimed its arrows of witness - in industrial processes, such as chlorine production, its use in the chemical industry and the source of virtually all toxic organic compounds, in fossil fuel burning, nuclear reprocessing, atomic weapons systems, forest destruction.... That is a tall order for a group that hitherto could do little more than point fingers and obstruct the leviathan. In those years, however, we have seen ocean dumping of radioactive and industrial wastes banned, incineration at sea phased out, sulphur emissions across Western Europe have been cut, and the Antarctic seas declared a Whale Sanctuary.

Elaine Lawrence now lives across Tremadoc Bay. I can see the end of the peninsula where she shares a cottage with her partner and their young son. She commutes one week on and one week off by train to the office in London, and is still active as an International Council member. She tells me there has been a great restructuring and re-analysis. In the past few years, despite a growth to over four million members worldwide, Greenpeace has taken a lot of criticism for having lost its edge, for being negative and unconstructive, and even for not taking the kind of risks it had done before when it had nothing to lose. The re-appraisal is taking these criticisms on board and new programmes will be developed that seek to be part of the solution and not merely signposting the problem. The role of science and 'scientism' will be challenged.

My life, however, is peaceful and relatively uninvolved. My work has become more internal. I have visions of a new mobilisation of consciousness, a reclaiming of our true relationship with planet Ocean and its landmasses that have for so long sustained and nurtured us.

Outside my door the season turns at Solstice. Only a few days ago, on December 12th, there were two warblers in the garden and the wood violets had bloomed. Robert phoned from Devon where he had watched Little Egrets on the Exe. The land broods. One moment it is gentle. The next fierce winds come straight off the warm Atlantic. Scientists pull the ears of ministers and warn of the warming. Already their computers hum with calculation of the expected degrees. They hone their linear models and talk only among themselves of mathematical chaos and its boundary.

The rains have been heavy. There is more I know now than then and which I should say before leaving you with this book. In the mid-seventies, the science journalist, John Gribbin, toured the world's meteorological institutes and in summary concluded that science was expecting a global cooling. Ten years on the expectation has changed radically. We fight so strongly against the global emissions of carbon dioxide, yet the quietest of questions surfaces: is Gaia, after all, a sentient mother protecting us from the next cooling?

And where carbon dioxide causes warming, sulphur emissions modulate the effect by increasing cloud seeding. However damaging the acid rain, could this be a stabilising influence?   And the global pollution by persistent organic chemicals - we suspect now that they impair immune systems and are part responsible for the viral epidemics in marine mammals, and that some are estrogenic and depress male fertility. How long before these effects begin to depress mankind's spiralling population growth? Even in our hideous error, there is a balancing.

And as for Plutonium. Succussed in the reactor and distributed in homeopathic doses by the bomb tests, such that not a bone on the planet is free of it! Poisonous as it may be in the doses around Windscale, as with all homeopathic poisons, may it not also possess healing powers, borne of Plutonic dimension, a preparation for rebirth, an awakener to higher consciousness?

Even that which we have opposed as evil, may have been Gaia attempting to help us! Oh, heresy! Is there no right action?

I have little wisdom, but am guided now by other motivations. There has been an unfolding here in the woods by Harlech. Here I met Pan. Here the mystery of the White Lady has unfolded. And of that I will one day write.

As the final editing of this manuscript closes (October 1994), David MacTaggart and two other ageing activists are taunting the same French militarists of ten years ago by hiding out on the atoll of Mururoa and disrupting the atom tests the French have insisted on completing despite the strides that have been made toward a worldwide moratorium. On the 10th anniversary of the sinking of the Rainbow Warrior, Fernando Pereira's daughter was interviewed in the newspapers, and finished with the question of 'why did they kill my father?', as if she knows it was not a simple manslaughter.

And Parliament has just announced a special inquiry into the practice of Freemasonry and its potential threats to democracy. In ten years, the issues have not gone away.

Postscript

Following the hard times of the 1980s, I retreated to the wildwood of North Wales. Surrounded by loving friends and children, another journey began. I have not forsaken science or political involvement, having worked a little toward the conservation and regeneration of wildlife and the countryside, as well as renewable energy and consequences of climate change. In the 1990s, though committed to more positive and creative work, I continued to harass the developments at Sellafield for improvements in safety, and worked with a consortium of six major northern cities including Manchester, Glasgow, and Newcastle; and also with lawyers working for the Irish government. I include below a list of relevant scientific publications for those who might wish to examine these issues in more depth. I am still occasionally consulted by our own government and even Greenpeace, and I sit on a national advisory group relating to the development of renewable energy in the countryside. My work can be seen on the Ethos-UK website.

To those who might be of a more spiritual and therapeutic leaning, I want to say – I have changed a lot! In the wildwood I underwent a re-education. I have written about this in a forthcoming book 'The Heart of Nature'. And as that book also weaves the personal and scientific, though more of the latter, I intend to write again on the quest for the White Lady. I lived close to where Robert Graves played as a child, and his White Goddess was still alive and well in those woods, though somewhat lonely!

And a little cautionary note about mind-altering substances. I have been very open about my experiences in the period leading up to 1984, and whatever people may make of those few episodes, I do not want to leave anyone with the impression that I regard them as an integral part of any spiritual path. I was very fortunate to have been secure in the company of loving and experienced friends. Since that time I have come to have a deep respect for the shamanic use of natural 'allies' from the plant kingdom, but only under circumstances of maximum respect and clear healing intention. Any other use, I have concluded, leaves people open to great dangers in ways that are beyond my own comprehension, but not observation.

Babaji, as ever, blesses my life.

233

A list of scientific publications on work referred to in the text

1994   Consequence Analysis of a catastrophic failure of Highly Active Liquid Waste Tanks serving the THORP and Magnox nuclear fuel reprocessing plants at Sellafield.
        Nuclear Free Local Authorities, Manchester City Council.

1993   The State of the Marine Environment 'A critique of the work and the role of the Joint Group of Experts on Scientific Aspects of Marine Pollution (GESAMP).
        Marine Pollution Bulletin 26, 3: 120-127.

1993   The Precautionary Principle and the Prevention of Marine Pollution. (with T.Jackson).
        Chemistry & Ecology, 7: (1-4), pp123-134.

1992   Non-governmental organisations and international treaties: the role of Greenpeace (with Kevin Stairs).
        in Hurrel & Kingsbury Ed. *The International Politics of the Environment* Oxford University Press.

1991   Radioactive discharges in the Irish Sea: a lesson in the principle of precautionary action.
        Proc.Symp. 'Cardigan Bay in Crisis', Snowdonia National Park Authority.

1988   Land use implications of radioactive contamination.
        Land Use Policy, Vol.5 No1 pp62-70.

1988   Environmental issues in nuclear risk assessment.
        Nuclear Technology International, 1988, pp219-223.

1988   Large Consequence Low Probability Accidents
        Standing Conference on Health & Safety in the Nuclear Age,
        CEC, Radiation Protection, Report EUR 11608 EN

1987   The interpretation of monitoring Results
        in *Radiation & Health*, ed. Southwood & Russell-Jones, Wiley. pp19-45.

1986   Risk decisions must involve the public
        Town & Country Planning, Vol 55 No 3.

1985   The disposal of nuclear waste in the deep ocean.
        PERG RR-15, Political Ecology Research Group, Oxford.

1985   Radionuclides in Cumbria: the international context.
        in *Pollution In Cumbria*. Institute of Terrestrial Ecology, Merlewood. HMSO.

1983   The health risks of nuclear and coal fired electricity generation.
        PERG RR-13 (with R.J.Kayes) Political Ecology Research Group, Oxford.

1982   Impact of nuclear waste disposals to the marine environment.
        PERG RR-8 Political Ecology Research Group, Oxford.

1979   Nuclear Energy: how the odds are stacked against the opponents
        Nature Vol 277 pp594-595.

1977   Nuclear Power in Central Europe,
        The Ecologist Vol 7 No 6 pp216-222.
        (Also used as a text for the Open University's 'Control of Technology Course)